History of Digital Games

History of Digital Games
Developments in Art, Design and Interaction

Andrew Williams

CRC Press
Taylor & Francis Group
Boca Raton London New York

CRC Press is an imprint of the
Taylor & Francis Group, an **informa** business

AN A K PETERS BOOK

CRC Press
Taylor & Francis Group
6000 Broken Sound Parkway NW, Suite 300
Boca Raton, FL 33487-2742

Printed on acid-free paper
Version Date: 20170127

International Standard Book Number-13: 978-1-138-88555-4 (Paperback) 978-1-138-88553-0 (Hardback)

Library of Congress Cataloging-in-Publication Data

Names: Williams, Andrew, 1981- author.
Title: History of digital games : developments in art, design and interaction
/ Andrew Williams.
Description: Boca Raton, FL : Taylor & Francis, 2017.
Identifiers: LCCN 2016035577| ISBN 9781138885554 (pbk. : alk. paper) | ISBN
9781138885530 (hardback : alk. paper)
Subjects: LCSH: Video games--Design--History. | Electronic
games--Design--History. | Video arcades--History. | Video art--History.
Classification: LCC GV1469.3 .W56 2017 | DDC 794.8--dc23
LC record available at https://lccn.loc.gov/2016035577

Visit the Taylor & Francis Web site at
http://www.taylorandfrancis.com

and the CRC Press Web site at
http://www.crcpress.com

Contents

Preface

Elements of digital game history abound in contemporary culture. References to Pac-Man, Mario, and 8-bit graphics appear on T-shirts, album covers, and other material objects. Internet memes commonly mix and remix historical game images and phrases like "all your base are belong to us" and "the princess is in another castle" for humorous effect. Recent feature films, meanwhile, have used game nostalgia as central plot points. While the presence of these game history elements are ubiquitous and promote recognition of the past, they frequently fail to serve as anything but references and treat history as little more than trivia. Thus, the central motivation for the creation of this book was to approach digital game history in a way that would be useful for a variety of disciplinary backgrounds in educational contexts; something to inform and promote a sense of appreciation beyond fandom.

Digital games are highly sensitive to technological changes due to their intimate connection to advancements in computer hardware and software. Indeed, one of the major themes in the history of digital games has been the struggle to fit a vision within the confines technological limitations. Thus, when we consider how and why digital games have developed in their manner, it may be tempting to look at their history as a strictly linear development in tune with Moore's Law: as processor speeds increase, so too do our abilities to put more into our games. While extremely important, this techno-centric view of game history can lead to an overemphasis on game hardware, a phenomenon particularly evident in the construct of "console generations." From this author's perspective, this ignores the continuity of game design ideas that exist outside of technological constraints and creates a missed opportunity for meaningful discussions. Another view of game history focuses on the evolution of the industry itself and the personalities behind the scenes. While this places a "human" face on a largely faceless industry, it can focus on intrigue. In their worst forms, both of these perspectives fixate on "firsts" and commercial success, leading to disconnected discussions that remove games from their contexts. As such the educational value for students of game history or individuals looking for broader perspectives becomes compromised.

This book uses elements of the previously mentioned approaches to game history but combines them with a consideration for historical design trends and the evolving practice of game development. It considers digital game history as a composite of the three main historical gaming contexts/platforms (arcades, home computers and consoles) while following a chronological and thematic organization. A key focus of this book centers on the reciprocal influences between these different contexts. At times they converge as seen in the close connections between the design of arcade games and home console games from the mid-1970s through the late 1990s. In other instances contexts became associated with distinctive forms of art, design, and interaction. These differences remained meaningful until the early 2000s as the Internet became a universal medium that began to break down barriers between platforms and blurred traditional boundaries between public and private space. This book is arranged chronologically as well as thematically as each period of time. Each chapter and section is centered on certain design problems and the solutions, both successful and unsuccessful, that were employed in the face of technological, economic, and cultural forces.

Acknowledgments

I thank my wife Chelsea, family, and friends for their support through the 2-year creation of this book. In particular I thank James Hague for his helpful comments as well as all of the other industry professionals, former hackers, and independent game developers who sat for interviews and granted image permissions. Additional thanks to Bill Loguidice and Matt Barton for providing other images.

Author

Andrew Williams, PhD, is an art and design historian at the University of Wisconsin-Stout in Menomonie, Wisconsin. He teaches graduate and undergraduate courses that cover a range of historical topics from digital games and film to fine art and general design history. Williams has also worked with the Minnesota Historical Society on the development of history-based educational games and has established a collection of vintage games, hardware and other related materials at the University of Wisconsin-Stout.

Chapter 1

Mechanical and Electromechanical Arcade Games (1870-1979)

Arcade Game Design

Nearly one-hundred years before the first appearances of digital arcade games, both mechanical engineers and artists created games designed to be visually attractive, easy to understand, and difficult or outright impossible to master. These design concepts were conditioned by a business model that centered on making money by having a high volume of customers pay low prices per trial. As such, the games would only be financially successful if play could start immediately and conclude quickly. While impossible to establish the absolute origin of these concepts, they are intimately connected to playing games in public spaces and are best illustrated by carnival games and games played on the midways of fairs. Combined with the very human desire to win or redeem one's self after failure, these ideas led to some of the most memorable, enjoyable, and profitable gameplay experiences of the nineteenth and twentieth centuries. This chapter explores the development of many of these ideas and discusses the companies, technologies, and personalities that helped hone a philosophy of game design that widely influenced the major gaming contexts of both the arcade and the home.

The Beginnings of Coin-Operated Amusement

The beginning of coin-operated machines dates to as early as the first century CE when the inventor Heron of Alexandria designed a device that used the force of a dropped coin to trigger a mechanism that dispensed water for purification rituals. While Heron's design was strikingly forward thinking, the classic coin-operated videogame arcades of the last quarter of the twentieth century relate more directly to the technological and economic changes brought about by the Second Industrial Revolution of the late 1800s and early 1900s. Three major types of coin-operated amusement machines emerged from this period: the first were noninteractive *working models* that brought kinetic delight to audiences; the second were monetized versions of testing devices designed for use in public spaces; and the third were viewers that allowed individuals to look at a series of two-dimensional (2D) still images, three-dimensional (3D) stereoscopic images, or early motion pictures. The creation of these new coin-op devices illustrated complex changes in the industrialized nations of the late nineteenth century as the public found itself increasingly able to not only spend money, but also spend money on quick bursts of amusement-related activities.

Automata and Coin-Op Working Models

Since the medieval period, European engineers applied the knowledge associated with clocks to create mechanically animated amusement devices called *automata*. The variety of automata was vast, ranging from mechanical birds that sang songs, to automated devils who made grotesque expressions to congregations of Christians. Over the course of several hundred years, the works became increasingly specialized and elaborate, leading to lifelike recreations of movement and behavior. The production of automata in the eighteenth and nineteenth centuries by Swiss, German, and French clockmakers was particularly noteworthy, as their creations displayed sophisticated mechanical programming stored on irregularly shaped discs called cams; an early form of read-only memory and a key component of later mechanical amusement devices.

Jacques de Vaucanson created the *Canard Digérateur* or "Digesting Duck" in 1739 that flapped its wings, ate, drank, and even simulated defecation. In 1785, Peter Kinzing and David Roentgen gifted France's queen Marie-Antoinette with an automaton that played a miniature dulcimer by actually striking the strings with a hammer, all the while making subtle movements with its head and eyes. Perhaps, most impressive was the *Draughtsman-Writer* created by Henri Maillardet around 1805, which drew four detailed scenes and wrote three poems in script; two of which were in French, the other in English. This automaton had the greatest amount of programming and memory capacity of any produced of the time, yet it, like the others, consisted solely of gears, cams, and wound springs. Such masterworks of science and invention served as amusements for the wealthiest European nobles. The larger public had relatively little experience with automata until they appeared as a part of magic show acts in the later nineteenth century. The full introduction of these devices to the public, however, came in the form of coin-operated working models.

Working models first appeared in England and then spread to the rest of Europe and the United States. They typically consisted of an animated scene or object, sometimes accompanied by music that created an audio-visual experience. One of the earliest designers of working models in the United States was William T. Smith who created *The Locomotive* in 1885 (Figure 1.1). Inserting a coin made the miniature locomotive come to life as music played while pistons drove the wheels and levers pulled a string to ring the engine's bell. Although entirely made by hand, the battery-powered model was produced in large quantities that allowed for wide distribution. Fitting the device's theme, Smith's working model was commonly placed in railroad stations to maximize exposure to a constant stream of potential customers.

Similar examples from Europe, such as coin-operated singing birds created by French automaton designer Blaise Bontemps, attracted people who frequented public spaces and emerging amusement centers. In addition to machines and animals, working models also featured elaborate scenes of animated puppets. In England, for instance, the Canova Model Company produced a number of working models employing sensationalism that illustrated scenes of drama and horror, much like British "penny dreadful" novels. One such example was *The French Execution* (1890), which showed the execution by guillotine of a convicted criminal. Another working model by

FIGURE 1.1 *The Locomotive*, **1885 by William T. Smith. (Courtesy of National Jukebox Exchange, Mayfield, New York, www.nationaljukebox.com)**

Canova Model Company showed animated figures suffering from opium addiction while being visited by horrific characters. Despite a sharp decline of popularity in the early 1900s, working models were produced well beyond the 1950s, with one of the most popular being the life-size animated "grandmother" or "gypsy" fortuneteller who consulted crystal balls or tarot cards before dispensing a written fortune.

Coin-Op Competitive Testers

At the same time that automata were fitted for coin operation, a similar phenomenon was happening to popular pub and saloon games. Although slot machines and other gambling games were by far the most popular types of machines in these establishments. Pubs and saloons also featured games that promoted competition or facilitated social interaction and spectatorship. The majority of these machines measured the results of lifting, pushing, pulling, gripping, and punching. For example, the P.M. Athletic Company's *Athletic Punching Machine* (1897) featured a large padded area designed to measure an individual's punching power while the early twentieth century *Perfect Muscle Developer* by Mills Novelty Co. used a plunger resisted by a large spring to measure lifting ability (Figure 1.2).

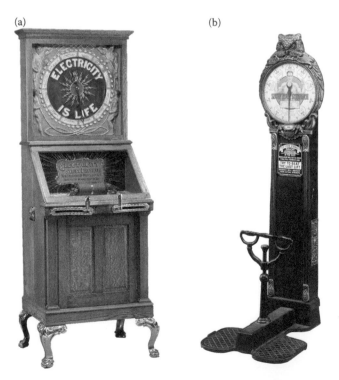

FIGURE 1.2 *Electricity is Life*, 1904 Mills Novelty (a) and *Perfect Muscle Developer*, early twentieth century C Mills Novelty (b). (Courtesy of James D. Julia Auctioneers, Fairfield, Maine, www.jamesdjulia.com)

Regardless of test type, these machines shared several characteristics: sturdy materials designed for repeated use and decoration representing the rich aesthetic vocabulary of the late nineteenth and early twentieth centuries. The *Perfect Muscle Developer*, for instance, used heavy iron in its plunger and platform where the competitor stood while the rest of the device's wooden exterior was embellished with decorative motifs and an elaborate image of the trademark Mills Novelty owl icon. The most important and prominent feature of nearly every strength tester, however, was its display. Displays measured effort numerically, providing an unambiguous, quantifiable, and *comparable* assessment of performance. They were also typically the largest part of the machine, making the readout visible to not just the user, but onlookers as well; a reflection of the social environment these devices inhabited. The competitive nature of these devices was explicit as the display of the *Perfect Muscle Developer* featured phrases like "Not so Good. Use me More" for a low score of 100 and "Great Stuff BIG BOY!" for a high score of 900, giving the competitor feedback on their performance even if not competing in front of a crowd. In addition, the machine continued to display the attempt's score until a new coin was inserted, providing motivation to the next challenger to leave a higher score.

In addition to the various forms of physical strength testers, devices that measured health as a reflection of strength were also extremely popular. Scales measured a person's weight, spirometers measured lung capacity, and machines that administered electric shocks as a "cure all" for headaches, rheumatism, and "all nervous disorders" appeared in cigar stores, post offices, drug stores, hotels, and saloons. Important in the promotion of many of these testers was the "scientific" basis for their health benefits, regardless of actual scientific proof. For example, the 1904 Mills Novelty Co. *Electricity is Life* boldly proclaimed "Electricity, the Silent Physician. Treats all forms of muscular ills. Good for the nervous system too." Here as well, the large dial contained messages for scores based on how long the person held on to the shocking machine; "Electricity if properly applied will benefit any one" was shown for a range of the lowest scores while "Exceptionally fine condition of the entire system" indicated the highest score (Figure 1.2). Spirometers that measured a user's lung capacity followed similar competitive health formats. As an extra incentive, many of these health-based testers returned the spent coin for exceptionally high scores of "healthiness."

A related form of tester was those that measured a person's accuracy with projectiles. Since at least the 1880s, several companies produced gun games for amusement purposes and used virtually anything for projectiles: coins, ball bearings, pellets, gumballs, and even live ammunition. All of these early gun games used realistic looking rifles or pistols for controls. They sometimes also featured highly detailed animated environments, an antecedent of the later electromechanical and digital gun games of the late twentieth

FIGURE 1.3 Simple early twentieth century gun game trade stimulator. (Courtesy of James D. Julia Auctioneers, Fairfield, Maine, www.jamesdjulia.com)

and early twenty-first centuries. A surprisingly advanced early gun game was the English-made *Electric Rifle* of 1901, which used wires and a sophisticated alignment system to send signals from a pedestal-mounted gun to a target area that, when properly aligned, caused bells to ring, figures to animate, and bullet holes to appear. More common, however, were small countertop-based shooting games called *trade stimulators* that distributed cigars, candy, or other small consumables. Figure 1.3 shows an early twentieth century gun game trade stimulator that used a penny as a projectile. A perfectly aimed shot sent the coin through the bull's eye where it rang a bell and returned the coin. More likely, however, the shot missed, resulting in a gumball for the player and a coin for the machine's owner.

Coin-Op Viewers at the Turn of the Century

Even more technologically sophisticated than working models or testing devices were the coin-operated amusements created by American inventor Thomas Alva Edison. Known as the "Wizard of Menlo Park" for his work in creating the incandescent light bulb, methods of distributing electricity to buildings and x-ray-related technologies, Edison's foray into coin-operated entertainment began with the invention of the phonograph. Edison's original intention was to create a machine to record business meetings. This concept, however, received a lackluster reception. One of Edison's investors, however, experimented by adding listening tubes and a coin slot to the phonograph. For a nickel, the user could hear a recording of music, speeches of public figures, or dramatic narratives filled with sound effects. Thus, the phonograph was brought in line with the growing number of late nineteenth century mechanical and electromechanical novelties in train stations, hotel lobbies, and resorts.

Edison's influence on the coin-operated industry was more profound with his next product, the *Kinetoscope*, prototyped in the late 1880s and put into production in 1894. Created by Edison's assistant, William Dickson, the *Kinetoscope* was capable of playing motion pictures from a strip of 35 mm film run between a peephole and a battery-powered light bulb. A user could watch 30–40 second movies of boxing matches, circus performers, or historical reenactments. Each machine was loaded with a different film produced at Edison's Black Maria Film Studio in West Orange, New Jersey.

Dedicated amusement spaces called *Kinetoscope* parlors first appeared in New York and spread to Chicago, San Francisco, Atlantic City and abroad to London and Paris where they were located in central business districts. To capitalize on Edison's reputation as a producer of technological marvels, many of the *Kinetoscope* parlors used his name on banners, named their parlors after him, and even incorporated Edison's likeness into decorative statues. *Kinetoscope* parlors, often decorated in the high style of the time, catered to the upper tiers of society. The interior of Peter Bacigalupi's *Kinetoscope* parlor in San Francisco, for example, featured a flamboyant peacock made of feathers and light bulbs, floor-to-ceiling wallpaper and lighting fixtures powered by gas and electricity—a luxury in 1895 that ensured continual lighting (Figure 1.4). The initial model of the *Kinetoscope* was not equipped with a coin slot. Patrons paid an admission fee and viewed as many of the short film segments as they desired, served by a staff of well-dressed attendants operating the machines. Like other devices, coin slots were quickly incorporated, reducing the need for as many attendants.

The *Kinetoscope* parlor was more than film; it often contained vending machines and a full array of other Edison gadgets including the phonograph and even x-ray machines that visitors used to view the bones in their hands. When it was realized how harmful x-rays actually were, as no shielding was used in any of the devices, the novelty x-ray machines were promptly removed. The *Kinetoscope* parlor helped create the concept of an "arcade" as a space of coin-operated amusement devices as seen in the proper name of Bacigalupi's *Kinetoscope* parlor: "Edison's Kinetoscope, Phonograph and Gramophone Arcade." From this point on, it became increasingly more common to see the word "arcade" in the titles of amusement spaces.

A Gathering of Games and Amusements at the Penny Arcade

Since many British and American games of the late nineteenth century cost a penny to operate, "penny arcade" became a common term to describe the

FIGURE 1.4 Patterned interior of Edison's Phonograph and Gramophone Arcade in San Francisco, California. (Courtesy of U.S. Dept. of the Interior, National Park Service, Thomas Edison National Historical Park.)

increasingly frequent clustering of low cost amusement games and devices. In the United States, permanent penny arcades first appeared on the East Coast in the early 1900s, especially in New York City, as the games needed a large audience to remain profitable. In England, permanent penny arcades were relatively rare until the 1920s as it was far more common to have machines placed sporadically along the piers of seaside resorts outside of London.

Like *Kinetoscope* parlors, penny arcades prominently featured motion picture machines. Edison's *Kinetoscope* had waned in popularity by the early 1900s, replaced by a new coin-operated movie viewer, the *Mutoscope*, created by *Kinetoscope* inventor and former Edison colleague William Dickson. This penny arcade "peep show" device was crank-powered and spun a series of sequential images on paper past an eyepiece. Cheaper to manufacture and maintain, with larger and clearer images, it was able to outperform Edison's *Kinetoscope*. The *Mutoscope* had a robust international presence, with business relations in the United States, England, France, and other European countries. The model most frequently associated with the penny arcades was the 1901 "Iron Horse" that featured an abundance of decorative elements

FIGURE 1.5 "Iron Horse" model *Mutoscope* (1901, International Mutoscope and Biography Company). (Courtesy of James D. Julia Auctioneers, Fairfield, Maine, www.jamesdjulia.com)

including a "clam shell" design on the viewer's side (Figure 1.5). Like the back glass and cabinet art of later pinball and videogame arcade machines, these aesthetic flourishes, along with electric lights and patterned wallpaper in the arcade's interior, were meant to create spaces of excitement that could lure potential customers off the street.

By 1907, penny arcades in the United States had narrowed their focus and provided less film-related amusements. After early filmmakers began to exploit the artistic and mass entertainment potential of film, showings moved out of peep show parlors and into specialized spaces designed for projection to large audiences. Despite competition between penny arcades and early movie houses, the penny arcade was still dominated by novelty viewing devices. According to the suggested layout of penny arcades in the 1907 Mills Novelty Company catalog, penny arcade owners were to set up as many as 25 stereoscopic peep show machines but carry only 15 other coin-op devices such as strength testers. Images of penny arcades from the period show row upon row of *Mutoscopes*, *Quartoscopes* (which showed non-animated 2D or 3D images), and other coin-operated viewing machines, with a few punching, lifting, and fortune-telling machines sprinkled in between.

Envisioned as spaces for families, with candy machines that randomly chose prizes for children, the ideal customers at early penny arcades were young men, which resulted in peep-show viewers with sexually suggestive titles like "For Men Only" and "Those Naughty Chorus Girls." While titillating in title, what was actually delivered (the occasional nudes not withstanding) often failed to live up to imagined expectations.

Sport-Based Games and the Roots of Digital Game Genres

In addition to viewers and testers, coin-op manufacturers also produced games based on organized sports. Early sports-based coin-op machines combined the elements of target shooting and strength testing games with detailed environments and animated characters seen in working models. This signaled a different approach to thinking about interacting with games as the player did not directly compete in the task, but did so through a surrogate entity that represented the player's presence and actions in the game space; a concept known as the *avatar* in digital games. A significant number of these sports-based games were intended for two players, a design feature of paramount importance for games used in public social spaces. Many machines also featured a large amount of glass, allowing crowds of spectators to enjoy the game as well.

Like other early coin-op devices, England was a major center for the manufacture and export of sports-based arcade games in the late 1800s and early 1900s. The London-based Automatic Sports Company manufactured a number of games based on British sport such as *Yacht Racer* (1900) and *The Cricket Match* (1903). Because of technical and practical limitations, these games did not recreate all of the dimensions, rules, and interactions of any one particular sport; rather they were abstractions of the sport's basic gameplay experience. *The Cricket Match*, for instance, focused on the batting and pitching portions of the game. The batting player attempted to hit a pitch into any one of a number of holes in the playfield, the most difficult of which returned the spent penny to the player. Administering a reward for a skilled or lucky performance, as seen in *The Cricket Match,* was common in other English arcade machines of the time as well (Figure 1.6). Considered in light of the game-based trade stimulators discussed earlier (Figure 1.3), the boundaries between coin-op vending machines, arcade games, and gambling machines were anything but fixed in the early 1900s.

Full Team Football, created by the London-based Full Team Football Company in 1925, featured a standard 11 on 11 game of soccer with red and blue players grouped at the forward, midfield, defender, and goalie positions. A brightly colored background of seated spectators completed the illusion. In a similar setup to a contemporary foosball table, each group of players was controlled by one of three levers that allowed them to kick a ball around the field until one side scored a goal. Even with the players fixed in place at each position, the game was able to recreate frantic ball movements by using a ridged field that could redirect the ball in an unpredictable manner. When a goal was scored, the game was finished and no payout was received.

Although England was the main manufacturer of arcade games throughout the early 1900s, penny arcades and their machines were more popular

FIGURE 1.6 An English "Climbing Fireman" coin-op game from the 1920s. (Courtesy of James D. Julia Auctioneers, Fairfield, Maine, www.jamesdjulia.com)

in the United States. By the late 1920s, American manufacturers were producing games in larger numbers, some of which were adaptions of English games. In 1926, the New York-based Chester-Pollard Amusement Company was granted the right to distribute *Full Team Football* in the United States and renamed it *Play Football* (Figure 1.7). This represented the beginning of a new line of games in the United States. American advertising of *Play Football* carried taglines like "Something New at Last," implying that the coin-op amusement industry was hungry for new ideas. The game, although similar in form to its English predecessor, was greatly modified in operation as the player pressed one, and only one lever to control the kicking motion of the figures. Although this greatly reduced the ability for the player to make meaningful gameplay decisions, the reduction in moving parts lowered the cost to manufacture the game and potentially meant less maintenance over its lifetime. The game, nonetheless, saw wide distribution. Its frantic and competitive matches made it popular in penny arcades.

NON-SPORT PENNY ARCADE GAMES

Not all competitive coin-op games were based on specific sports, as seen in the English "Climbing Fireman" arcade cabinet from the 1920s (Figure 1.6). The game required each player to insert a coin and furiously turn the machine's dial to ascend his or her fireman as fast as possible to reach the top of the ladder first. The winner's fireman signaled a bell and triggered the machine to return one of the coins, presumably to the winner. The visual details in the firemen's clothing and building's curtains as well as the animated figures show common elements between working models and early arcade games.

The Chester-Pollard Amusement Company followed the success of *Play Football* with other sport-based games such as *Play the Derby* (1929). *Play the Derby*, featured a miniature horseracing field complete with track, trees, buildings, and railings, painted in bright colors. Much like the controls in the *Climbing Fireman* game (Figure 1.6), *Play the Derby* used a hand crank to drive each player's horse around the track in a two-lap race. To prevent the game from devolving into a mere competition of spinning the handle

FIGURE 1.7 *Play Football* (1926, Chester-Pollard Co.). (Courtesy of James D. Julia Auctioneers, Fairfield, Maine, www.jamesdjulia.com)

the fastest, the game's mechanical engineers devised a clutch that slipped if a player spun too fast, resulting in a horse that came to an abrupt stop. This encouraged not only a more interesting form of gameplay, as players had to contend with the crank's speed threshold, but also helped ensure that the machine's mechanism would receive less physical abuse from overexcited players.

Penny arcade game design in the 1920s and 1930s was also influenced by the popularization of radio. The technology for radio developed throughout the 1800s, but the medium came into proper form during the 1920s as the number of stations (and thus radio programs) grew at an exponential rate. The broadcasts that drew the largest crowds and most captivated the public's interest were those featuring live sporting events, particularly boxing matches and baseball games. The 1926 boxing match between the heavyweight champion Jack Dempsey and challenger Gene Tunney, and its rematch a year later, was one of the most anticipated and listened to broadcasts of the day, carried on 74 radio stations and drawing an estimated crowd of 15 million listeners. Although first appearing in late 1800s England, American companies continuously created boxing games from the 1920s to the 1970s in an attempt to capitalize on the continued excitement generated by the real-life matches. Most used similar formats of small, articulated figures maneuvered by players in a miniature-boxing ring. Rather than tabulating points for each punch landed, as in the actual sport of boxing, the game concept attempted to recreate the most dramatic portion of the match: the knockout punch to the chin. This proved pragmatic for the design of the device, as it provided a decisive and exciting signal of victory. In *K.O. Fighters* (1928, National Novelty), the players moved two boxers in

FIGURE 1.8 *Knock Out Fighters* **(1928, National Novelty). (Courtesy of National Jukebox Exchange, Mayfield, New York, www.nationaljukebox.com)**

and out of punching distance through pistol-grip handles that allowed for individual control of the right and left arms (Figure 1.8). The player who connected a punch to a trigger on their opponent's chin caused the defeated player's boxer to fall to the mat.

Baseball, however, was more difficult to execute in a coin-operated arcade game due to the complexity of the sport's rules. Since the sport of baseball only allows the team at bat to score points, the majority of designers of arcade games chose to focus on hitting the ball. George H. Miner, an automobile mechanic working for the Amusement Machine Corporation of America, created the highly sophisticated electromechanical *All-American Automatic Baseball Game* (1929) which replicated nearly all the rules of baseball related to pitching, batting, and scoring runs. The player, as the batter, attempted to hit a ball bearing past basemen and outfielders to the stadium wall where it fell into various chutes that counted as a single, double, triple, or home run. The game's impressive pitching system allowed the mechanically controlled pitcher to actually throw the ball bearing a short distance before it rolled to the batter. An irregular-shaped cam caused the pitcher to subtly change direction before each throw, giving a great degree of variety and making pitches seem unpredictable. A series of hidden slots behind the batter registered an un-hit bearing as either a ball or strike and then computed it so that three strikes converted to an out, three outs ended the game, and foul balls counted as strikes. As a final aesthetic flourish, the game's umpire, located behind the pitcher, gave a signal for each ball or strike by raising his left or right arm. The rights to Miner's game were eventually purchased by the influential pinball and arcade game designer, Harry Williams, who modified it to include a display that automatically updated the positions of men on base and cleared the bases in the instance of a homerun or final out. Williams' game was released to coincide with the highly anticipated 1937 World Series between the New York Yankees and New York Giants, in a game appropriately called *1937 World Series* (1937, Rock-Ola) (Figures 1.9 and 1.10).

Early Developments in Pinball

It may be tempting to create a connection between Miner's 1929 baseball game and the gameplay of pinball, with the bat serving as a proto-flipper and Williams' involvement as one of the preeminent pinball designers of the twentieth century. While they do share some similarities in mechanical elements, the state of the game of pinball was vastly different. The game of pinball emerged in the late 1920s and early 1930s after undergoing a number of changes from its ancestor, the eighteenth century French game, *bagatelle*. Bagatelle was played on a rectangular felt-covered table and used a cue stick to sink a ball into a pattern of holes at the opposite end of the

FIGURE 1.9 *1937 World Series* (1937, Rock-Ola). Note the rounded edges of the case and decorative stripe that shows the influence of the Art Deco design movement. (Courtesy of James D. Julia Auctioneers, Fairfield, Maine, www.jamesdjulia.com)

FIGURE 1.10 The Pitcher was able to throw the ball bearing as far as the black padded circle, after which it rolled to the batter. (Courtesy of James D. Julia Auctioneers, Fairfield, Maine, www.jamesdjulia.com)

board. The slight incline of the table caused any balls that missed their target to roll back down to the table's base. To enliven the game, the playing surface frequently included small upright nails that randomly redirected the movement of the ball. This game proved popular among upper class members of French society and was eventually brought to the United States where it was miniaturized for use on countertops in saloons and other places.

The game in its miniature form remained essentially unchanged until 1871 when the American, Montague Redgrave, filed a patent entitled "Improvements in Bagatelle" which replaced the miniature cue stick with a spring-loaded plunger and added several obstacles to the playing field. These features included small gates that slowed ball momentum, cups that funneled the ball to different areas, and bells that rang when game balls collided with them. From the standpoint of gameplay, Redgrave's introduction of the spring-loaded plunger promoted accessibility: by equalizing skill across players, the fine art of using the miniature cue sticks was no longer necessary. The game's inclusion of bells created not only a multisensory gaming experience, but also an unambiguous indication of point score.

Interest in bagatelle or "pin games," as they grew to be known, came and went until a major surge of interest occurred in the 1920s and 1930s, the same period that saw the expansion of game offerings in arcades. One of the first successful pinball game designers of the period was David Gottlieb, a man with a background in the design of carnival games and the exhibition of film. Using this experience, he founded D. Gottlieb & Co. in Chicago, which began by manufacturing various amusement devices such as grip testers and shooting trade stimulators. Turning his attention to pinball games, David Gottlieb saw success with *Baffle Ball* (1931), a completely mechanical game that combined a brightly colored playfield with an interesting placement of pins and cups. Costing a penny for seven to ten shots with steel balls, the player needed to gauge the amount of force used to pull back the lever and direct the balls to the high-scoring areas. Balls that did not make it into one of the four main scoring cups or the coveted "Baffle Point" cup, rolled down to the bottom of the board. Gottlieb, like many other early pin game designers, understood the probability of the ball reaching any one area of the board. As such, the game's highest scoring areas were located in the places least likely to intersect with the path of the ball. Even with practiced use of the plunger, the pins in the playfield randomly redirected the rolling ball.

Like most games of the early 1930s *Baffle Ball* did not automatically tabulate score; instead, points were counted manually as the balls remained in their scoring areas after play finished. In this way, the previous score was displayed as a challenge to the next player much like that of strength testers produced 30 years earlier. When the next player inserted a penny into

FIGURE 1.11 *Five Star Final* **(1932, Gottlieb & Co.). The game used the same design philosophy of** *Baffle Ball* **as it placed the highest scoring cups in the most difficult to reach areas and left the balls in place until a new coin was inserted.** *Five Star Final* **also shows the variety of playfield designs as it was based on a figure of eight. (Courtesy of James D. Julia Auctioneers, Fairfield, Maine, www. jamesdjulia.com)**

Baffle Ball, the balls would then fall through a series of trap doors, clearing the score. Every game was thus different and often concluded with the unfulfilled desire of reaching the high score targets or beating the previous score. Gottlieb helped popularize the game of pinball in the United States, producing 400 machines a day at peak, and strengthened the presence of coin-operated games (Figure 1.11). Although not explicit, the largely random path taken by the ball's descent made early pin games ideal for gambling as location owners created game rules that existed outside of those contained within the device itself. This helped pinball games collect pennies and nickels even in the midst of America's Great Depression.

A New Emphasis on Art and Design

As the pinball industry grew in both the United States and Europe in the 1930s, the need to gain attention in an increasingly crowded field pressured designers to add new, and sometimes unusual, gameplay features. In addition, artists played an increasingly important role by enhancing playfields with colorful images and characters that distinguished the games from one another. An example of the interplay between new game design and art can be found in Rock-Ola's *World's Fair Jigsaw* (1933), an entirely mechanical game that, as its title suggested, featured a colorful jigsaw puzzle of the 1933 World's Fair fairgrounds. Sinking the ball into various holes in the playfield allowed the player to accumulate points and caused the pieces of the jigsaw puzzle to flip over one by one, or if lucky, to fill in an entire row. Special holes also flipped random pieces or modified the score by doubling the value of points. Completing the puzzle was extremely difficult: the player was given 10 balls to flip 20 pieces, each ball had to be fired with enough energy to circle the entire table almost one and a half times and the pins, springs, and gates dotting the playfield effectively removed any amount of control by the player.

Another novel mechanical pinball game by Rock-Ola, was *World's Series* (1934). A similar design to *World's Fair Jigsaw*, the playfield was divided into upper and lower spaces and required the ball to be shot completely around the board before entering the pin-studded playfield. The board's center had a set of channels marked strike, out, ball, or hit. As in the rules of baseball, the game's complicated mechanisms were able to convert three strikes into an out and four balls into a walk through weight sensitive trap doors. After three outs, the game was over. A ball that went through the channel signifying a hit would fall into the lower portion of the board, which was decorated as a brightly colored baseball diamond. Here the ball was caught in a pocket and rotated in a predetermined sequence, signifying anything from a base hit to a home run. "Runners" who made the trip around the diamond were ejected at the end, clearing the bases and falling into a slot that displayed the number of runs. The design of the playfield assured it was much more likely that the jostled ball would result in an out rather than a hit. Thus, player control in both *World's Series* and *World's Fair Jigsaw*, like all pre-World War II pinball tables, was minimal at best.

New technologies also helped produce novel game designs for pinball, the most significant being the adoption of electricity in the 1930s. Solenoid-powered kickers shot the ball out of holes and decorative cannons, score totalizers provided unambiguous tallies of points, and Nick Nelson created the first bumpers in the appropriately named, *Bumper* (1937, Bally). But perhaps the most influential and industry-shaping ideas in pinball came from Harry Williams. Harry Williams (1906–1983) known for the design of innovative features in pinball and for designing arcade machines like *1937 World Series* (1937, Rock-Ola), had a degree in engineering and professional experience as a commercial artist. Williams began his game design career refurbishing pinball machines by reconfiguring the arrangement of pins in the playfield. In addition to founding three companies, one of which eventually became Williams Electronics, Harry Williams' expertise in game design allowed him to work with some of the largest amusement machine companies of the twentieth century, spreading his designs and innovations throughout the entire pinball and arcade game industry. Williams was the first pinball designer to use electricity, creating the "kick out hole" which allowed the ball to fall into a hole and be kicked back into the playfield by a solenoid-powered plunger, a revolutionary idea that was instantly adopted by other designers.

Harry Williams' influence was also seen in the "tilt" mechanism that prevented players from cheating. Since pinball games were largely chance-based, players created strategies such as hitting or nudging the table to change the course of the ball's path or lifting the table end to put spent balls back in play. Pinball game designers were largely aware of this and devised a number of anti-cheat methods such as making scoring pockets deeper or weighing the machine down with sandbags. To combat cheating in his games, Harry Williams experimented with a number of design ideas, including placing nails on the bottom of machines. Williams, however, eventually devised the electromechanical "pendulum tilt" in 1935, which consisted of a weight at the end of a rod surrounded by a metal ring. When shaken or jostled too hard, the pendulum swayed and made contact with the ring, creating a circuit and triggering a mechanism that prevented score bonuses or halted gameplay depending on its configuration. Williams' tilt mechanism was widely adopted and became the standard anti-cheat device in pinball machines at a time when pinball's expansion appeared limitless.

The Prohibition of Pinball

As discussed earlier, payout for high scores was a common and informal practice between the player and the pinball machine's owner, as it increased a game's earning power and skirted the label of gambling. This charade came to an end when manufacturers made gambling functions explicit by introducing payout pin machines in the mid-1930s. Games like *Tycoon* (1936, Mills Novelty Co.), for example, featured a typical bagatelle-style playfield with seven slots at the board's bottom. The gambling component came in the form of betting on which slot the game's single ball would land. If the ball passed through certain gates, it would increase the amount of payout. This single ball gameplay was common among payout pin tables.

Concerns about gambling, meanwhile, swept across the United States resulting in a heavy crack down on all forms of chance-based amusements. During the 1930s and 1940s, Los Angeles, New York, and even Chicago, the center of the US coin-operated industry, enacted severe restrictions on slot machines, payout machines, and regular pinball machines. The situation was further complicated as non-gambling pinball machines in the 1930s began offering a "free replay" or "free game" for players who reached a specified score threshold. This concept was widely adopted and allowed a skilled or more likely, lucky player, to play another game. Pinball was implicated in the gambling crackdown not only for its informal payout practices and heavy reliance on randomized gameplay, but also for this ability to win a free game, as this was considered something of value.

In 1941, at the request of Mayor Fiorello LaGuardia, the Commissioner of Investigation in New York City drafted a report entitled "Operation of Pinball Machines in the City of New York." In its summary, the report stated, "…pinball machines serve no useful purpose and are inherently detrimental to the public welfare. Fundamentally, the operation of the machines in this city presents the same problems as those formerly presented by slot machines."[*] As a result, pinball machines in New York City were seized and publicly destroyed by sledgehammer-wielding police as well as Mayor LaGuardia himself, the shattered machines dumped over the sides of boats and barges into the Atlantic Ocean. A patchwork of pinball-related laws spread across cities throughout the United States, ranging from specific requirements that balls had to be rolled by hand instead of being launched by plunger, to a ban of the game outright. In spite of it all, pinball machines still operated in many places, as anti-pinball laws were generally only lightly enforced.

Postwar Mechanical and Electromechanical Game Design

During World War II, many game manufacturers ceased production and joined others in the conversion of their facilities to the production of war materials. Those that did produce games were forced to rely on used parts from prewar games, as new parts were virtually impossible to acquire. Innovation in game design slowed, but existing types saw sudden changes in theme and meaning. British and American shooting galleries, pinball games and trade stimulators sported bright national colors and featured images that dehumanized leaders in Germany, Japan, and Italy, motivating players to humiliate or otherwise destroy them. By late summer of 1945, with the war in Europe and the Pacific concluded, American game companies picked up almost immediately where they had left off, rekindling the coin-op industry. While the American coin-op industry bounced back quickly, the European and East Asian industries were not able to reestablish their momentum until the later 1940s and 1950s. Nonetheless, in the 25-year period after World War II, arcade games of all genres largely transitioned from mechanical to electromechanical operation.

One feature that saw expanded use in postwar electromechanical games was the timer. Timed gameplay helped to even out the rate at which a machine could collect coins, as novice and skilled players played for predictable periods of time. This feature was applied to several existing game

---

[*] Herlands, W. B. 1941. *Operation of Pinball Machines in the City of New York.* New York: Department of Investigation.

FIGURE 1.12 *K.O. Champ* **(1955, International Mutoscope Reel Co.). (Courtesy of National Jukebox Exchange, Mayfield, New York, www.nationaljukebox.com)**

genres such as target shooting games like *Captain Kid Gun* (1966, Midway Manufacturing Co.) and boxing games like *K.O. Champ* (1955, International Mutoscope Reel Co.) (Figure 1.12). In each case, the experience of gameplay became more stressful and exciting; players were required to not only complete a challenge, but also do so within a limited period of time. The presence of the timer in *K.O. Champ*, in particular, effectively created a different game as each player was given a minute to score as many knockouts as possible. This led to more frantic matches of flailing shots to the opponent's chin as opposed to the one-hit knockout boxing games produced 30 years earlier (Figure 1.8).

Driving and Racing Games after World War II

Driving was highly popular in arcade games in the postwar period. Particularly in the United States, the act of driving became a potent symbol of adventure, status, and recreation as families engaged in summer driving vacations and drive-in movie theaters saw their greatest popularity. From the 1950s through the 1970s, coin-op game manufacturers produced a significant number of vehicle-based amusements with timed gameplay operated by steering wheels and pedals. Initially, racing was not a widely implemented concept. More common were games that purported to measure a player's safe driving skills through their ability to react to changes in the road or the playfield; the better the driver, the higher the score.

The array of technologies used to create the experience of driving was impressive. From 1954 to 1959, Capitol Projector Corp. used film projection of recorded driving footage in various versions of *Auto Test*. More a simulator than a game, *Auto Test* awarded the player for making proper driving decisions like avoiding collisions and maintaining the speed limit. Failure to perform these actions resulted in a loss of points. In Genco's *Motorama* (1957), the player directed a detailed model car to perform U-turns, parking maneuvers, and other driving exercises in an environment resembling a parking lot in the city. Players of Williams Electric's *Road Racer* (1962) controlled a model car suspended over a rotating drum with images of a winding road; the objective was to follow a set of metal studs embedded in the road to gain enough points to be considered a "perfect driver" by the machine (Figures 1.13 and 1.14).

In the late 1960s and early 1970s, game designers added more tension and enlivened the gameplay of driving by adding proper racing elements

FIGURE 1.13 *Road Racer,* (1962, Williams Electric Mfg. Co.). In order to view the rotating drum, the player needed to look down into the machine. (Courtesy of Musée Mécanique, San Francisco, California, www.museemecaniquesf.com)

FIGURE 1.14   Game space over a rotating drum. (Courtesy of Musée Mécanique, San Francisco, California, www.museemecaniquesf.com)

and representing speed in more sensational ways. Chicago Coin's *Speedway* (1969) and *Motorcycle* (1970) featured an endlessly curving racetrack populated by six other rival vehicles moving at different speeds (Figure 1.15). Although avoiding accidents was a significant part of the game, going as fast as possible was even more important as the longer one drove, the more points they earned. Both *Speedway* and *Motorcycle* used a method of producing graphics based on shining light through a series of translucent animated discs. The final image seen by the player was projected on a screen using mirrors to create a pseudo-3D perspective.

One of the most sophisticated racing games of the electromechanical era was *Road Runner* (1971, Bally). In *Road Runner*, the player controlled a model car with a steering wheel and accumulated points for passing other cars in a vast, three-lane space that appeared much larger than the game's cabinet. If the player's car collided with another on the track, it would tumble end over end through the air and reset on a starting strip outside of the main lanes, where the player could not score points. The combination of timer and nonscoring starting strip encouraged the player to go as fast as possible in order to accumulate maximum points, a marked difference in gameplay from the driving games produced 20 years earlier.

From a technological standpoint, the game space of *Road Runner* was made possible by a vertical playfield consisting of model cars on conveyor belts mirrored into position. This allowed the player to see a much longer game space than appeared possible from the cabinet's outside. In addition, the player's car and rival cars occupied different places within the cabinet and used mirrors, again, to create the illusion of one racetrack. A sensor tracked the player's car movement and was able to detect if any collisions happened, triggering a mechanical arm to spin the car.

FIGURE 1.15 *Motorcycle* (1970, Chicago Coin). Note the distortion of the otherwise round disc caused by the projection technique. (Courtesy of Arcadia, McLean, IL, www.vintagevideogames.com)

Missile-Launching Games in Japan and the United States

Japan was a vastly different place at the conclusion of World War II as the United States installed permanent military bases and businessmen from around the world moved to Japan looking for new markets. As a result, Japan witnessed different models of behavior, attitudes, habits, and patterns of recreation. The aftermath of the war also saw the creation of a number of major Japanese companies such as Sony, which initially specialized in telecommunications equipment. The combination of these complex and interwoven factors contributed to the "economic miracle" that was Japan in the 1950s and 1960s. It is from this postwar period that significant aspects of Japan's gaming industry originated.

At the opening of the 1950s, numerous vending machine companies were founded or moved to Japan with the intent of catering to the presence of American soldiers: in 1951, American entrepreneurs Marty Bromley, Irving Bromberg, and James Humpert moved their Hawaii-based coin-op company Service Games (previously named Standard Games) to Japan to provide US bases with various types of vending and slot machines; the Taito Trading Company, founded in 1953 by Russian businessman Michael Kogan, imported jukeboxes as well as other vending machines in Tokyo; and American David Rosen established Rosen Enterprises in 1954, which imported coin-operated photo booths that soldiers used for making ID cards. Starting in the mid-1950s, Rosen Enterprises began importing used arcade games from the United States into Japan, creating the first vestiges of Western-style arcade spaces. By 1960, arcades appeared in major cities all over the country, a sign of the growing demand for leisure activities among the population of Japan. The competition between Rosen Enterprises and Service Games eventually led to a merger in 1965. This new company was headed by Rosen and named Sega, a shortened version of Service Games.

The first arcade game produced under the Sega name was *Periscope* (1966). Using a mock-up submarine periscope, the player launched torpedoes at sets of model ships powered by a motorized conveyor belt. A series of lights that sequentially turned on and off represented the path of the torpedo to its target. The machine played an explosion sound effect when a ship was hit and flashed a bright red light across the background. The simplicity and fun of *Periscope* made it immediately successful, as it became the first Japanese game imported to the United States.

Periscope represented a larger trend in the late 1960s and 1970s of missile-launching gameplay. Most of the games featured several postwar electromechanical game design elements already discussed; timed gameplay and vertical playfields that used mirrors to create an artificial sense of depth. The games, expressed in submarine or land-based turret themes, used the basic concept of a shooting gallery but restricted player movement to the lateral plane. This forced players to carefully time their shots against the moving targets since the player had to wait a few seconds between each shot. Several turret-based missile-launching games like Sega's *Missile* (1969), created the illusion of missile movement by using film projection on the backdrop (Figure 1.16). The player rotated a brightly lit missile left and right, waiting for proper alignment against a constant stream of planes flying overhead in different formations. Once fired, the light in the missile tuned off and a missile in flight was projected receding into the background, creating a convincing illusion. In the United States, Midway Manufacturing became a major producer of several submarine-themed missile-launching games like *Sea Raider* (1969), *Sea* Devil (1970), and *Submarine* (1979), in addition to land-based turret games like *S.A.M.I—Surface to Air Missile Interceptor* (1970).

FIGURE 1.16 *Missile* **(1966, Sega). (Courtesy of Arcadia, McLean, IL, www.vintagevideogames.com)**

Pinball as a Game of Skill

By the mid-1970s, pinball machines had changed markedly from those produced in the 1930s, and were for all practical purposes, a different game. Pinball's playfields became more colorful and complicated, while back glass art displayed the work of numerous comic book artists and tallied the game's score as targets were hit. Solenoid-powered flippers first implemented in Gottlieb's 1947 *Humpty Dumpty* and refined over the decades, allowed the player more control over the ball, a feature entirely lacking in earlier pinball tables (Figure 1.17). The idea of "winning" a free game was replaced by the "add-a-ball" game mechanic in 1960, which allowed skilled players to earn multiple extra balls for meeting certain objectives. This extended playtime without violating anti-gambling laws. Created by David Gottlieb's son Alvin Gottlieb, the add-a-ball concept was first implemented in *Flipper* (1960, D Gottlieb & Company) and was widely adopted by other pinball manufacturers, a prototype of the extra life in digital games.

These changes were significant enough to help distinguish the differences between gambling machines and pinball machines. The culminating event

FIGURE 1.17 *Covergirl* **(1947, Keeney). Note the position of the flippers along the sides of the table that pushed the ball into the center of the game space rather than saving it from rolling out the bottom. United States. (Courtesy of Arcadia, McLean, IL, www.vintagevideogames.com)**

for pinball occurred on April 2, 1976. Rodger Sharpe, as a respected pinball game designer and skilled player, testified to the New York City Council. His testimony consisted of not only a verbal argument, but also a demonstration of the skill-based elements of the game performed in front of council members in the council chambers. During play, he was able to call his shots with sufficient accuracy and skill that members of the committee immediately took a vote to end the ban following the demonstration. After the decision by New York, other cities followed with the most symbolically important being Chicago, the main city where the American coin-operated industry was centered.

The Sunset of Electromechanical Games

While the removal of pinball bans across the United States was cause for celebration among manufacturers and owners, the nature of game arcades had already changed, as digital coin-op games were flourishing in the late 1970s. Although early digital arcade games lacked the visual detail and the feeling of space found in electromechanical arcade games, they also lacked the maintenance problems caused by complex arrays of moving parts and dirt buildup. Relative to the size of the more elaborate electromechanical pinball and arcade games, coin-op video games were smaller, meaning more machines could occupy a space and collect more coins. Further, electromechanical games were limited by the speed of a rolling ball or the time it took for a solenoid to turn a model missile turret.

The type of games that could be designed digitally presented more dynamic possibilities in gameplay than electromechanical games. Their biggest advantage was the ability to implement a system of progressive difficulty, as it ensured that the game would be constantly attractive to both new and experienced players. In pinball of the 1970s and 1980s, the board always stayed the same and operated at a fixed level of difficulty as they relied solely on the probability of player error increasing with playtime. By the time more dynamic pinball systems were introduced, digital games had become the preference of the majority of game players. Nonetheless, the design knowledge gained in the previous 100 years was invaluable, as it was used to form the basis for arcade games in the early digital era, a topic continued in Chapter 3.

Chapter **2**

Games as Experiments (1912–1977)

Electronic Computers and Games

Engineers of the 1930s and 1940s from Germany, England, and the United States independently developed electromechanical and electronic computing devices capable of performing a variety of mathematical calculations and problem-solving functions.[*] Early machines such as the American-built Electronic Numerical Integrator and Computer (ENIAC) and English Colossus computers calculated firing tables for artillery and deciphered encrypted messages, operations driven by the military needs of World War II. These mid-century behemoths weighed several tons, occupied entire rooms, and utilized physical switches or vacuum tubes to denote the binary computer logic states of "on" and "off." Computers such as these were almost exclusively found in specialized research labs housed in universities or government facilities. Access to them was highly restricted. In the decades after World War II, technologies became faster, smaller, and, crucially, more affordable. Small transistors replaced large vacuum tubes, creating a new class of refrigerator-sized "minicomputers." In addition to the differences in size and cost, access to minicomputers was considerably less restrictive allowing for the formation and proliferation of the computer hacker culture in universities in the 1960s and 1970s.

---

[*] Unrealized projects such as Babbage's mid-nineteenth century Analytical Engine, however, showed that the concept of general purpose computing had been in existence for at least 100 years prior.

Computer games were important within this context as they illustrated theories of artificial intelligence and provided a focus for radical innovation that was applied to other areas. Although games were particularly associated with microcomputers, few people outside of research and educational contexts had familiarity with them. The games that developed within this noncommercialized context did, however, help create a knowledge base from which many video arcade and home computer game designers drew.

Early Games in Research and Scientific Demonstration

Chess and Artificial Intelligence

One of the first, and most common, appearances of computer games occurred in research related to artificial intelligence. Chess programs were a favorite of early computer scientists and have a history with machines that stretches to at least the eighteenth century with Wolfgang von Kempelen's chess playing, "Turk" automaton hoax. In order for a computer to win against a human player, the computer needed to strategize by planning several moves in advance, constantly reevaluate its position on a changing board, and dynamically adjust to the moves of its opponent; criteria that were deemed sufficient for the demonstration of "intelligence." Chess, however, may not have been the most ideal game to test artificial intelligence. Its rules were difficult for early computers to model, and required several concessions like simpler games with limited moves and fewer choices, variants that seemed to diminish the "intelligent" behavior desired.

The use of chess as a test for artificial intelligence, however, revealed an early uneasiness on the part of computer scientists to use the most technologically sophisticated equipment for game play. Many vigorously declared that game-based computer applications were strictly for research and demonstration purposes only. Serious work demanded a serious game. Thus, they felt chess was ideal as it was associated with sophistication and intelligence rather than entertainment and fun, a cultural perception that helped legitimize the work.

One of the first truly autonomous chess-playing machines was built by Leonardo Torres y Quevedo (1852–1936), an early twentieth century Spanish inventor who specialized in the creation of intelligent electromechanical devices. Torres built "el Ajedrecista" (the chess player) in 1912 (Figure 2.1) based on his experiments of the 1890s. The device could not play a full game of chess, but it was capable of a more manageable "end game" variation that used a king and a rook controlled by the computer against a single king controlled by a human player. Each piece was plugged into a small chessboard with a metal peg, which sent a signal to the machine. Since checkmate for

FIGURE 2.1 Leonardo Torres y Quevedo's 1912 "el Ajedrecista." (Scientific American. (1915, November 6). Torres and his remarkable automatic devices. *Scientific American*. **Supplement 80. No. 2079, 296–298.)**

the single human-controlled king was inevitable in this particular setup, the machine was always able to eventually beat its opponent. Torres' design, however, was still sophisticated as it signaled game states of "check" and "checkmate" to the player via a set of individual light bulbs. It could also detect and signal an illegal move. Gonzalo Torres, son of Leonardo Torres y Quevedo, created in 1920, the more refined "el Ajedrecista II" that used a phonograph to "speak" the words "check" and "checkmate" to the player. Instead of pieces that plugged into a board, it used magnets to move its pieces, as if miraculously directed by an invisible hand.

Chess continued to be used for testing the theoretical and actual capabilities of computers after World War II. In the late 1940s, Alan Turing in England and Claude Shannon in the United States designed theoretical computer programs centered on decision-making and strategy implementation, illustrated by chess. The early to mid-1950s saw limited chess programs played on early commercialized computers like the Ferranti Mark

I in England and purpose-built research computers like the Los Alamos-based Mathematical and Numerical Integrator and Computer (MANIAC). The chess program for MANIAC, for example, was only capable of playing an "anti-clerical" game of chess on a 6×6 board that excluded the diagonally moving bishops.

Computers were able to play a full game of chess without modification by the late 1950s. Although still playing at a simple skill level, the programs became more efficient and began utilizing computation-saving strategies that eliminated certain decisions with unfavorable outcomes, allowing the computer to concentrate on more productive moves. From this point on, the skill level of chess-playing programs grew greater as the number of possible decisions a computer could evaluate per second grew to the hundreds and thousands, outpacing human capabilities. Programmers looking to test the capabilities of their programs began competing against one another through computer-only chess tournaments that began at the 1970 Association for Computing Machinery (ACM) annual meeting. The culmination of these experiments was a famous 1997 chess match in which the IBM supercomputer "Deep Blue" defeated reigning chess champion Garry Kasparov.

Beyond Chess

Chess was not the only game that computer pioneers used to test theories of artificial intelligence. The game of Nim involved players taking turns at selecting a certain number of small objects from one of three heaps. By selecting a different number of objects each turn, players forced their opponent to take the last remaining object from the last pile. The game's inherent design, like chess, required planning and the ability to react to an unknown variable—the opponent's choice. The British computer company, Ferranti, used the game of Nim to demonstrate the capabilities of its "Nimrod" digital computer at the 1951 Festival of Britain's Exhibition of Science. The gigantic vacuum tube-run Nimrod, like many computers of the time, measured 12 feet wide, 5 feet tall, and 9 feet deep. Although the computer required oversight by an operator, Nimrod played Nim using a simple lighted board of circles to display the number of virtual objects left in each pile. The demonstration of this "electric brain" captivated the public. After the fair's conclusion, the Nim-playing computer was put on tour before being disassembled. Ferranti continued to manufacture computers for scientific purposes but never returned to making games.

Also in England, at the University of Cambridge, far from public display, was the Electronic Delay Storage Automatic Calculator (EDSAC). The gigantic EDSAC, built in 1947, carried out typical computer functions of the time such as calculating tables and discovering prime numbers. Its bank of three, 9-inch round cathode ray tube (CRT) displays, however, provided the means for graphic output that gave simple, but immediate, feedback. Alexander S. Douglass' "OXO" or "Noughts and Crosses" program of 1952 used the game tic-tac-toe to illustrate his PhD thesis that related to human/computer interaction. Douglas' program used a rotary phone dial where each digit represented one of the spaces on the nine square game grid. Since the game was displayed on a CRT monitor, OXO was the first digital game to use computer-generated imagery. Douglas' involvement with computers and games, like Ferranti, was limited: he did not return to games after proving his thesis and the program was essentially forgotten. The quest to demonstrate artificial intelligence was also taken up by others such as American researcher Arthur Samuel of IBM, who created a checkers game program in 1953, as well as scientists at the Atomic Energy Laboratory at Los Alamos who, in 1954, simulated the card game, blackjack.

Turing's Imitation Game and Artificial Intelligence

Demonstrations of artificial intelligence included other game-like systems. Alan Turing, in a 1950 paper, proposed one of the most famous game-based tests for indicating artificial intelligence, the Imitation Game.[*] The first version of the theoretical game involved two participants, a male and female, who sent messages to a judge whose role was to guess their sex based solely on their responses to various questions. The game was complicated in that one of the participants was to lie about their sex, while the other was instructed to help the judge. Turing's second version of the game replaced one of the two participants with a computer. Turing reasoned, if the judge misidentified the computer as a human at the same rate that the respondent's sex was misidentified in the first game, then the computer might be considered "intelligent." Although Turing's Imitation Game generated considerable debate as a valid measure of intelligence, it nonetheless served as inspiration for computer scientists and became an important concept in the field of artificial intelligence.

In the decades after Turing, researchers created computer programs that could actually provide responses to questions. Most were unsatisfactory, but Joseph Wiezenbaum's ELIZA program, created at the Massachusetts Institute of Technology (MIT) between 1964 and 1966, was one of the first programs capable of holding a general conversation. ELIZA consisted of a language analyzer and a script that the program could reference. The most famous script of ELIZA was "doctor," which mimicked a Rogerian psychotherapist as it scanned the content of typed responses and asked passive, but leading, questions based on certain key words. Any responses that

---

[*] Turing, A. 1950. Computing machinery and intelligence. *Mind: A Quarterly Review of Psychology and Philosophy*, 236, 433–460. doi: 10.1093/mind/LIX.236.433.

were outside of ELIZA's limited scripts returned a generic question, hoping that it would lead the conversation to subjects more easily addressed by the computer. ELIZA's design, thus, made the user responsible for driving the conversation and required less complexity in programming than other similar experiments.

The ELIZA program and others inspired by it spread to other institutions in the United States and became, as Weizenbaum described, a "national plaything."[*] Weizenbaum, however, was shocked by the unexpected responses to the program: some psychiatrists believed it could automate therapy; people using ELIZA anthropomorphized it and became highly emotional with the computer despite knowing it was not human; others claimed that ELIZA was the general solution to computers understanding human natural language. Although Wizenbaum never intended for ELIZA to have any value to psychotherapy, it initiated interest in later experiments such as PERRY, a program created in 1972 by Kenneth Colby of the Stanford Psychiatry Department, which simulated a paranoid schizophrenic. Taking the notion of computer-based conversations to their logical end, Vint Cef, a pioneer in Internet technologies then at Stanford University, later arranged a "conversation" between ELIZA and PERRY held over the ARPAnet (see below) in 1973. More entertaining than anything else, the conversation revealed the relative weaknesses of each program as ELIZA repeated the same questions over and over, while PERRY, despite simulating anger at the repetition, always responded to the questions and inevitably returned to the main topic.

Tennis for Two and the Beginning of Entertainment Applications for Computer Games

The New York-based Brookhaven National Laboratory sponsored an annual visitors' day, opening its doors for the public to learn about recent advancements in science. The goal, as part of a larger Cold War-era focus, was to inspire young people to pursue careers in science and strengthen American technological dominance. William Higinbotham, a nuclear physicist who had worked on the atomic bomb during World War II, felt that past displays at the event were unengaging and decided to create something more interactive. Higinbotham's solution was an electronic game called *Tennis for Two*, which debuted at the 1958 visitors' day (Figure 2.2). The game represented a significant departure from the previous games created within a scientific context as it did not solve specific scientific problems or demonstrate

---

[*] Weizenbaum, J. 2003. Computer power and human reason: From judgment to calculation. *The New Media Reader*, N. Wardrip-Fruin and N. Montfort (eds.), pp. 368–375, MIT Press.

FIGURE 2.2 **William Higinbotham's** *Tennis for Two* **at the 1958 visitors' day (second machine from the left). (Courtesy of Brookhaven National Laboratory.)**

advances in artificial intelligence: instead it entertained and inspired through its unique, competitive, two-player format.

The simple, but engaging, game featured a tennis match, seen from a sideway perspective with a vertical line representing the net and a horizontal line representing the playing field. *Tennis for Two* was based on an analog computer able to simulate the trajectory of ballistic missiles and other types of objects. The setup used a 9-inch oscilloscope for a display and featured two custom-built, single button, rotary-dial controllers. Players adjusted the trajectory of a ball through the knob controller and sent it to their opponent with a press of the controller's single button. Each time the player volleyed the ball, the computer's electromechanical switches created a loud clacking noise, which, although unintended, provided an element of sound feedback for the virtual actions. Players took turns batting the ball back and forth, trying to force their opponent to hit the ball at an awkward angle.

The game was inspired by and named after the sport of tennis, but it did not actually simulate a full game, much like earlier chess-playing games. In *Tennis for Two*, players would never miss if they pressed the controller's button while the ball was on their side of the court; effectively players existed everywhere simultaneously. This inherent violation of reality led to an experience that was only possible in an electronic format; a concept that was explored to a greater extent in the games created by computer hackers in the 1960s and 1970s. *Tennis for Two* reappeared the following year before the

EARLY EXPERIMENTS IN AUGMENTED AND VIRTUAL REALITY

Ivan Sutherland, in a famous 1965 essay entitled *The Ultimate Display,*[*] speculated on a number of display and control schemes for computers including non-vector, "filled" images made of colored areas and computers capable of being controlled by eye movement. Taking these concepts to their theoretical extreme, Sutherland described the ultimate display as a computer that could control matter in a room leading to "[a] chair displayed in such a room would be good enough to sit in. Handcuffs displayed in such a room would be confining, and a bullet displayed in such a room would be fatal."

Although the ultimate display was entirely theoretical as it literally created "virtual reality," Sutherland and others, nonetheless, pursued the simulation of spaces using the rapidly advancing computer technologies of the late 1960s and 1970s. Through a series of individual experiments and improvements, Sutherland, along with several student assistants, created the first head-mounted display (HMD) to show 3D objects in 1968. Using a wireframe vector display that drew straight lines from a series of coordinates, the HMD produced a simple 3D cube overlaid on the physical environment, which allowed users to see a computer-generated object in space. Sutherland's HMD coevolved with his theories of kinetic computer control introduced in *The Ultimate Display,* as the user adjusted the perspective of the image by turning his or her head. The HMD was attached to a mechanical arm suspended from the ceiling of the lab, which both tracked head movement and helped alleviate strain on the user's neck caused by the unit's considerable weight. Its intimidating appearance and the precarious nature of the setup earned the HMD the nickname, the "Sword of Damocles," an allusion to the ancient Roman parable involving a sword suspended by a single horsehair over a man's head. Sutherland's "Sword of Damocles" became a major source for later research into both virtual reality and augmented reality that would emerge in the consumer realm in the later 1980s and reemerge in the early 2010s (see Chapter 8).

[*] Sutherland, I. 1965. The ultimate display. In *Information processing 1965: Proceedings of IFIP Congress 65,* W. A. Kalenich (Ed.), Vol. 2, pp. 506–508, London: Macmillan and Co.

computer powering it, like many early game-playing computers, was disassembled for parts.

A modified version of *Tennis for Two* under the name *"Computer Tennis,"* however, was created and displayed at the 1961 visitors' day.

The Hacker Ethic and Games

"Hacking" is a form of experimentation and solution-finding centered on cycles of creating, deconstructing, and tinkering that naturally lent itself to expression on programming electronic computers. Although highly technical, hacking was an art among early programmers, as computers were made to perform in new, often unexpected ways. The desire to iterate and improve on programs led to a vibrant, collaborative hacking scene that originated in the later 1950s, after behemoth-sized electronic computers found their way into university labs and research institutes. Creating games was a logical extension of these ideas. Hackers explored the technical and artistic capacities of computers through hands-on experimentation in the ultimate "sandbox" environment. Although earlier engineers and computer programmers used games, such as chess, in the course of their research to test various theories and procedures, hacking was born of and motivated by a different mindset, one that extended into a system of values.

Steven Levy's 1984 book, *Hackers: Heroes of the Computer Revolution*, (Levy, 2010)[*] chronicled the contributions of individual hackers active between the 1950s through the early 1980s who helped build the knowledge base that led to the home computer revolution (see Chapter 6). Levy's understanding of the attitude of these individuals led him to formulate a set of hacker principles known as "the hacker ethic." The hacker ethic, as Levy outlines, is a set of beliefs and values governing people, their relationship to computers, and relationships to each other. Key concepts include the unrestricted sharing of information, a mistrust of authority, the imperative to demonstrate one's abilities, the prospect that computers are capable of creating art and beauty, and that computers can lead to the betterment of mankind.

Much of the hacker ethic was derived from the practices surrounding computers in the immediate post-World War II era. A person who wanted to run a program or compute a mathematical equation on a computer was unable to directly do so as early computers required specialized technicians to run them due to their complexity and relative fragility. As such access was strictly limited to a few. This hierarchical "priesthood" of technicians surrounding the operation of computers was intolerable for individuals driven to understand how computers worked and what their capabilities were. Many of the underlying attitudes of the hacker ethic also comingled with the counter-culture movement of the 1960s and 1970s in the United States. Hackers in and around the California computer scene and the developing Silicon Valley, were occasionally described as having long hair and strong antiwar views. Although not all hackers fully articulated or even subscribed to these ideas, this unspoken attitude was an underlying presence in many of the games produced in the 1960s and 1970s.

The Spread and Modification of *Spacewar!*

The MIT in Cambridge, Massachusetts became one of the earliest havens for computer hackers of the late 1950s and early 1960s. During late night hours, when computers were not reserved for "real" research applications, the unorthodox and curious computer science students of MIT engaged in their own,

---

[*] Levey, S. 2010. *Hackers: Heroes of the Computer Revolution*. Sebastopol, CA: O'Reilly Media, Inc.

more playful form of research. They built their own assembler and debugger programs, which allowed them to engage in more experimental endeavors such as programs that played music as well as various "display hacks." Display hacks took advantage of the visual output capabilities of newer computers through a CRT display. Hackers devised everything from noninteractive dynamic imagery to user-created mazes populated by computer-controlled mice. MIT student Steve "Slug" Russell, along with Martin Graetz and Wayne Witaenem, looking to create an impressive display hack, decided on a game.

Russell, Graetz, and Witaenem were members of a fictional research lab called the Hingham Institute, named after their Hingham Street apartment—a mocking reference to the grandiose air of buildings at Harvard University, MIT's Cambridge rival. The group's interest in space operas filled with battles between space ships, written by science fiction novelist, Edward Elmer "Doc" Smith, led them toward a space-based game and the formation of the tongue-in-cheek, Hingham Institute Study Group on Space Warfare. While searching for ways to implement the idea of outer space battles into a game, the group formulated the first articulated theory of video game design, the Hingham Institute Study Group on Space Warfare's Theory of Computer Toys, which read as follows:

1. It should demonstrate as many of the computer's resources as possible, and tax those resources to the limit
2. Within a consistent framework, it should be interesting, which means that every run should be different
3. It should make the viewer a participant[*]

Guided by these principles, Steve Russell began to program *Spacewar!* in late 1961. The game was written on the Programmed Data Processor-1 (PDP-1), a minicomputer with a CRT display manufactured by Digital Equipment Corporation (DEC). Russell's progress on the game was slow and prone to long periods of inactivity, as the code to manipulate the ships was difficult to create. Fellow MIT hacker Alan Kotok, through his connection to programmers at DEC, was able to acquire the code necessary to calculate the ship's motions. Significant progress was then made and the initial version of *Spacewar!* was completed in early 1962.

Spacewar! was a dueling game in which two players attempted to shoot the other's wedge-shaped or needle-like spaceship. Players could rotate each ship in a clockwise or counter-clockwise circle and initiate a thrust of the engines using toggle switches on the control panel of the PDP-1. The first version of *Spacewar!* took place in outer space with a few random dots representing stars and featured inertia: ships continued to glide through the screen space even when the engines were not firing (Figure 2.3).

---

[*] Graetz, J. M. 1981. The origin of spacewar. *Creative Computing*, 5, 61.

FIGURE 2.3 *Spacewar!* **played on a PDP-1 minicomputer. The trails of green and yellow left by the ships in the image are phosphorescent artifacts of the PDP-1's CRT scope. (Photo by Joi Ito. CC BY 2.0. Level adjustment from original.)**

The program spawned a flurry of activity among hackers at MIT, as each added to or modified both the game design and its visuals. Peter Samson replaced the random background stars with astronomically accurate star positions that slowly rotated; Dan Edwards added a large star in the center of the playfield, which exerted a constant gravitational tug on the ships and drew them toward destruction if they collided; Martin Graetz added a limited-use hyperspace feature that randomly placed the ship in a new position, one that had the possibility of landing the player in the path of the flying space torpedoes or next to the star—a mechanic accompanied by the spectacular visual effect of a "warp-induced photonic stress emission."[*] Further, the hyperspace mechanic became unstable overtime and had the potential to destroy a player's ship. Alan Kotok and Bob Saunders addressed the problem of skinned elbows developed from the excited gameplay on the machine's toggle switches by creating two controllers from requisitioned parts. The wooden, box-like controller consisted of two switches that regulated the rotation and amount of thrust of the ships, as well as a single button used to fire. The controller triggered the hyperspace jump through pushing the thrust lever forward and releasing. Later versions of the controller were "enhanced" with feedback in the form of an electric shock on player death.

---

[*] Graetz, J. M. 1981. The origin of spacewar. *Creative Computing*, 5, 66.

Spacewar! spread to universities, research labs, and commercial companies throughout the 1960s and early 1970s. Steve Russell himself ported *Spacewar!* from the PDP-1 to the PDP-6 in 1966 after arriving at Stanford University's newly founded Artificial Intelligence Laboratory, while other hackers created versions for other computers. Following the tenets of the hacker ethic, the ports of *Spacewar!* were further modified by later users with new mechanics that resulted in significantly different gameplay. A 1972 version of *Spacewar!* modified by Ralph Gorin and played at the Stanford Artificial Intelligence Laboratory (SAIL) featured five simultaneous players, space mines, partial damage, and two torpedo tubes. Just as at MIT, the hackers of SAIL created their own controllers. Other variants of the game included a "2 ½-D" version of *Spacewar!* in which the entire playfield was presented from a first person perspective—a setup that required the use of two CRT scopes, one for each player.

In addition to physically sharing the paper tape code for games like *Spacewar!*, DEC itself, the manufacturer of the PDP-1 computer, facilitated the distribution of games. *Spacewar!* for example, was used as a final testing tool for the PDP-1 and was left in the computer's memory during shipping. When the PDP-1 arrived at its destination, the game was initialized as a check to ensure that the delicate computer had arrived intact. In 1961, a group of computer users representing various technology companies and university research labs formed the Digital Equipment Computer Users Society (DECUS) with the goal of creating a community knowledge base for computer programming. Principally important was the program library established by the DECUS, which allowed its members free access to everything from utility programs to games. The DECUS library, through the 1970s, distributed demonstration packages that, in addition to the *ELIZA* program, included small collections of games such as chess, word games, tic-tac-toe, simulations of board games like *Monopoly* and *Battleship* and *Spacewar!*, among others.

Computer Networks and Games

The advent of minicomputers like the PDP-1 led to important developments in computer science that helped define the way computers are used and experienced today. In the early 1960s, minicomputers adopted a multiple user model of computing called *time-sharing* that replaced the *batch processing* model of the 1950s. Time-sharing systems used a single central computer that powered a number of user terminals. Programs were centrally run on the computer, while the terminals provided input as well as output via a visual display or through a printer. As opposed to the earlier batch processing, which consisted of a single user's program intermittently using computer resources, time-sharing allotted a portion of processing power to each terminal. With multiple users working simultaneously, the time-sharing model created continuous activity on the computer and minimized any down time. The demand for computers grew throughout the 1960s and 1970s, with time-sharing systems proliferating at universities, research institutions, and government agencies.

The ARPAnet

The Advanced Research Products Agency (ARPA), created in 1958, was a special organization within the United States Department of Defense tasked with developing new science and technology. Initially focused on missile and space technologies, ARPA became increasingly involved with developing computer technology in the 1960s and helped support the building of time-sharing networks at MIT, UC Berkley, and the Systems Development Corporation. Each site was connected to ARPA via an individual terminal in order to easily share research advancements and facilitate communication. Seeing the growth of these and other small, local time-sharing networks, Bob Taylor, then head of the Information Processing Techniques Office at ARPA, began a project in 1966 to link individual networks together. The project eventually became known as the ARPAnet.

The initial phase of the ARPAnet was completed in 1969 and linked four time-sharing networks at UC Santa Barbara, UCLA, Stratford Research Institute, and the University of Utah, allowing users to access multiple computer mainframes. By 1971, the ARPAnet linked more than 20 locations, connecting the east and west coasts of the United States directly as well as through a major link at the University of Illinois at Urbana-Champaign. Two years later the ARPAnet had grown to 30 locations including international connections to University College of London and the Royal Radar Establishment in Norway. By 1975, the number of locations grew 61 and continued to grow exponentially as the ARPAnet infrastructure became increasingly known as the Internet, a network of networks connecting computers. The software-based World Wide Web, however, did not develop until the late 1980s to early 1990s, with commercial forces powering much of its development.

Programmed Logic for Automated Teaching Operations and Multiplayer Games

One of the largest time-sharing systems was Programmed Logic for Automated Teaching Operations (PLATO), centered at the University of Illinois at Urbana-Champaign. From its 1961 conception, PLATO was intended as a low-cost way to deliver automated educational content to students from kindergarten to college, using computer terminals. PLATO evolved rapidly from the late 1960s to early 1970s. Its TUTOR programming language allowed instructors to easily formulate lessons with interactive features. A new generation of terminals for the 1972 PLATO IV system featured highly responsive, touch screen plasma panel displays capable of producing sound and high quality visuals in monochrome orange. Email, instant message, chat rooms, and a host of other virtual communication tools were developed for PLATO, creating the first true online community and a model of things to come with the World Wide Web.

The open environment associated with PLATO encouraged experimentation leading some instructors to develop early educational games. Paul Tenczar, who wrote the TUTOR programming language for PLATO, created two simple programs to teach concepts of computer programming. In them, animated figures were instructed to pick up objects on the screen. Bonnie Seiler's elementary mathematics game *How the West Was One + Three x Four* (1971) was particularly popular and resulted in continued development for other computer platforms through the 1990s. Instructors, however, were not the only content creators on the PLATO system, as students from a range of ages used the responsiveness of the system and high-resolution displays to create animations as well as their own games.

The PLATO network's inherent connectivity between users led to a number of games designed specifically for multiple players. One of the first multiplayer games on PLATO was a version of *Spacewar!* written in the late 1960s. Another was a version of chess. Although *Spacewar!* and chess were played between two players, later games in the 1970s incorporated a larger number of players as amateur programmers began to explore the system's capabilities. John Daleske's 1973 *Empire* grew from a project for an education class while he was attending Iowa State University. The game, unlike others on the PLATO system, allowed for eight players. Each represented one of the races from the television series, *Star Trek,* in a strategic game involving the management of a planet's economy and population, as well as directing space ships to conduct trade and diplomacy. Daleske, looking to add more action, redesigned *Empire* later in 1973 to exclusively focus on *Spacewar!*-like battles across a larger multiscreen game space. Players used a variety of keyboard commands, independent of each other, to adjust the ship's heading and direction of fire. Daleske continued to modify the game through 1981. He eventually combined the strategic elements of the first game with the space combat of the second, allowing a wide range of roles for up to 50 players, rivaling the complexity of later commercialized online games. Development of more complex versions of *Empire* continued. Each new version added and refined features based on Daleske's vision as well as suggestions from programmers and players, making it one of the earliest community-driven multiplayer games.

The code and concept of *Empire* spawned a number of network-based games developed by other individuals. Silas Warner was a well-respected and prolific PLATO programmer at Indiana University responsible for the creation of a number of games on PLATO. One of his early projects was the 1973 strategy game *Conquest,* developed from the original strategic version of *Empire*. Other *Empire*-based programs included various "Trek" titled games of the 1980s that retained *Empire*'s original Star Trek alien races. Perhaps, the best known descendent of the "Trek" titled *Empire* games was *Netrek*, a game designed in the late 1980s and popular on university campuses through the early 1990s.

Adapting Dungeons & Dragons *to PLATO*

PLATO also featured a number of games inspired by the tabletop roleplaying game, *Dungeons & Dragons*. Heavily based on themes from J.R.R. Tolkien's *Lord of the Rings* book trilogy and game systems from tabletop war gaming, *Dungeons & Dragons* was created in 1974 by Gary Gygax of Wisconsin and Dave Arneson of Minnesota. Unlike other games both physical and digital, play of *Dungeons & Dragons* began with the creation of a character. Players chose from a list of classes/professions, such as fighter, wizard, or thief, and determined the character's physical and mental attributes by rolling dice (Figure 2.4). The setup of play was unique relative to other games, as a group of players worked together to complete episodic adventures that continued from session to session. Characters created by the players grew and changed overtime, becoming stronger and gaining new abilities. A crucial component of *Dungeons & Dragons* was the player who served as the Dungeon Master, a storyteller/director who provided information to the other players about the game world and its characters. Players interacted with the fantasy world in a variety of ways, many of which required rolling dice to simulate outcomes beyond player control.

The PLATO computer network was particularly well-suited for the adaption of games like *Dungeons & Dragons*. The mathematical systems of probability and random number generation were easily ported to computers while the social gameplay involving a group of players could rely on PLATO's well-developed communication capabilities and vibrant

FIGURE 2.4 Typical types of dice used to generate ability scores and simulate event outcomes in *Dungeons & Dragons*.

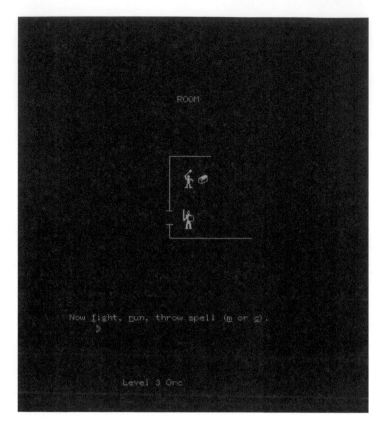

FIGURE 2.5   Encounter in *pedit5/The Dungeon*. (Courtesy of Paul Resch and Cyber1.org.)

community. One of the first PLATO games inspired by *Dungeons & Dragons* was a single player game called *pedit5*, created in 1975 by Rusty Rutherford of the University of Illinois at Urbana-Champaign (Figure 2.5). The gameplay of *pedit5* involved navigating a maze-like dungeon space of 40–50 rooms, with randomly generated locations that housed monsters and treasure. The game's ultimate goal was to accumulate 20,000 experience points, which, like *Dungeons & Dragons*, was gained through combat with monsters and collecting treasure.

Not all *Dungeons & Dragons* systems were fully replicated in *pedit5*, but it did use the game's core elements such as experience points and monster levels. Rather than distinct classes, as in *Dungeons & Dragons*, players played a character that combined the attributes of the warrior, mage, and cleric. *Pedit5* was widely played on the PLATO system, but it was unreliable because system administrators constantly deleted it to free memory resources for more "academic" applications, forcing Rutherford to rewrite the program each time.

---

* "Pedit5" was the original file name for the program and intentionally kept nondescript to prevent it from being deleted. It was also known as *The Dungeon*.

Gary Wisenhunt and Ray Wood of Southern Illinois University, tired of the erratic availability of *pedit5*, decided to write their own dungeon-based game called, *The Game of Dungeons*, better known as *dnd*.* The likelihood of *dnd* being deleted was slim, as Wisenhunt and Wood were PLATO system administrators at SIU. Relative to *pedit5*, *dnd* was more expansive. Players could venture into multiple dungeon levels, each featuring monsters of increasing difficulty. As players progressed, they ultimately encountered the "boss" character in the form of a dragon, one of the first instances of this staple element in digital games. Boss characters are particularly strong adversaries with different behaviors requiring the player to abruptly change tactics. This punctuation in gameplay was a signal in *dnd* to indicate the player was close to completing the game.

As with *Empire*, the player community was involved in the development of *dnd*. Features and improvements to the game were constantly considered and implemented. Part of the game's appeal, in addition to its quirky humor, was the inclusion of a visual maze editor, a rare feature for games of the time. It allowed both the designers and the members of the PLATO community to quickly and easily create their own dungeons. Wisenhunt and Wood eventually handed off further development of *dnd* to the brothers Dirk and Flint Pellett, who had previously created a number of add-ons and other features to the game. Another *pedit5*-inspired game was *Orthanc*, created in 1975 by Paul Resch, Larry Kemp, and Eric

DESIGNING FOR EFFICIENCY

PLATO terminals were connected through a phone line-based network capable of transmitting 1200 bits per second out and 300 bits per second in. Although PLATO was significantly faster than other network connections of the time and the terminals themselves stored text data, games needed to minimize the amount of data transmitted during gameplay to ensure a playable speed. *Pedit5* and *Oubliette*, for example, sent the player only the minimum amount of information necessary to play: i.e. the lines making the walls of the dungeon maze and the title of the space. Information about player health, player stats, or monsters was only transmitted and displayed when absolutely necessary. Thus, the screen was largely empty, but gameplay remained responsive. The designers of *Orthanc*, however, grew tired of constantly needing to request information in *pedit5* and designed the game's interface to constantly display all relevant information. To keep the gameplay fast, the entire screen was drawn once and then kept static. The game then updated individual pieces of the screen as needed, with the maze receiving the most frequent refreshes.

---

* Not to be confused with the very similar mainframe game, *DND* written in the BASIC programming language by Daniel Lawrence of Purdue University in the late 1970s, nor the DOS game, *DND*, developed by Bill Knight of R O Software in 1984.

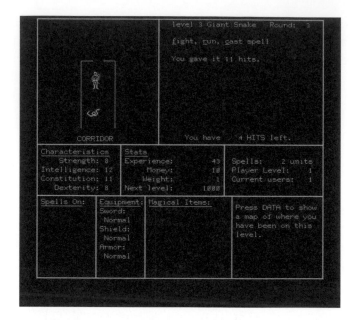

FIGURE 2.6 **Traveling through the dungeon in *Orthanc*. The reference to the map in the lower right corner of the screen was added to the game much later during its continuous development. (Courtesy of Paul Resch and Cyber1.org.)**

Hagstrom of the University of Illinois at Urbana-Champaign (Figure 2.6). *Orthanc* included elements intended for *pedit5* but never implemented, such as multiple level dungeons as well as certain improvements like the ability to choose a different randomized starting character if the first was undesirable.

Other dungeon exploration games on PLATO granted players the ability to form a party and play as a group. The 1975 game *Moria*,* by Kevet Duncombe and Jim Battin of the University of Illinois at Urbana-Champaign, was distinctive as one of the first multiplayer games with a *persistent game world*, where events and actions continued to take place even when the player was not playing. *Moria* also moved away from the top-down mazes of earlier dungeon-based games and replaced them with line drawings of rooms in a first person perspective. Another major distinction was the game's systems. According to *Moria*'s authors, the game was created not from *Dungeons & Dragons*, but from talking about design problems encountered in the formation of *dnd* with its creators. This allowed a greater degree of freedom in design, as the game lacked many *Dungeons & Dragons*-inspired mechanics, such as experience points and character levels to measure growth, leading to more innovative mechanics such as character progression through practicing certain skill-related actions.

---

* Not to be confused with the commercial release of the 1988 game *Moria*, a roguelike dungeon game (see Chapter 6).

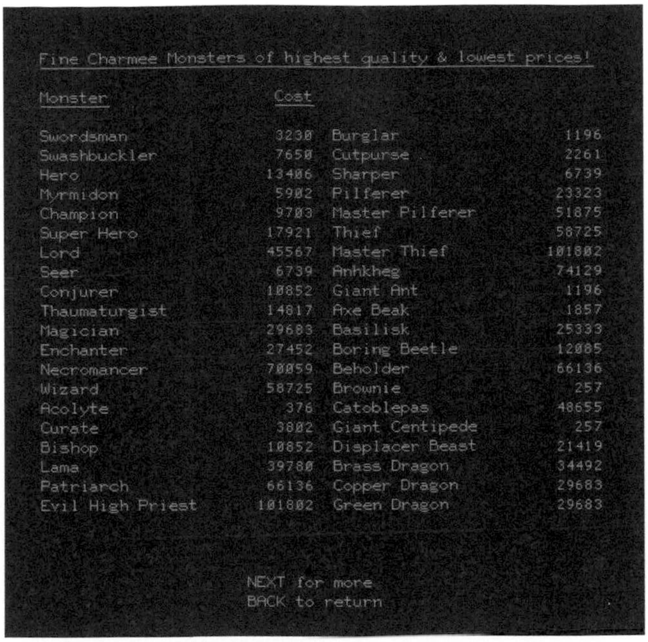

FIGURE 2.7   Selections from the Monster Store in *Oubliette*. (Courtesy of Jim Schwaiger and Cyber1.org.)

Oubliette (1977) was one of the most developed and popular roleplaying games on the PLATO system. The game was originally designed by Jim Schwaiger along with John Gaby and Bancherd DeLong out of a desire to automate the tedious dice rolling associated with *Dungeons & Dragons*. The scope of *Oubliette* was massive. Players were able to choose form 15 character races and 15 classes depending on ability scores. Prior to venturing into the game's dungeon, players roamed the streets of a large castle and shopped in multiple stores, outfitting their characters with everything from simple items to monster companions (Figure 2.7). Players could join various profession-based guilds, gamble, deposit money in banks, and socialize with other players in a chat room-like tavern. *Oubliette* was also extremely difficult for single players as the game was designed for parties of adventurers. The dungeon was full of traps and secret doors. Monsters were frequently encountered in large numbers (Figure 2.8) and death was permanent unless another player found and retrieved one's body from the dungeon.

The combination of multiplayer gameplay, robust communication capabilities, a developed game economy, character generation choices, and spell systems of *Oubliette* and the later attempt to outdo *Oubliette*, *Avatar* (1979), were not surpassed in commercialized computer games until the 1990s and 2000s when Internet infrastructure allowed visually complex massive multiplayer online roleplaying games. *Moria, Oubliette*, and *Avatar* established many of the design, gameplay, and keyboard command conventions seen in

FIGURE 2.8 Encounter with seven mediums in *Oubliette*. (Courtesy of Jim Schwaiger and Cyber1.org.)

EARLY MONETARY TRANSACTIONS

Games on PLATO occupied resources intended for educational and research purposes. This created some misgiving, since the microbiology department of the University of Illinois at Urbana-Champaign sponsored the space for *Oubliette*. *Oubliette* creator Jim Schwaiger, thus devised one of the first monetization strategies for multiplayer online games in which he "paid" the microbiology department for the game space using funds collected by the players. Players were free to play the game, but if they desired to keep their characters through the regular system purges, they would need to pay a fee of $3 per year. This unprecedented notion was met with criticism by the player base, however, those who had invested a great amount of time into their characters feared losing their progress and paid the fee. Other monetary exchanges in *Oubliette* centered on an underground economy in which players sold high-level characters and rare in-game magic items for real money in amounts in excess of $100. Although this phenomenon is typically associated with more recent massively multiplayer online role-playing games (MMORPGs), games like *Oubliette* provided one of the earliest examples of these transactions.

later commercialized computer roleplaying games. In particular, games like *Wizardry: Proving Grounds of the Mad Overlord* (Sir-tech, 1981) drew significantly from *Oubliette* and became influential in their own right by shaping the development of computer roleplaying games in the 1980s (see Chapter 6).

Early 3D and Networked Games

The early 1960s saw the first experiments that involved 3D computer graphics to illustrate scientific work. One of the first examples was a 1963 computer-generated animation by Edward Zajac of Bell Laboratories showing the movement of a rectangular satellite in space around a wireframe sphere. Each minute of animation took the computer 3–8 minutes to compute, so playback was not done on the computer but was printed to film, frame by frame. Computers were able to compute and animate wireframe images in real time and present them on CRT displays by the early 1970s.

Hackers not only jumped at the opportunity to explore the capabilities of 3D imagery through games, but also some did so in conjunction with emerging computer networks. The 1973 game, *Maze War*, or simply *Maze*, developed from a project in which Steve Colley, a high school intern at the NASA Ames Research Center, desired to create a program to utilize hidden line removal on a rotating wireframe 3D cube. Colley, assisted by fellow high school intern, Howard Palmer, elaborated on the original idea by creating a maze that was explored from a first person perspective. Players moved through the game space one square at a time, making right angle turns, looking for the exit. Another high school intern, Greg Thompson, helped add more action to the game by creating a multiplayer version that linked two Imlac PDS-1 computers, with each player represented by a large eyeball avatar. Players had the ability to shoot each other in a manner that predated the "Deathmatch" multiplayer modes of first person shooters in the 1990s (see Chapter 8).

Maze War accompanied Greg Thompson to college at MIT in 1974. There, Thompson and Dave Liebling, a member of MIT's Dynamic Modeling Group, co-created a version of the game that was playable over the ARPAnet and allowed more simultaneous players. Although the initial ARPAnet-based gameplay suffered from high latency, the problem was eventually remedied.

The PLATO system also featured games that used wireframe 3D images with multiplayer capabilities. Most important was Jim Bowery's 1974 *Spasim* (pronounced "space sim"), a game in which 32 players piloted space ships from a first person perspective and fought in 3D space. *Spasim*'s unique 3D perspective was based on an earlier program co-written by computer image pioneer, Ron Resch, that Bowery obtained while studying at the University of Iowa. Using Resch's program as a basis, Bowery crafted *Spasim* to be a 3D version of *Empire*. Players maneuvered through space using both polar and Cartesian coordinate systems, a feature that Bowery used to justify the game's presence on the network because of its educational nature. Later in 1974, Bowery deleted the initial competition-focused version of *Spasim* and replaced it with a more cooperative game that discouraged warfare and instead, focused on the strategic management of resources in order to stabilize a planet. Like *Spacewar!* and other early computer games of the 1960s and 1970s, Bowery distributed the code for *Spasim* to other hackers who modified it to create their own games, resulting in a number of other 3D games on PLATO and beyond. Silas Warner modified *Spasim* into the 3D airplane simulator, *Airace*, which, in turn, led to the 3D combat-oriented *Airfight* of 1974 by Brand Fortner. *Spasim*'s code was also the basis for the 1975 first person tank game, *Panzer,* by John Daleske and Derek Ward.

Into the Commercial Realm

To many hackers of the 1960s and 1970s, games like *Spacewar!* were a means to an end, an interactive learning project that challenged their abilities and furthered their knowledge about computers. A number of these programmers, however, did pursue games as a profession. Silas Warner, was part of the first wave of programmers to create commercialized games for early home computers. His most noted works were those he designed and created under Muse Software: *Castle Wolfenstein* (1981) and *Beyond Castle Wolfenstein* (1983). Warner executed the programming for the Amiga version of the submarine simulation game, *Silent Service* (1986, MicroProse) as well as other contributions to console games of the early 1990s. Dave Liebling helped create the text-based interactive fiction game *Zork* while still in school, which eventually became a flagship commercial franchise of Infocom, a company he helped found (see Chapter 6). *Orthanc* programmer Paul Resch briefly worked for Atari's coin-op and home computer divisions just prior to the North American video game industry crash (see Chapter 5), while *Oubliette* creators Jim Schwaiger and John Gaby eventually entered the mobile game market (see Chapter 9). As discussed in Chapters 3 and 6, some of the earliest video arcade and home computer games of the 1970s were either inspired by or directly adapted from these experiments. Thus, the collective work of early computer hackers was crucial in establishing the commercial digital game industry.

Chapter 3

Early Commercialized Digital Games (1971–1977)

New Technology in the Consumer Market

The 1970s was a decade of technological revolution in the consumer sector that reshaped the nature of entertainment and productivity. Microprocessors and microcontrollers appeared in calculators, microwave ovens, automobiles, and more enabling new degrees of speed and automation. Computer-manipulated and computer-generated imagery first appeared in films such as *Willy Wonka and the Chocolate Factory* (1971), *Westworld* (1973), and *Star Wars* (1977). Compact cassette tapes for recording audio gained significant traction leading to Sony's 1979 Walkman, which launched the beginning of portable and individualized music listening. The 1970s saw the first "microcomputers," which brought computers into homes and launched a wave of hobbyist programmers (see Chapter 6). Adding to this context were the first all-electronic video games in arcades and the home.

Approaches to Commercialized Digital Games

The first commercialized digital games, in general, followed one of two approaches to game design. The first adapted familiar mechanical and electromechanical games to an electronic medium. This strategy provided these products the cache of the "new" while limiting conceptual barriers about electronic games for consumers. Game developers, however, were not afraid to work beyond the edges of accepted conventions to create new types of games and experiences. The tension between developing modes of play unique to the electronic format verses updating the tried and true was significant for a number of game developers at the time; however, the most successful games were able to incorporate both approaches by providing the familiar in a novel way.

Monetizing *Spacewar!*

The code for *Spacewar!*, as discussed in Chapter 2, spread through universities and research labs, often leading to tweaks and modifications by various hackers. Although, the programmers responsible for *Spacewar!* initially considered copywriting and selling their creation, the relative lack of computers able to run the game in the early 1960s made this idea impractical. As a result, *Spacewar!* inhabited a separate and exclusive context for nearly 10 years. The game's popularity, however, prompted others to consider bringing *Spacewar!* to the larger public and monetizing it as an arcade game.

In 1971 two Stanford University graduates, Bill Pitts and Hugh Tuck, modified code from *Spacewar!* to play on a smaller PDP-11 computer that was specially designed for coin-operation and housed in a fiberglass cabinet. Their creation, *Galaxy Game*, allowed two players to duel in a one round match for a dime or spend a quarter for a "best two out of three" bout. As the winner of each duel was awarded another play at the game, *Galaxy Game* promoted continuous competition and the potential to receive a continuous flow of coins. While *Galaxy Game* marked the first instance of commercialized digital games, it still remained part of a context separate from the general public as the single unit was placed in Stanford University's student union. Additionally, the cost to manufacture the single unit effectively eliminated the possibility of mass production.

The debut of more widespread digital games occurred with the efforts of two electrical engineers, Nolan Bushnell and Ted Dabney. While working for the electronics company Ampex, and later the coin machine manufacturer Nutting Associates, Bushnell and Dabney informally founded a digital game company called Syzygy. Bushnell, a visionary inspired by *Spacewar!*, attempted to bring the excitement of the dueling game to the public with *Computer Space* (1971, Syzygy Co.) (Figure 3.1). *Computer Space* used a single circuit board designed solely to run the game and displayed it in an off-the-shelf television set. Although it was not as visually detailed as the original *Spacewar!* or *Galaxy Game*, *Computer Space* had an advantage in that it was relatively inexpensive to mass produce.

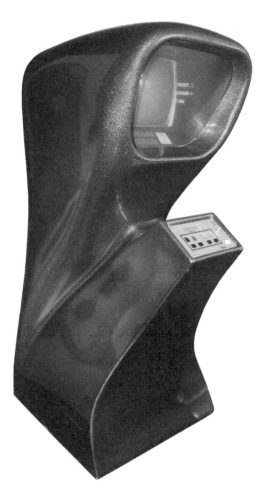

FIGURE 3.1 *Computer Space*. **(1971, Syzygy Co.) (Courtesy of Arcadia, McLean, IL, www.vintagevideogames.com)**

The design of the gameplay in *Computer Space* combined the basic shooting mechanics and inertia of *Spacewar!* with conventions seen in electrome-chanical arcade games. The player inserted a coin and received a time limit of 2.5 minutes to score as many points as possible against two computer-controlled flying saucers. Each successful hit on either the flying saucers or the player's ship resulted in a point for the opposing side; competitive gameplay inherited from *Spacewar!* A 1973 edition of the game unaffiliated with Bushnell and Dabney included controls for two players: one the space ship, the other the UFO.

Many of the design features of *Computer Space* can be linked to Bushnell's past as he was experienced in the maintenance of carnival games and had served as a barker. Carnival barking is a time-honored part of fairs in which a person attracted game players through instigation tactics ranging from peaking one's curiosity to hurling insults. In *Computer Space*, Bushnell effectively automated the role of the barker by creating the first instance of an *attract mode* as flying saucers moved across the screen in formation when the machine was not in use, a method to gain attention and entice play. *Computer Space* also employed sound. The destruction of the ships triggered an explosive sound effect, a feature absent in the original *Spacewar!* This, along with a brightly colored, futuristic cabinet design, ensured that the game would not go unnoticed when placed in public spaces.

Computer Space had all the potential for an exciting and successful game, but interest from the public was lukewarm possibly due to a lack of familiarity with the game concepts and controls. In comparison, part of the success of Harry Williams' *1939 World Series* was due to the player's familiarity with the rules of baseball. *Computer Space* used concepts of inertia and simulated gravity that, while fun for computer scientists with a passion for science fiction, would have been less captivating for members of the general public at the time. A set of instructions explaining these concepts and how to work the controls accompanied the game but their length and relative complexity likely dulled the game's otherwise impressive presentation. Further, Nutting Associates was cautious about the new venture and produced a limited run of the machines, reducing the game's exposure to potential customers.

Computer Space, nonetheless, encouraged Bushnell and Dabney to continue developing digital arcade games. Bushnell particularly was convinced of digital games' superiority over electromechanical games as they had less moving parts to service and would thus require less maintenance, a feature pitched to location owners more than players. Looking to formally incorporate their business, the two discovered that another company already had trademarked the name "Syzygy." Instead they incorporated under the name "Atari," a term analogous to the word "check" in the Japanese board game of *Go*, a favorite pastime of Bushnell and Dabney's. Thus Atari Incorporated

LATER COMMERCIALIZED VARIANTS OF *SPACEWAR!*

Dueling in the void of space, introduced by *Spacewar!*, continued as a basis for coin-op, home console, and computer games. In 1978, Atari created the coin-op game *Orbit*, which featured an array of selectable game variations ranging from changes to the game speed to the use of space stations. Larry Rosenthal recreated *Spacewar!* using vector beams in *Space Wars* (1978, Cinematronics). *Spacewar!* was released on the Atari VCS as *Space War* (1978, Atari) complete with 17 game variations. Later elements of the game appeared on the PC space strategy game, *Star Control* (1990, Toys for Bob Inc.) and its adventure role-playing sequel, *Star Control 2: The Ur-Quan Masters* (1992, Toys for Bob Inc.). Both games featured segments of gameplay that recalled *Spacewar!*-style duels complete with a gravity-inducing planet. One of the alien races even utilized the hyperspace feature introduced in the original game.

was officially founded on June 27th 1972 where it began work on the creation of a digital game distinctly different from *Computer Space*.

The Magnavox Odyssey and Divided Game Space

From the 1950s to the 1980s Ralph Baer worked as an engineer at American defense contractor Sanders Associates. In 1966 Baer and a handful of engineers began to work on an unofficial side project that used a television screen to display interactive squares of light. Their work quickly directed them to the creation of a novel consumer product that would allow people to play games on their home television sets. After producing several prototype units, Baer revealed the work to his superiors who supported further development of the project. The official backing from Sanders Associates allowed the capabilities and scope of the project to rapidly grow. Prototype units sported color graphics, utilized random number generation, included a light gun and golf putter accessory, projected different shapes on the screen, and incorporated a ball-like projectile that could change velocity. Despite these impressive capabilities, all of the prototypes relied on illustrated, semi-transparent, plastic overlays placed on the television screen which marked the location of scoring areas and set the general context of gameplay. Having the machine produce the detailed graphics would have made it too expensive for the consumer market. The experiments culminated in 1968 with a prototype TV game unit that Baer and his engineers dubbed the "Brown Box," named for the unit's wood-grained, vinyl tape exterior. Magnavox eventually purchased the design, gave the unit a cosmetic makeover and released it to the public as the Odyssey in 1972 (Figure 3.2).

The Odyssey was the initial entry in what became known as the first generation of home videogames. The unit used a home television set to display two squares of light and a projectile on the screen. The two squares moved on the x and y axis, using knobs on the game controller. A third knob labeled "english," a term borrowed from pool and billiards to indicate side-spin, allowed the projectile, when used, to curve eccentrically. The Odyssey omitted many features of Baer's prototypes, most notably color graphics, in order to further reduce manufacturing costs. The result was a unit capable of only a few simple interactions: a player's square could be removed from the screen by colliding with the opponent's square and a projectile could be shot or "bounced" between the squares. The optional rifle accessory could also remove a square from the screen. These basic capabilities, along with constant use of the "reset" button, formed the core game mechanics of the Odyssey's games.

The games offered by the Odyssey represented a diverse cross-section of genres including sports, analytical/educational, and gambling games. With the exception of shooting gallery games, none of the Odyssey's offerings

FIGURE 3.2   The consumer model of the Magnavox Odyssey. (Photo Evan Amos.)

had any connection to the electromechanical arcade games of the day. Each game was played using one or more "game cards." Unlike later cartridge-based systems, such as the Atari VCS and Nintendo Entertainment System, the Odyssey's game cards contained no data: instead, they modified the logic of the unit itself. Certain games such as *Football* (1972, Magnavox) (Figure 3.3) required players to switch between multiple game cards. The overlays, a feature inherited from Baer's prototypes, made up for limited graphics capabilities and provided crucial information for gameplay. Thus, changing the overlay rather than the game card could, and often did, create a new game.

The Odyssey's diverse game catalog, however, did not always pair well with the unit's capabilities leading to a number of awkward experiences. Several games divided the game space between the television overlay, a game board, playing cards, and verbal cues between players. *Football*, for example, required a game board, dice, and decks of cards printed with different foot-ball plays (Figure 3.3). Players on offense and defense chose their play from the deck of cards, used the Odyssey to determine if the play succeeded or failed in a tag-like game on the television screen, then rolled the dice and consulted a chart to determine the success or failure in yards. The over-all game was strikingly similar in design to popular football-themed board games of the 1960s and 1970s.

Many of the Odyssey's games incorporated role-playing elements through "in character" words or phrases, spoken at key points in game-play. The rifle game, *Shootout* (1972, Magnavox), pitted the player with the electronic rifle accessory (the sheriff) against another player controlling the movement of the white square target (a member of the Dalton Gang). Using an overlay that evoked buildings in the American Old West, the Dalton Gang player, from behind cover, was to pop the light square up and shout, "You'll never get me, Sheriff!" before being allowed to hide again (Figure 3.4). *Football* instructed the player on offense to verbally call out signals and yell, "Hike!" before the play was allowed to start; *Haunted House* (1972, Magnavox), meanwhile, culminated when one player shouted "Boo!" at the other player while simultaneously revealing their hidden "ghost" on the

FIGURE 3.3 The overlay and game board for *Football* **(1972, Magnavox). The game required two game cards to play; one for passing plays, the other for running plays.**

screen. These role-paying elements, odd by contemporary video gaming standards, were crucial for creating structure as the Odyssey and its television overlays could not actually enforce most game rules. Additionally, since players were free to break the rules of the games, unlike contemporary digital games, many included detailed instructions for how to settle penalties or other violations.

The reach of the Odyssey was limited largely due to a mishandling of marketing, which suggested that the unit would only work with a Magnavox television set. Thus, the unit did not see its greatest commercial potential. Regardless, the Odyssey introduced a crucial game concept that led to a more elegant and unified approach to digital game design. *Table Tennis* (1972, Magnavox), one of Ralph Baer's original prototype

FIGURE 3.4 Overlays for *Shootout* **(1972, Magnavox) and** *Haunted House* **(1972, Magnavox).**

games, was the only game for the Odyssey that did not explicitly require an overlay and could be played entirely on the television screen without extra game boards or cards. The two-player ping-pong game presented the game space from above, as each player volleyed a small square of light over a centerline. *Table Tennis* utilized an interesting gameplay feature whereby a player could control the path of the ball using the Odyssey's "english" control knob after hitting it. As such, the game did not truly simulate physics.

Simple as it was, *Table Tennis*, like William Higinbotham's unrelated *Tennis for Two*, presented gameplay that could only occur electronically and showcased the potential of the new medium. This game, among others, was publically demonstrated in several American cities as part of a promotional campaign for Magnavox in May of 1972. Nolan Bushnell, while working for Nutting Associates, played the Odyssey at an exhibition in Burlingame, CA near San Francisco. In November of 1972, Atari began producing *Pong*, a table tennis game that strongly resembled Baer's concepts. This eventually led to a 1974 lawsuit and a 1976 out-of-court settlement over patent infringement.

Pong and Variations on Ball and Paddle Game Design

Atari's first game, *Pong* (1972), was an unexpected success as it was initially intended as a project to help familiarize Atari engineer, Al Alcorn, with the process used to create digital games. *Pong* was a digital abstraction of table tennis that focused on playing the trajectory of a volleying ball between two players' paddles (Figure 3.5). *Pong* delivered intuitive and engaging gameplay through simple rotary dial controls, making it ideal for coin operation in public spaces. Its design featured paddles that were very short relative to the goal area, leading to exciting play through constant scoring. Alcorn added variability to the game by dividing each paddle into eight segments; the further away the ball made contact from the paddle's center, the more extreme the angle of return. The speed of the ball also increased on the fourth and twelfth volleys, preventing any one match from lasting too long and creating an increasingly difficult, but fun-filled experience. The game's successful test run at a local tavern convinced Atari to manufacture the game itself, rather than sell it to an established game company, as was the case with *Computer Space*. *Pong* was such a phenomenal, nearly instantaneous hit that it required Atari to expand its facilities and workforce to meet the demand by eager location owners.

The operation and work culture of Atari's first years resembled, at times, a fly-by-night operation rather than a company at the cutting edge of digital game design. The workforce, primarily high school and college-aged people, was not the shirt and tie-wearing crew found in other technology companies

FIGURE 3.5 *Pong* **(Atari, 1972). (Courtesy of Jordan Stolz.)**

such as IBM. Theft of electronics and smoking marijuana on the job were common occurrences, in addition to regular parties sponsored by the management as a reward for meeting quotas. Bushnell, ever the carnival barker and charismatic salesman, was notorious for telling half-truths in order to put on a good show and expand the company. For example, many distributers demanded Atari's exclusivity, ensuring that rival distributers would not have access to Atari arcade games. Looking to make as many as possible, Bushnell orchestrated the creation of a bogus competitor to Atari named Kee Games in 1973. Kee Games, as a secret subsidiary, sold Atari arcade games under new titles, effectively overriding exclusivity agreements and doubling potential orders for machines.

Despite questionable business practices at times, Atari's effect on the early video arcade industry cannot be overstated, as *Pong* inspired several electromechanical game companies around the world to venture into the creation of digital games. Japanese and American companies such as Taito, Sega, Williams Electronics, Midway, and Chicago Coin created their first digital games in 1973, many based on *Pong*. To keep ahead of competition, Atari rapidly iterated on the *Pong* concept, developing first *Pong Doubles*

(1973), a two-on-two *Pong* match for four-players, then *Quadrapong* (1974), which introduced an elimination format that penalized a "life" from the player who missing the ball. *Breakout* (1976), meanwhile, adapted the competitive multiplayer gameplay of *Pong* to a single player game that involved clearing rows of blocks by using a paddle and ricocheting ball. Like most games of the early to mid-1970s, the graphics of *Breakout* were black and white. However, many cabinets added color to the game though using overlays not unlike those of the Magnavox Odyssey since the game space largely remained static during play. *Breakout* was also notable for the individuals involved in its creation as 19-year old Atari employee, Steve Jobs, called on his friend Steve Wozniak to complete the electrical design of the *Breakout* game board. Wozniak's design showed a mastery of technical sophistication beyond what most thought was possible. Nonetheless, unbeknownst to Wozniak, Jobs took the credit when he presented the finished product to Atari. Later that year, Jobs and Wozniak went on to found Apple Computers, which was instrumental in establishing the home computer market (see Chapter 6). *Pong* also served as the basis for a variety of other sport games such as *Rebound* (1974, Atari), a volleyball game played from the side with two paddles on the ground, bouncing a ball up and over a net. All used the same basic ball and paddle mechanic of *Pong*; the point of contact on the paddle determined the angle of return and the ball increased speed after several hits.

While other companies created clones or other iterations of *Pong*, Atari was entangled in a legal battle with Magnavox. Magnavox alleged that Bushnell copied the concept of TV ping-pong from the Odyssey's *Table Tennis* game based on the fact that Bushnell played it at the 1972 trade show in California. That fact, coupled with Ralph Baer's meticulous notes and patents filed during the development of the Brown Box, made for a prolonged legal fight ending in 1976 with an out-of-court settlement. In it, Atari became Magnavox's sole licensee in the production of video ping pong games. This allowed Atari the legal basis to proceed, unimpeded, in the creation of *Pong* games. With Magnavox in pursuit of legal action against the steady stream of worldwide *Pong* clones, Atari's position in the digital game industry was strengthened even further.

Late Ball and Paddle Games

Although ball and paddle games saw their popularity significantly diminish by the late 1970s, the basic game mechanics continued to find success in *Gee Bee* (1978, Namco) and *Warlords* (1980, Atari). *Gee Bee* by Tōru Iwatani, was game manufacturer Namco's first internally developed digital game. It combined the brick-breaking gameplay of *Breakout* with a pinball playfield as players used a double-decker set of paddles to accumulate points and bonuses earned by hitting various targets represented in full color graphics.

SPACES OF PLAY: CONVENTIONAL AND UNCONVENTIONAL

Much like their mechanical and electromechanical forbearers, video arcade games were commonly placed in public waiting spaces. As a flyer for Atari's *Super Pong* (1974) describes, "Attractive Superpong packaging fits any location…fine restaurants, hotel or reception room lobbies, lounges, game centers, department stores, or anywhere four square feet of floor space can be put to work making money for you!" Atari also created a special kiosk made of wedge-shaped modules called "The Atari Theater," which contained upward of six games that could be arranged in a column for use in public spaces. Similar to William T. Smith placing his working model, *The Locomotive*, in train stations, Atari placed a six-sided kiosk on the waiting platform of the Montgomery Street Bay-Area Rapid Transit (BART) station in San Francisco.

Several manufacturers in the mid-1970s also produced round cocktail format cabinets, which combined the functionality of a table with money-making potential. Geared for a different audience, the cocktail format cabinets were initially intended to entertain adults in lounges and restaurants and generally featured a more sophisticated approach to surface decoration. To guard against drink spills and to protect the game's electronics, the surfaces were sealed behind a heavy layer of glass (Figure 3.6). By the early 1980s, the cocktail cabinet was commonly manufactured in a rectangular format that could be played from either end and featured a number of games designed to take advantage of this oppositional game space.

Not everything was as blatantly commercially oriented, however, as *Pong* targeted pediatric waiting rooms with *Doctor Pong* and *Puppy Pong*, both 1974. The games did not include coin slots as they were intended to keep children entertained while waiting for appointments. *Puppy Pong*, in particular, featured a happy-looking cartoon dog on top of a bright yellow doghouse, with monitor and rotary dials at a lower level on the cabinet's side. *Puppy Pong*, however, was not well received by doctors and soon went out of production.

Another ball and paddle game, *Warlords*, combined the elimination format of *Quadrapong* with the brick-breaking mechanic of *Breakout*. Using a medieval fantasy theme, the game featured a castle made of blocks in each corner. In front of each castle, players controlled a shield that could bounce or catch a fireball and knock down the walls of opponent's castles. The game included an elaborate overlay that colored each player's castle and provided the illusion of three-dimensions as the image was rendered in perspective. As players, both human and computer-controlled, were eliminated, the game introduced additional fireballs that increased in speed, bringing the gameplay to a dramatic and timely end.

FIGURE 3.6 An advertisement featuring adults enjoying the nightlife and playing *Electromotion IV* (1975, Electromotion), a stylish *Pong* clone in a round cocktail table format. (Courtesy of The Arcade Flyer Archive, The International Arcade Museum. flyers.arcade-museum.com)

Adapting Electromechanical Games to the Digital Arcade

Since the graphical capabilities of early digital arcade games were limited, being monochromatic or producing color through transparent plastic pieces, electromechanical games continued to offer much more detailed imagery. Rather than competing visually, many digital games of the early to mid-1970s focused on enhancing gameplay of familiar mechanical and electromechanical arcade games. One way this was achieved involved using dynamic behaviors that could make a game more challenging in ways that would have been cost prohibitive or outright impossible in electromechanical games.

Chicago Coin created a digital version of pinball, *TV Pingame* (1973), which used a vertical playfield with a paddle at the bottom of the screen, controlled by a rotary dial. The game space, like pinball, was filled with obstacles, bumpers, and pockets along the side, represented by simple squares. The game also included a moving rectangle at the top of the playfield which served as a skill shot. Other manufacturers quickly picked up digital pinball as well: Midway with *TV Flipper* (1973), Exidy with *TV Pinball* (1974), and Atari with *Pin Pong* (1974), which digitally represented flippers controlled by buttons, rather than a paddle and rotary dial.

Midway's *Tornado Baseball* (1976) meanwhile, closely resembled Harry Williams' *1937 World Series* as it employed the same gameplay of hitting the ball past the outfielders to the stadium wall, marked with "Home Run," "Triple," "Double," "Single," and represented the player as a swinging bat. The digital format of *Tornado Baseball*, however, had an advantage: it could be played by one or two people and used simple but effective animations to move players around the bases. Other translations of electromechanical games into digital ones included missile-launching games like Midway's *Guided Missile* (1977), which recalled Sega's earlier *Missile*.

Racing Games in the Early Digital Arcade

The model for digital racing games was also rooted in electromechanical games. Players of Atari's *Gran Trak 10* (1974), for example, controlled a race-car from a top-down perspective using a steering wheel and pedals. Racing against a timer on a dotted track the player accumulated points by passing scoring gates denoted by colored overlays (Figure 3.7). As with *Pong*, Atari iterated on the design basics of *Gran Trak 10*, adding more players in subsequent versions ranging from two in *Gran Trak 20* (1975) to eight in *Indy 800* (1975). Later Atari racing games like *Le Mans* (1976) used the same gameplay, but added realistic vehicle handling: if a high-speed turn was taken too quickly, the car would skid.

Racing games made a significant jump toward simulation with a series of first person perspective driving games in the mid-1970s including *Nürburgring 1* (1976) by German engineer Reiner Foerst, *Midnite Racer/ Datsun 280 Zzzap* (1976, Bally/Midway), and *Night Racer* (1977, Micronetics). Although not the first, the most well-known first person driving game was Atari's *Night Driver* (1976) by Dave Shepperd (Figure 3.8). The player, driving at night, raced against the clock on a long track that smoothly curved left and right. As with the more realistic handling in the top-down *Le Mans*, a quick turn of the wheel at high speeds would cause a skid into the road markers and force the player to briefly stop, losing precious game time.

Night Driver and the other first person games that immediately preceded it were creative solutions to a practical set of limitations, as displaying a solid racetrack with curves and turns from a first person perspective required computation beyond what was practical at the time. For *Night Driver*, Shepperd implied the presence of the track through sets of rectangles that represented highway reflector markers, going so far as driving his actual car at night to observe and replicate the effect. *Night Driver* was an early adopter of the microprocessor, allowing the final product to display road markers

FIGURE 3.7 Atari's fake competitor, Kee Games, produced *Sprint 2* in 1976, a microprocessor-based, two-player racing game similar to *Gran Trak 20*. (Courtesy of Arcadia, McLean, IL, www.vintagevideogames.com)

that smoothly grew in size and flowed back and forth with the curve of the road.

Racing games also experimented with ideas that moved them away from earlier, non-digital arcade games. *Space Race* (1973, Atari) consisted of a drag race through an asteroid field. Each time an individual player made it through the drag strip without a collision, they received a point and began at the start line again, hoping to outscore their opponent in the allotted time. A number of "demolition derby" games experimented with reversing the conventions of racing games by making collisions with objects the main part of gameplay. These games appeared in the mid-1970s and attempted to capitalize on the peak popularity of demolition derbies in the United States.

FIGURE 3.8 *Night Driver* **(1976, Atari) with simulated overlay of the car's hood.**

Exidy's *Destruction Derby* (1975) and *Car Polo* (1977), Atari's *Crash 'N Score* (1975) and Chicago Coin's *Demolition Derby* (1977) combined the top-down perspective and steering wheel controls familiar from earlier racing games with an arena-like space filled with moving cars or other targets. While some electromechanical games employed a concept similar to ramming cars as seen in Sega's *Stunt Car* (1970) and *Dodgem Crazy* (1972), the dynamically changing open arena of digital games set them apart.

The most famous example of the demolition derby-type game was Exidy's *Death Race* (1976). The game's concept was drawn from Paul Bartel's 1975 cult film, *Death Race 2000,* as one or two players scored points by running their cars into pedestrians (Figures 3.9 and 3.10). The design of *Death Race,* however, was more complex: each time a pedestrian was hit, an immovable tombstone appeared in his place. Each game, thus, was unique. Additionally, as the score climbed higher, the game space became incrementally more difficult to navigate, an ideal system for an arcade game that helped prevent outright mastery.

The gameplay of *Death Race* caused concern and led to the first of several public debates on violence in video games. Some feared that the game would lead players to commit acts of violence. Newspapers and television shows discussed the game, using it as an example of societal corruption, much like that experienced by pinball games 30 years earlier. The result, however, was not a ban on digital games. Although some locations did refuse to carry the game, the controversy and media exposure caused an uptick in sales, making *Death Race* one of the most popular games of its time.

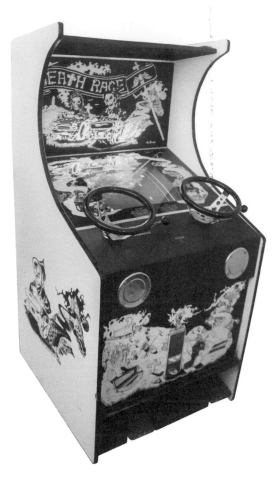

FIGURE 3.9 Cabinet for *Death Race* (1976, Exidy). (Courtesy of Arcadia, McLean, IL, www.vintagevideogames.com)

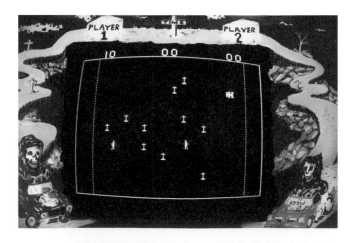

FIGURE 3.10 Screen and bezel of *Death Race* (1976, Exidy). (Courtesy of Arcadia, McLean, IL, www.vintagevideogames.com)

**FROM TRANSISTOR–TRANSISTOR LOGIC
TO MICROPROCESSORS**

The earliest digital arcade games were assembled by electrical engineers and functioned through a process known as transistor–transistor logic. Effectively the game rules and behaviors on screen were physically constructed out of separate circuits that were custom placed for each game. Thus a *Pong* cabinet would have a completely different board layout and types of parts than *Gran Trak 10* as each game has different rules. In a microprocessor-driven game, the rules and behaviors of the game exist as software, which gives instructions to more standardized hardware. Compared to transistor–transistor logic, microprocessors were significantly faster, allowing games to immediately grow in complexity. The adoption of microprocessors brought a number of changes in the physical design and development of games as manufacturers could create more uniform sets of boards, resulting in games that could be produced much faster. Most significantly, it shifted the responsibilities of designing the game from engineers to computer programmers. From the late 1970s through the 1980s, programmers were commonly tasked with creating not only the game, but the graphics and animation as well.

Early Variants of Maze and Shooting Games

Although games designed around the concept of a ball and paddle were some of the most prolific game types of the 1970s, game developers explored a number of creative ideas using mazes for the construction of space. Many of the concepts found in these maze games would become signature elements of the Golden Age arcade games of the late 1970s and early 1980s.

Penny arcades of the early to mid-1900s occasionally featured mechanical games centered on navigating a ball through a vertical or horizontal maze. The player typically manipulated the field with dials, while avoiding faults like holes or an edge of the game space. Manipulating the maze itself was typical in mechanical games, but digital game designers more commonly focused on manipulating elements *within* the maze. The first of many early digital maze games was Atari's *Gotcha* (1973), a competitive cat-and-mouse-like game where one player chased the other through a maze that was in constant motion. *Gotcha* represented an early attempt at using sound to affect the player's performance; as the pursuer came closer to the target, the game steadily increased the rate of a beeping noise. Although the noise proved to be more of an annoyance, a more successful version of the concept would appear in the Golden Age arcade games *Space Invaders* (1978, Taito) and *Pac-Man* (1980, Namco). *Gotcha* was more notable for the controversy it stirred than for the sound it made, as the controllers were not joysticks or dials, but pink, breast-like hemispheres. Atari, prompted by negative reaction to the controllers, redesigned later versions to use joysticks for maneuvering through the maze.

Another maze-based game was *The Amazing Maze* (1976, Midway). Here, the player competed against either a computer-controlled opponent or another player, in a race to complete the maze in the fastest time. While the game did not use a countdown, the computer-controlled opponent always moved at a constant speed and never deviated from the path to the exit, creating a more elegant timer. The game was supposedly capable of creating over one million variations through random constructions of each maze, ensuring that the player would not be able to memorize the patterns. Other competitive maze games included *Blockade* (1976, Gremlin) in which players controlled the head end of an ever-growing wall of bricks that progressively filled the game space. Players were awarded points when opponents ran into a brick wall, regardless of who laid it. *Blockade*, like *Pong*, was designed to become progressively more difficult with time, as the space for maneuvering became limited and magnified player mistakes. This simple game concept was used in the light cycle battle in the CGI-pioneering Disney film, *Tron* (1982), and also found its way onto Nokia cellular telephones through the game, *Snake* (1997).

Mazes became the structure of choice as they maximized the single-screen game space and provided numerous opportunities for the player to make meaningful choices with consequences. A number of games released in the mid-1970s employed maze-based levels but combined them with shooting mechanics. *Tank* (1974) by Atari's bogus competitor, Kee Games, grounded the outer space duels of *Spacewar!* in a maze. The fast-paced nature of the duel coupled with significant strategic elements provided by the maze, was perfectly suited for the gameplay preferred by designers of early digital arcade games.

Western Gun (1975, Taito), by Tomohiro Nishikado, featured dueling cowboys in a maze-like American Old West landscape of rocks and cacti. As bullets could ricochet off rocks, gameplay focused on a strategic use of angles. *Western Gun* was the first Japanese-designed digital game adapted for play in the United States. The American version of the game, *Gun Fight* (1975, Midway) by Dave Nutting, featured another notable first; it was the first arcade game to employ a microprocessor. Nishikado, impressed with the more advanced animations and speed made possible by the microprocessor, decided to utilize the technology in his follow-up game, *Space Invaders* (1978, Taito), discussed in Chapter 4.

Dedicated Consoles in the Home and Signs of Trouble

As the popularity of *Pong* grew and microprocessor became more affordable, dozens of major and minor game companies broke into the nascent

**RIDING THE SUCCESS OF POPULAR
TELEVISION SHOWS AND FILM**

Many digital arcade games, like *Death Race*, looked to film for new ideas. *Shark Jaws* (1975), produced by Atari under the name Horror Games, drew on Steven Spielberg's 1975 film *Jaws*. It was a cat-and-mouse-style game where the player earned points by catching a fish while avoiding a shark that opened and closed its jaws. A game by Project Systems Engineering called *Man-eater* (1975) used a similar style but allowed two players to compete against each other. The game's most distinctive element was the cabinet: a large shark's mouth made of fiberglass. Pinball machines, still struggling with legal issues in some places, also took cues from film with Bally's *Wizard* (1975), which was based on the Ken Russell film of the same year, *Tommy*, featuring music by The Who. One of the most blatant media tie-in of the period, however, was Sega's *Fonz* (1976) a motorcycle racing game that featured The Fonz character from the television show, *Happy Days*.

home market in the mid- to late 1970s with a number of *dedicated consoles*. Unlike later cartridge-based consoles, dedicated consoles featured a fixed number of built-in games. These later first-generation home consoles overwhelmingly consisted of *Pong* variants with dials integrated directly into the surface. Most units used the "*Pong*-on-a-chip" AY-3-8500 integrated circuit by General Instruments, which resulted in a flood of nearly identical home video game units. A few, however, featured driving games.

In 1975 Magnavox discontinued the Odyssey and replaced it with a dedicated console, the Odyssey 100. The Odyssey 100 shed the minimalist, boxy white form of the original Odyssey, and was molded in a more aerodynamic form in bright red-orange. It moved completely away from television overlays and included basic sound capabilities. Despite these changes, the Odyssey 100 retained the knob controls of its predecessor: one each for the x and y axis and a third for the "english" knob that controlled the path of the projectile. It contained two games, tennis and hockey, which differed little from each other. A physical counter that slid on top of the unit tracked scoring. Magnavox released five dedicated consoles between 1975 and 1976, including the AY-3-8500 powered Odyssey 300, which ironically, played an almost identical copy of Al Alcorn's *Pong* arcade game, complete with onscreen digital scoring and a variety of sound blips (Figure 3.11).

Meanwhile, Bushnell, Alcorn, and others at Atari, still fighting the lawsuit by Magnavox at the time, worked on bringing *Pong* to the home by creating their own chip. Through a partnership with Sears in 1975, Atari released a dedicated console that perfectly recreated *Pong*, but with color graphics. Atari, like other companies, continued to release new, dedicated home consoles with arcade adaptions, Pong Doubles and Super Pong in

FIGURE 3.11 The Odyssey 300 dedicated console. (Photo Evan Amos. CC BY-SA 3.0.)

1976. Other companies throughout the United States, Europe, and Japan also scrambled to produce home versions of *Pong*. Between 1976 and 1977, digital game newcomer Coleco released over a dozen models of its Telstar home console, consisting of *Pong* variants and light gun games. Japanese toy manufacturer Nintendo released its first home game systems, the Color TV Game 6 and Color TV Game 15 in 1977 and 1978.

These dedicated consoles, together with a steady stream of *Pong* clones in the arcade, flooded home and arcade markets, leading to a general slow down and stagnation of ball and paddle games by 1977. Other genres such as racing games, also suffered from oversaturation, leading to the industry's first crash. The 1977 crash, though not as devastating as the later crash of 1983, was significant enough to put many clone game producers out of business. Atari and the larger electromechanical game manufacturers were able to endure due to their size; nonetheless, without genuine innovation in game design, it was clear that the nascent home and arcade game industry would not survive.

New concepts for arcade games and home consoles, however, came quickly. In the late 1970s and early 1980s arcade games entered an exceptionally creative period in art and design, launching a Golden Age that carried the industry to new heights. At the same time a second generation of home consoles began utilizing cartridges, providing an almost limitless library of games. These two contexts of arcades and home consoles are addressed individually in Chapters 4 and 5.

Chapter 4

The Golden Age Arcade (1978-1984)

The Golden Age Arcade

The concept of a "Golden Age" is used to describe a mythical time in the past notable for great technological and cultural accomplishments but followed by an inevitable decline. This is an apt metaphor for the arcades of the late 1970s and early 1980s as game designers created some of the most iconic concepts, characters, and visuals in the history of digital games: inevitable death from descending aliens in *Space Invaders*, the "Jump Man" character, and multicolor vector beam graphics. Game designers explored abstract and unconventional concepts such as claiming territory against a randomly moving enemy by drawing rectilinear outlines in *Qix* (1981, Taito) and competing in surreal contests against ostrich-mounted knights in *Joust* (1982, Williams Electronics).

These creative, non-sport, game concepts flowered in this context largely due to the public's increased ability to understand and play digital games. Additionally, game manufacturers found better ways to teach people how to play as simple instructions were placed near the controls and attract modes walked the player through the game's rules step by step like an animated manual. This, accompanied by massively successful films like *Star Wars* and other popular science fiction media, helped provide a new set of references for the public and game designers alike. Whereas *Computer Space* failed to connect with the general public in 1971, a scant 8 years later, *Asteroids* (1979, Atari) using the same controls and being a more complex game proved to be a positive hit.

Nonetheless, it is important to remember that many of these great accomplishments took place against a background of aggressive expansion as companies consolidated resources to strengthen their position and weaken others in an increasingly competitive market. Sega acquired Gremlin in 1978 and produced games as Sega/Gremlin until 1981, when the name Gremlin was dropped from the title. The pinball division of Bally merged with Midway in 1982, producing arcade games under the name Bally/Midway. Atari as the undisputed leader in coin-op added to its worldwide presence with Atari Ireland, which manufactured and shipped games throughout Europe.

Tendencies and New Concepts in the Golden Age

One of the key distinctions between the games of the Golden Age and those of the early digital arcade was the pace of gameplay. With a few notable exceptions, gameplay in the early digital arcade tended to be continuous and was limited to a specific amount of time regardless of performance; features inherited from postwar electromechanical arcade games. Gameplay in Golden Age arcade games, however, tended to be delivered in smaller but more intense segments as it was divided into stages or levels. This allowed the game to become more difficult, as each level could introduce new rules, enemy types, or spatial layouts. Combined with the ability to dynamically change the speed of enemies throughout the course of any one stage, designers relied more on attrition than a timer to end a player's game. The use of increasingly difficult stages to frame gameplay allowed the player to feel a sense of accomplishment in the early stages but fail quickly later, ideally limiting the game time to 90 seconds or less.

Overlays were replaced with color graphics, which brought new vibrancy to the Golden Age. Color first appeared in 1975 and was used to differentiate vehicles and scores in Atari's eight-player racing game, *Indy 800*. Color was also a major component of Exidy's *Car Polo* (1977), but it was not widely used until 1980, after game hardware could more efficiently process the graphics and after the cost of color monitors had fallen. Game designers outpaced the practicality of overlays as they worked best with static gamespaces with preset, predictable, movements of game objects. Games like *Asteroids*, thus, would have been impossible to create with overlays due to the great amount of change the player could enact on the floating asteroids.

The Golden Age also saw the brief, but widespread use of a new method to create imagery in vector graphics. Vector graphics were not new to computers—university computers like those that ran the original *Spacewar!* used them extensively—but they were new to the arcades. Vector displays used sets of points connected by a thin beam of light that refreshed at a high speed to create the outlines of shapes. Visually, vector graphics differed from the predominant raster-type graphics primarily in their clarity and ability to create intensely bright imagery, displaying razor-sharp lines at a resolution of nearly 1024×768 pixels. The image resolution of most raster-based visuals in arcade games of the period, by contrast, was around 200×180 pixels, which prevented games from producing the visual detail often desired by game designers. Since vector graphics created straight lines measuring the width of a single pixel, the vast majority of the screen was black, favoring outer-space themes. Initially black and white, vector graphics too transitioned to color in the early 1980s.

Shooting and Shoot 'em Ups in the Golden Age

As discussed in Chapter 3, Taito designer Tomohiro Nishikado saw how microprocessors improved the performance of games in the conversion of his transistor–transistor logic-based *Western Gun* to the microprocessor-driven *Gun Fight*. This experience left him with a desire to build his next game using microprocessors. Taking inspiration from a variety of sources including the 1977 film *Star Wars*, Atari's *Breakout* (1976), and earlier electromechanical shooting galleries, Nishikado created *Space Invaders* (Taito, 1978). Since Nishikado felt that shooting other humans was immoral, he used alien characters as a substitute.

Space Invaders consisted of 55 space aliens that unleashed a constant barrage of projectiles from the top of the screen while methodically marching to the opposite edges of the screen before descending one row. This pattern of encroachment continued until they reached the screen's bottom; after which the game automatically ended. The player, as a lone laser turret, took a single shot at a time against the slowly descending block of aliens while seeking cover behind three shield-like structures that became progressively more damaged with each hit, an element reminiscent of the destructible cacti in Nishikado's earlier *Western Gun*. Each invader destroyed caused the remaining group to move incrementally faster eventually causing the last remaining invader to move at high speed and descend quicker. If the last invader was destroyed, the game began anew with a complete block of aliens slowly moving from the top of the screen.

The design of *Space Invaders* was well suited within the context of coin-operated arcade games. Although the game did not have a timer, the descending aliens themselves effectively fulfilled this function as the closer they came, the less time the player had left. Further, the game featured a dynamically adjusting difficulty as the player actively shrank their window of time to play with each successful hit. Thus, the game would conclude quickly, even for highly skilled players. *Space Invaders*, like nearly all Golden Age arcade games, placed a heavy emphasis on the collection of points. Each invader the player shot awarded points. To help players accumulate points faster, Nishikado included a UFO that flew across the top of the screen and awarded special bonus points when shot. Although achieving a high score and being featured on the game's high score board were powerful motivators, points served a more direct function of extending playtime through awarding extra lives; a feature similar to Gottlieb's "add a ball" game mechanic for pinball (see Chapter 1). Also like many games of pinball, the player began the game with three chances.

Space Invaders pieced together a number of aesthetic elements from earlier games and other sources to create a memorable play experience. Unlike adversaries in many earlier digital games, Nishikado's aliens were differentiated by various morphological characteristics, a hint of the wealth of characters and narrative elements that were soon to find their way into digital games. In many of the cabinet versions, the natively black and white graphics were enhanced with color overlays and mirrors that created a 3D effect of playing over a cratered moon in space (Figure 4.1). The game's most significant aesthetic flourish, however, was a low, four-note minor key sequence that sped up in time with the movement of the invaders. Although this idea was first seen in Atari's two-player, coin-op chase game, *Gottcha*, the simple but unsettling music track of *Space Invaders* proved both more appealing and effective at increasing tension.

The "shoot or be shot" gameplay of *Space Invaders* created a sensation in the arcades at precisely the right time. By 1977 many arcades and dedicated home consoles experienced a significant slump in sales, convincing

FIGURE 4.1 *Space Invaders* (1978, Taito).

SPACE INVADERS AND COIN SHORTAGES

An often-repeated story related to *Space Invaders* states that the game was so popular it caused a shortage of 100 yen coins in Japan. The story continues by stating that the Japanese Mint reacted to this *Space Invaders*-caused shortage by doubling, tripling or, in some versions, quadrupling the number of 100 yen coins it minted. This legendary tale is often used to dramatically illustrate the magnitude of *Space Invaders'* success, and by extension, the power of video games. The underlying circumstances of this sensational story and the relationship between *Space Invaders* and the Japanese Mint, however, are more than questionable.

First, while *Space Invaders* certainly did collect a massive amount of 100 yen coins in its day, location owners likely would have cashed in their profits as soon as possible, thus putting the coins back into circulation. Second, while the Japanese Mint did briefly increase production after 1979, it is unlikely that *Space Invaders* was the culprit. One plausible alternative to explain the increase in production could be related to the silver content in 100 yen coins and subsequent coin hoarding. From 1957 to 1967, 100 yen coins were minted in 60% silver. After the value of silver rose sharply in the late 1960s, the Japanese Mint ceased using silver to make coins due to the high cost of production. This also triggered coin hoarding and the smuggling of the silver coins out of Japan to be melted down for sale on the silver market. Further, the number of 100 yen coins minted from the mid- to late 1970s actually *decreased*, from 680,000,000 in 1973 to 292,000,000 in 1978 according to the *Krause Standard Catalog of World Coins: 1901–2000*, which may have been an attempt to control economic inflation. While not devastating to the national Japanese economy, it is possible that this combination of factors may have caused some localized shortages. Nonetheless, from 1979 to 1980 the Japanese Mint increased its coin output, but at a significantly lower rate than that of 1973. Thus, *Space Invaders* was launched at the end of a period of low coin mintage that was complicated by a context where older coins were less likely to be openly circulated.

some that digital games had been a passing fad. *Space Invaders*, with its unique gameplay and intuitive concept allowed it to sell more than 100,000 machines in its Japanese debut. Dedicated "Invader Houses" which housed cocktail and upright cabinet versions of the game, sprang up throughout the country in addition to appearing in stores and other public spaces. Its phenomenal success rejuvenated the coin-op industry worldwide as American manufacturer Midway, along with Taito, distributed the game in the United States and in other countries.

Part of the reason *Space Invaders* was able to help revive the industry as a whole, was due to the flood of games inspired by, or directly cloned from it. Every major and minor game platform, whether arcade, home computer, or home console of the time, featured some variant of a lone turret or other vehicle dodging left and right while shooting at a block of enemies. Games like *Space Fever* (1978, Nintendo), *Space Attack* (1979, Sega), *TI Invaders* (1981, Texas Instruments), and others all directly replicated this successful formula.

The basic concept of *Space Invaders* was pervasive particularly in Japanese shooting games and was quickly modified into a format known as vertically scrolling, "shoot 'em ups." The incremental iterations seen in the games produced by Namco show this progression: in *Galaxian* (1979), enemies broke formation and "dive bombed" the player; in *Galaga* (1981) players could shoot multiple shots at one time and upgrade their ship; in *Xevious* (1982), players could move in all four directions, fly over a vertically scrolling landscape, and fight level bosses. Although it should be noted that these ideas did not necessarily originate with these games, they illustrate the growing complexity of the genre as gameplay become faster, the number and types of projectiles on the screen multiplied, and the player's chances of survival dwindled. As the concepts evolved in later vehicle-based shoot 'em ups such as *1942* (1984, Capcom) and *Raiden* (1990, Seibu Kaihatsu), successful gameplay required players to memorize increasingly complex patterns as game designers contended with a skilled player base.

Although games with shooting elements were dominant in the Golden Age arcade, not all were as directly derived from the *Space Invaders* formula. *Spacewar!* remained influential as many of the new generation of game designers had played it in university computer labs. The game *Space Wars* (1977, Cinematronics), translated much of the original 1963 dueling game to the arcade and even preserved the hacker-esque ability to modify it through various toggles that governed elements such as game difficulty, whether the space wrapped around or was bounded, and the effects of gravity. It was also the first coin-op game to implement a cost-effective method to display vector graphics, a feature that would rapidly spread through coin-op games. Atari's *Asteroids* (1979), designed by Lyle Rains and Ed Logg, also built on these ideas as players zoomed through a wraparound gamespace and shot floating vector graphic asteroids into progressively smaller pieces. Other games like *Gorf* (1981, Midway) combined many concepts of shooters, as the game offered five distinct variations on the theme.

Other Directions in Shooter Design, Input, and Theme

Game creators in the 1980s made a number of departures from existing concepts pursuing not only different directions in design, but also novel methods of interaction. Dave Theurer's *Tempest* (1981, Atari), for example, began as an attempt to create a first-person version of *Space Invaders*. As development progressed, however, it was melded with Theurer's reoccurring nightmare of monsters crawling out of a hole. The end result was a game based on maneuvering around the outline of an extruded polygon and shooting creatures that came toward the player (Figure 4.2). When the creatures reached

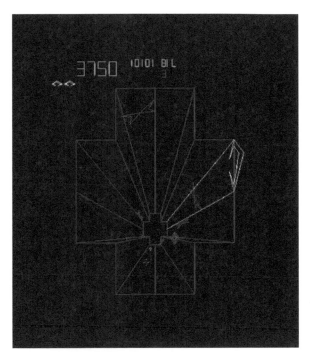

FIGURE 4.2 *Tempest* **(Atari, 1981). Although the technology for color vector graphics had been developed for the game** *Space Duel, Tempest* **was published first.**

the edge, they flipped end over end toward the player and dragged them down. While games like *Space Invaders*, *Space Wars*, and *Asteroids* utilized buttons to issue all commands, including moving or turning left and right, Theurer used a dial similar to *Pong*. This reduced the number of inputs and allowed the player to more intuitively maneuver clockwise or counterclockwise around the gamespace.

At times, the themes of many shooter games of the 1980s strongly resonated with the anxieties of the period, providing a deeper meaning to play. Eugene Jarvis' *Robotron 2084* (1982, Williams Electronics) used a smoothly designed twin joystick setup that allowed the player to move in one direction while shooting in another (Figure 4.3). Jarvis' concept centered on the player protecting the last remaining human family in the world against a robot uprising; a similar theme for gameplay he used to justify the constant shooting in his earlier side-scrolling shoot 'em up, *Defender* (1981, Williams Electronics). Each completed level in *Robotron 2084* resulted in larger waves and more varieties of enemies surrounding the player and the fleeing family. The frantic gameplay continued until either all the members of the family died or the player was overwhelmed. Like *Space Invaders*, the game was unwinnable. Jarvis' game resonated with a growing technophobia in much of the industrialized world as computers *had* caused a revolution in daily life. Although the concept of the creation turning on its creator is an old and

FIGURE 4.3 *Robotron 2084* **(1982, Williams Electronics). (Courtesy of Arcadia, McLean, IL, www.vintagevideogames.com)**

familiar theme in the literature, it was particularly strong in the science fiction of the period with films including *Westworld, Blade Runner,* and *The Terminator.*

One of the strongest connections between game design and context, however, was Dave Theurer's *Missile Command* (1980, Atari). *Missile Command* took on a shooting concept reminiscent of earlier electromechanical missile-launching games. The player, using a track ball rather than a joystick, maneuvered a crosshair in the sky above a planet's surface and attempted to intercept enemy missiles raining down on six cities. The game, like the majority of arcade games in the late 1970s and early 1980s, was based on attrition and had no way to "win." Enemy missiles moved faster and appeared in greater numbers with each new stage until the player lost all of the cities. Also typical of the period's arcade games, skilled players were rewarded with extended game time through earning a bonus city that replaced a destroyed city.

The theme and design of *Missile Command,* however revealed a nakedly nihilistic undertone: there was no way to win once missiles started falling from the sky. The large number of nuclear weapons in the United States and USSR during the Cold War created an extremely tense context where neither nation would launch the first missile, but both were prepared to retaliate. This context provided the basis for the game, however, Theurer did not like the idea of launching missiles at an opposing city and, like Tomohiro Nishikado and Eugene Jarvis, shifted the gameplay to defensive action. In early development, the game's cities were named after cities on the California coast. Further, if the player ran out of missiles or had their silos destroyed, the game did not end. Instead, the player was forced to helplessly watch the destruction of the cities. Once the last city was gone, the game flashed the words "THE END," implying an end to more than just gameplay.

Stronger Characters and Narrative in Arcade Games

In general, the history of coin-operated games featured little in terms of developed characters and complete narratives. Part of the issue with narrative was that coin-op games were designed for only around 90 seconds of play, while plot and character development often required more time to unfold. Manufacturing costs, time constraints, and gameplay, instead, took precedent. Nonetheless, coin-op game designers of the 1980s began to give their characters and settings greater personality and distinction. Early methods included expanding the game's attract mode to include text that explained the reason for the game's conflict as seen in *Robotron 2084*; others used simple noninteractive animated sequences. The inclusion of narrative ultimately allowed designers to explore more of the medium's expressive qualities and break away from the constraints of earlier coin-op electromechanical games.

Coin-op game developers from Japan were particularly successful in integrating character and narrative into games. *Pac-Man* (1980, Namco) created by Toru Iwatani was based on eating small dots in a maze. It featured the character Pac-Man, a yellow circle with a wedge-shaped mouth who was pursued by four brightly colored ghosts (Figure 4.4). *Pac-Man* was not the first game to feature collecting dots while avoiding pursuers in a maze as *Head On* (1979, Sega/Gremlin) and *Space Chaser* (1979, Taito) had used the concept before. *Pac-Man*, however, was a more compelling game through a refined use of color, sound, and interesting mechanics.

Consuming one of the maze's four power pellets caused all of the ghosts to turn bright blue, abruptly change their patterns of movement, and to move slower. This change in the game state granted Pac-Man the temporary ability to eat the ghosts. The shift was also accompanied by a change in the game's dominant sound effect, which became a sequence of rapid beeping. Each ghost began to flash blue and white near the end of the pellet's

FIGURE 4.4 **The iconic *Pac-Man* arcade cabinet by Namco's North American distributer, Midway. (Courtesy of Arcadia, McLean, IL, www.vintagevideogames.com)**

effect, after which the color of the ghosts and the background sound effect returned to their original states. Iwatani's use of color and sound in *Pac-Man*, thus, served a crucial role in communicating changes in the game state to the player.

Iwatani individualized the four ghosts, giving each a unique color, name, and nickname. It further suggested unique personalities through the simple programming that governed the movement of the ghosts as each tracked Pac-Man through the maze differently. The game was also the first to make use of cut scenes that built on each other to create a small narrative. The scenes highlighted the playfully antagonistic relationship between Pac-Man and the red ghost named Blinky. Each cut scene began with Blinky chasing Pac-Man off screen only to fall victim to a humorous twist of some sort. In the first segment, Blinky chases Pac-Man off screen but quickly reappears in blue form running away from a giant version of Pac-Man. In another scene, Blinky tears his red "sheet" after catching it on a post, while the final scene shows Blinky with a patched sheet, chasing

Pac-Man off screen only to reappear running away and dragging the red sheet behind completely "naked."

Pac-Man, was followed by a wave of "maze games" such as *Lock "n" Chase* (1981, Data East) as well as cloned games, most of which did not provide the level of refinement or characterization of the original. *Ms. Pac-Man* (1982), created by Namco's American distributer, Midway, proved to be an exception to the rule (Figure 4.5). *Ms. Pac-Man* initially began as a conversion kit for *Pac-Man* machines named *Crazy Otto* (1981, General Computer Corporation) that added more maze layouts, increased the game's speed, and changed the game's sprites. A lawsuit by Atari over *Missile Command* conversion kits, however, barred General Computer Corporation from creating any further kits without permission from the original creator. Looking to use *Crazy Otto*, the company presented it to Midway, which rebranded it as *Ms. Pac-Man*. It became one of the most successful games of the Golden Age arcade. The game followed the narrative precedent set by *Pac-Man* as it featured a story in which Pac-Man and Ms. Pac-Man met, fell in love, and had a baby in three acts. Midway further continued the trend with *Jr. Pac-Man* (1983), which utilized a scrolling approach to space as well as the telling of the romance between Jr. Pac-Man and the daughter of red ghost, Blinky.

FIGURE 4.5 *Ms. Pac-Man* **(1982, Midway).**

While the cinematic sections of the *Pac-Man* games existed as entirely separate entities from the gameplay, Shigeru Miyamoto of Nintendo found ways to more cohesively integrate narrative with *Donkey Kong* (1981). Miyamoto, unlike other contemporary game designers, was not a computer programmer. Instead, he was formally trained in industrial design and became familiar with approaching design problems from the user's perspective. Although many of the earlier successful game designers intuitively understood these ideas, Miyamoto's approach also drew on his ability as an artist. This art and design background, coupled with his childhood experiences of exploring spaces in rural Japan eventually lead to a signature style of games full of whimsical characters and playful exploration.

Miyamoto's work at Nintendo began in the planning department where he designed the product housing and interfaces for two dedicated consoles as well as creating character artwork for a number of games. His demonstrated design sensibility put him in a position to create a game for Nintendo that became *Donkey Kong* (Figure 4.6). Unlike other game designers, Miyamoto

FIGURE 4.6 *Donkey Kong* **(1981, Nintendo). (Courtesy of Arcadia, McLean, IL, www.vintagevideogames.com)**

began to build his characters and story first, instead of constructing them to fit a pre-defined format of gameplay. He drew inspiration from the fairytale, *Beauty and the Beast*, the film, *King Kong*, and the animated cartoon, *Popeye*. Miyamoto then created a scenario that more blended characters and behaviors with a unique game design. After inserting a quarter into the machine, *Donkey Kong* opened with a short cut scene of a large gorilla carrying a woman Miyamoto named "Lady" (later renamed Pauline) up a building while ominous music played in the background. Once at the top, the gorilla stomped, deforming the building's various platforms. This framework provided the player, the everyman Miyamoto called "Jump-Man," (later known as Mario), with an immediate understanding of the characters and the goal of ascending the building to rescue Lady—a narrative that directed gameplay.

Donkey Kong also represented a significant change for the content of arcade games. Prior games typically presented the player with a single task for each stage that became progressively more difficult as seen in *Space Invaders* and *Pac-Man*. Since *Donkey Kong* was based on a set of narrative concepts, Miyamoto envisioned the gameplay unfolding in four parts. A player who reached Lady at the top of the screen within the game's time limit saw the gorilla pick her up and climb higher. After a brief pause and a graphic indicating a height of 25 meters, the game resumed and placed the player at the bottom of an entirely different game level. This sequence was repeated three times, effectively creating four separate games, each with a different theme and unique set of jumping and climbing-based challenges. The player needed to jump over barrels in the first stage, navigate elevators in the second, maneuver past conveyor belts in the third, and disconnect pegs holding up a platform in the game's final stage. At the conclusion of the final stage, the player saw a short sequence of the platforms collapsing while Jump Man and Lady shared a romantic moment, bringing the story to an end—a first for coin-operated arcade games. The player then played through the levels again, each time more difficult due to slight changes in the patterns of behavior and faster adversaries. *Donkey Kong* was immediately successful the world over, marking the beginning of Nintendo's dominance and demonstrating the importance of art and narrative in games, two areas that had previously received little attention.

Donkey Kong's sequel, *Donkey Kong Jr.* (1982, Nintendo), cast the player in the role of Donkey Kong's son on a quest to free his father from captivity by Mario. Like its predecessor, the game was based on jumping, climbing, and avoiding traps across four different stages ranging from Donkey Kong's home to Mario's secret hideout. The game explored a wider range of emotions as Donkey Kong Jr. showed elation when reunited with his "papa" each time he reached the top of a stage and visibly saddened after Mario pushed the cage off screen leaving him alone. The game's final level involved Donkey Kong Jr. unlocking his father's cage and the two of them happily bouncing off screen together with Mario in pursuit. Once off screen,

Donkey Kong's large foot humorously kicked Mario into the air, causing him to run away.

What followed in the wake of *Pac-Man* and *Donkey Kong* was a wave of successful character-centric climbing or maze-based arcade games: *Q*bert* (1982, Gottlieb), *Dig Dug* (1982, Namco), *Pengo* (1982, Sega), *Burgertime* (1982, Bally/Midway), *Mario Bros.* (1983, Nintendo), *Ghosts 'n Goblins* (1985, Capcom), and *Bubble Bobble* (1986, Taito) among others. In the late 1980s and 1990s, new arcade genres such as beat 'em ups and head to head fighting games continued this trend as they built their identity on unique characters (see Chapter 7).

Laserdiscs, Narrative, and Gameplay

Inserting cut scenes between stages of gameplay, as seen in *Pac-Man* and refined in *Donkey Kong*, became the dominant approach to dealing with narrative. Coin-op games like *Dragon's Lair* (1983, Cinematronics), however, represented the brief pursuit of an alternative approach to integrating story and gameplay (Figure 4.7). As opposed to the period's typical raster or vector graphics, *Dragon's Lair* used visuals created through hand-drawn animation by the studio of former Disney animator, Don Bluth. The game's story centered on a knight named Dirk the Daring and his efforts to survive the challenges of a danger-filled castle to rescue the Princess Daphne from a fire-breathing dragon. Its medium and the talent in Bluth's studio made the characters in *Dragon's Lair* some of the most developed personalities in digital games.

In *Dragon's Lair*, the player watched animated segments and used the joystick and action button to react to flashing segments on the screen at key times. For instance, the game's opening featured Dirk walking across

FIGURE 4.7 *Dragon's Lair* **(1983, Cinematronics). (Courtesy of Digital Leisure Inc./ Dragon's Lair LLC.)**

a drawbridge and falling through a weak area. Below his dangling feet, a tentacled monster reached for Dirk; the player needed to press the "sword" button to fend the monster off. A player who failed to react in the appropriate way or was too slow, saw Dirk the Daring perish in darkly comedic ways. A player who succeeded, saw Dirk triumph via skill or luck, humanizing the character through nuanced actions. Since the gameplay needed to be fast and intense, the narrative of *Dragon's Lair* was punctuated with a constant sequence of threats, more than was typical for an animated film.

The design of *Dragon's Lair* was shaped by newly available laserdisc technology. Laserdiscs stored information in segments that could be accessed quickly and non-sequentially, as opposed to the linear format of film-based media. This setup allowed the player to almost immediately witness the consequences of the action, providing a feeling of control over the animated character. The gameplay was, nonetheless, entirely linear: the player either made the right choice and advanced the story, or the wrong choice and died. Despite this, the strength of the game's characters and the desire to see the story play out proved compelling enough to make *Dragon's Lair* a successful game. It led to a brief fad for "interactive film" games such as the animated *Space Ace* (1984, Cinematronics) and others during the Golden Age arcade.

Laserdisc technology was also used in conjunction with traditional raster graphics to give a fresh look to tried and true game concepts. Shoot 'em up games *Astron Belt* (1983, Sega) and *M.A.C.H 3* (1983, Mylstar Electronics) used raster graphic space ships and fighter jets superimposed over different environments captured by film to provide an unparalleled feeling of movement through space as the player shot at waves of enemies. Another action-flight simulator, *Firefox* (1984, Atari), used footage from the 1982 Clint Eastwood film of the same name. Problems with laserdisc players, caused by hours of searching for the proper scene to play, as well as the lack of replay value, however, limited the long-term viability of these games.

Eclectic Approaches to Arcade Game Design

Arcade games of the early 1980s faced increasing competition from home consoles and home computers as these platforms were able to deliver longer periods of gameplay with more variety of content (see Chapters 5 and 6). This need to remain competitive along with the desires of several seasoned coin-op game designers to tackle new challenges, resulted in a brief period of experimentation with "multi-genre" games. Multi-genre games combined several distinctive game types into a rapid-fire set of sequential play experiences that prevented the player from becoming settled in any one mode of gameplay for too long.

The eclectic approach was particularly strong between 1982 and 1983 and included games like *Tron* (1982, Bally/Midway), based on the

FIGURE 4.8 *Tron* **(1982, Bally/Midway). The cabinet for *Tron* featured black lights and high-quality graphics taken from the film for the cabinet art. (Courtesy of Arcadia, McLean, IL, www.vintagevideogames.com)**

Disney-produced film of the same name (Figure 4.8). The game presented the player with four different game types all loosely inspired by sequences from the film. Each of the four games used an existing genre: a light cycle battle similar to Gremlin's early arcade game *Blockade*, a tank and maze-based game evocative of Kee Games' *Tank*, and two shooting games similar to a single-player version of Taito's *Western Gun*.

One of Atari's last vector games was *Major Havoc* (1983) by Owen Rubin (Figure 4.9). *Major Havoc* combined three distinct types: a shoot 'em up against robot alien ships guarding a space station, a landing game on the space station's surface, and a low-gravity maze/platformer game within the space station. All of these sequences were smoothly linked together through a brief series of animated transitions. Each time the player completed the three-phased level, the robot ships became more aggressive, the landing space became smaller, and the maze grew more dangerous. Other examples

FIGURE 4.9 *Major Havoc* **(1983, Atari). The distinctive cabinet style for** *Major Havoc* **reflected the "high-tech" aesthetics of 1980s electronics. Custom designed for** *Major Havoc*, **the cabinet style was also used in Atari's other games of the period:** *Firefox, I, Robot,* **and** *Return of the Jedi.* **(Courtesy of Arcadia, McLean, IL, www.vintagevideogames.com)**

from the period included the manic *Zoo Keeper* (1982, Taito) and *Journey* (1983, Bally/Midway), a game based on the rock band Journey which featured digitized faces of the band's members.

Dave Theurer's *I, Robot* (1983, Atari) represented the height of Golden Age coin-op complexity: it consisted of three game genres and included a purely artistic mode that allowed players to create art using the game's visual assets. Additionally, *I, Robot* was the first arcade game to utilize solid 3D computer-generated imagery (Figure 4.10). These elements led to a surreal, unusually complex multi-genre game where the player, as an "Interface Robot," fought a rebellion against "Big Brother" and his "Evil Eyes." The first game segment involved running and jumping in a maze-like space to turn red squares blue, while avoiding flying birds, sharks, buzz saws, and the gaze of the Evil

CONTROLS IN MULTI-GENRE GAMES

Multi-genre games posed an interesting design challenge: how did one create a control scheme that would work for each of the games while remaining intuitive enough to not confuse the player? Additionally, designers needed to make sure that each game used all of the controls as "dead" inputs on any one game would unfairly confuse the player. A game like *Gorf* more easily bridged game and interface since each game was a shoot 'em up and only required a joystick for movement and a button to fire. *Tron* used a joystick with buttons and a dial controller for all but one of the four games—the light cycle battle used only the joystick. *Major Havoc*, however, found a method of universal input between its three very different game types by using a different controller type. The game's designer, Owen Rubin, utilized a single "action" button and a unique cylindrical roller control that could spin left or right. The roller allowed the player to move the ship left and right in the shoot 'em up sequence, maneuver into a landing position for the following segment, and direct Major Havoc to run left or right through the maze/platforming section.

Eye. Once completed, the game's second section contained a scrolling space shooter, viewed from behind the player's character as it shot at enemy units and polygons. Following this, the player needed to safely land on a platform to begin the cycle again. Both Theurer's *I, Robot* and Rubin's *Major Havoc* required the player to learn ever more complicated patterns of gameplay as each level introduced a new enemy behavior or pattern of movement. While still fundamentally based on attrition, this provided an alternative way to increase the game's difficulty beyond simply speeding up the enemies.

As mentioned above, *I, Robot* was the first coin-op game to use solid 3D computer-generated imagery. This avoided the problem of hidden line removal seen in earlier 3D vector-based games like *Tempest, Battlezone* (1980, Atari), and *Star Wars* (1983, Atari). Theurer, however, used this visual capability for more than novelty and integrated it in a way that effected gameplay. In *I, Robot* the player could cycle through different perspective views of the gamespace at any time, each at various heights and distances from the player's avatar. Since a view from farther away gave more information to the player, thereby making it easier to play, Theurer programmed the game to reduce the number of points awarded. The opposite was also true as closer views of the gamespace made the game more difficult, but awarded a greater amount of points. The 3D capabilities of the hardware saw other applications beyond games. The player could engage in what *I, Robot* identified as an "ungame" called *Doodle City* rather than play the game itself. In it, the player "painted" the screen for 3 minutes, using the game's visual assets. The works created were surreal as each object left a paint trail and could be rotated from a number of angles.

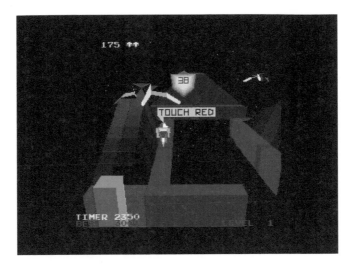

FIGURE 4.10 *I, Robot* **(1984, Atari).**

The innovative attempts to push multi-genre, coin-op games into new, experimental territory, however, were financially both hits and misses. Games like *Gorf* and *Tron* were critically acclaimed and successful in their time, but *Major Havoc* and *I, Robot*, were panned, as their design was considered too esoteric for coin-op audiences. Few of these games were produced, thus obscuring their accomplishments. The solid 3D geometry of *I, Robot*, for instance, would not return to the coin-op world until the late 1980s.

The End of the Golden Age Arcade

The stellar potential for profit in arcade games led many to believe arcades were a source of nearly limitless earning potential—a fallacy soon proven wrong. When the home console market in North America imploded in 1983 (see Chapter 5), the damage spilled over into coin-op games, significantly weakening it. In the late 1980s the home console game market recovered and home computers began to show greater gaming potential, signaling a decisive shift away from gaming in public spaces. Nonetheless, without the requirements to constantly generate money like arcade games, console and computer games were free to work with a wider variety of game design concepts that could appeal to more audiences. Although arcade-based beat 'em ups, head to head fighting games, and 3D racing games exerted significant influence on the other gaming contexts of the late 1980s and early 1990s (see Chapter 7), coin-op games were unable to recapture their former standard-bearing status. Thus the Golden Age signified both the height and the beginning of the end of the coin-op era that began in the late 1800s. Nonetheless, the ideas associated with games from the Golden Age arcade exerted a tremendous influence on a number of independent game designers, who worked to resurrect ideas long forgotten (see Chapter 10).

Chapter 5

Cartridges and Home Consoles (1976-1984)

The Second Generation of Home Consoles

Dedicated units that played variations of ping-pong dominated the first generation of home consoles. A major drawback of these machines, however, revolved around their inability to offer new content; once the novelty of playing the game wore off, players quickly tired of them. As discussed in Chapter 3, these machines flooded consumer outlets in the mid- to late 1970s and contributed to the market crash of 1977. Just prior to this slowdown, however, Fairchild Semiconductor followed by Atari each explored an alternative approach to home consoles (Figure 5.1). This approach took inspiration from computers as a single program could be switched into and out of the console's memory, potentially allowed for an infinite library of games. Other companies later followed this design concept as well, resulting in fierce competition as the home console market expanded rapidly in the early 1980s. Spanning approximately from 1976 to 1983, these "second-generation" consoles introduced game concepts and business practices that shaped the industry's development for decades.

Like prior dedicated consoles, arcade titles helped drive the popularity of the second generation. Atari, the largest coin-op game developer, particularly benefitted from porting its catalog of arcade hits to its home consoles, while Coleco pursued exclusive licenses with arcade game developers. Even games not originating in the arcade were commonly designed with arcade game-like

FIGURE 5.1 Fairchild Semiconductor released the first true cartridge-based home console in 1976. The main unit, designed by engineer Jerry Lawson, contained a number of built-in games as well as a cartridge port. The most notable feature of the unit was its unconventional controllers that combined a push button and rotary-like directional controller on a stick. (Photo Evan Amos. CC BY-SA 3.0.)

qualities. Despite the dominance of design ideas inherited from the arcades, the period saw the early development of a new approach to games that were more suited for play at home. These games utilized larger, more complex game spaces and centered their play on exploration and the discovery of the unknown. As such, their length of gameplay was measured in increments of tens of minutes, or in the most extreme cases, hours, as opposed to the 90 seconds of gameplay favored by arcade game designers.

New ideas in game design coupled with arcade hits reconfigured for home use, accelerated the young industry's growth in the early 1980s. By 1982, the industry had reached unprecedented heights only to be followed by a dramatic reversal. Multiple attempts at fast grabs for profit resulted in poorly designed games and created instability that weakened consumer demand and led to a collapse of the North American game industry in 1983. Companies like Atari saw its divisions spun off while many others, like Coleco and Mattel, exited the videogame market entirely. The void left behind allowed Japanese companies like Nintendo, Sega, and eventually Sony, to dominate the home console market from the late 1980s through much of the present day.

Atari and the VCS

Following the success of its home Pong unit, Atari released a cartridge-based console in 1977 called the "Video Computer System" or VCS (later renamed the 2600 after its product number). Since the console was intended for use in the home living room, the unit, like the Odyssey and Channel F, was designed with a faux wood front that matched home electronic trends of the 1970s. It was the unit's most iconic physical feature (Figure 5.2). Atari's arcade game background was apparent in the design of the unit's two main

FIGURE 5.2 **The first of several models of Atari's Video Computer System known as the "Heavy Sixer." Like Atari's Pong console, Sears released a version of the VCS as well as numerous cartridges under its "Telegames" brand. (Photo by Evan Amos.)**

controllers: one a rotary-dial paddle and the other, a single-button joystick. The joystick, however, was not particularly well-suited for operation in the home as a player needed to hold its base in one hand and manipulate the stick with the other. While this awkwardness led to frequent hand cramping, it nonetheless allowed game designers to more easily translate the basic controls of arcade games to home units.

The VCS, like other consoles of the time, was presented to the public as a machine capable of many applications. Its launch titles ranged from *Basic Math* (1977, Atari), an educational program centered on solving elementary-level math problems, to a simulation of the card game, *Blackjack* (1977, Atari). The majority of the launch titles, however, consisted of games either directly ported from or inspired by popular arcade games: *Surround* (1977, Atari) was effectively the dueling maze game *Blockade*, *Indy 500* (1977, Atari) included a port of Atari's *Crash n' Score* as well as a game similar to *Gran Trak 10*, *Combat* (1977, Atari) contained versions of *Tank* (1974) and *Jet Fighter* (1975), while *Video Olympics* (1977, Atari) featured a number of Atari's *Pong* variants. The debut of the VCS, however, was not met with immediate success: issues in production quality plagued the system and the glut of dedicated consoles slowed sales of home video games. In 1980, fortunes reversed as the VCS saw major gains, becoming the leader in the home market and overshadowing the Fairchild Channel F.

Game Design for the VCS

The majority of development time for VCS games was spent primarily on finding ways to display the game and achieve the programmer's goals as the machine had a strict set of limitations. From its earliest conception, the VCS was designed to play ball and paddle games like *Pong* and *Quadrapong* and dueling/shooting games like *Tank* and *Jet Fighter*. As such, the unit's hardware was designed to produce two projectiles, a ball and two player-controlled *sprites*—independently moving objects placed on top of a background. Additionally the cartridges loaded into the unit initially held only 2–4 kilobytes of memory, while the VCS could only hold a maximum of 128 bytes of data.

Despite these limitations, the VCS was remarkably flexible once its unique properties were mastered resulting in greater longevity than expected. *Video Chess* (1979, Atari), for example, presented a particularly clever set of solutions to these limitations. Although it took programmer Larry Wagner two years to write an algorithm to play chess on the VCS, one of the most difficult parts was representing the pieces on the screen. A standard game of chess gives each player 16 pieces to control distributed in two rows of eight. Translating this to the VCS meant placing eight sprites in a row. While certain techniques allowed programmers to place more sprites on the screen, eight sprites placed next to each other exceeded the unit's capabilities. Aiding Wagner was fellow Atari programmer Bob Whitehead who developed a graphical technique called *venetian blinds*, which broke each chess piece into segments of horizontal lines and horizontal spaces. Every other piece was then offset relative to its neighbors, creating a slight wave-like pattern among the rows of pieces. This technique reduced the number of sprites per row from eight to four, which when combined with other techniques, allowed the VCS to display a full game of chess. The venetian blinds technique was employed in several other games and is noticeable in the score readout for the VCS version of *Space Invaders* (1980, Atari) (Figure 5.3). *Video Chess*, however, was so taxing on the machine that it did not have enough resources to calculate the computer opponent's move and display the pieces at the same time. This resulted in a random sequence of colors briefly flashing across the screen between turns.

The development of *Video Chess* also led programmers to employ *bank switching* on the VCS. Although the final version of *Video Chess* did not utilize it, bank switching was a solution that allowed programmers to utilize a double-sized, 8-kilobyte cartridge. With more space, games could feature more game content, higher quality animations, and greater variety of visuals. The 1981 VCS port of *Asteroids* first made use of the technique. As the price of the higher capacity cartridges had become more cost-effective, both Atari and its competitors utilized this technique.

Changes at Atari

A number of changes occurred at Atari in the mid- to late 1970s. Atari needed a significant injection of capital to produce the VCS, resulting in the company's sale to Warner Communications in 1976. With Warner's backing, Atari's facilities expanded and its already impressive international presence grew even larger. The purchase, however, eventually led to friction as Warner Communications' traditional management structure clashed with the loose business culture at Atari. This, along with Nolan Bushnell becoming increasingly distracted by his new side venture, Chuck E. Cheese's Pizza Time Theatre, forced Warner Communications to initiate change. Bushnell was removed from executive functions and left Atari in 1979. After

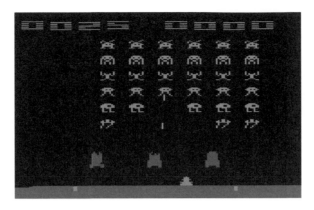

FIGURE 5.3 *Space Invaders* **(1980, Atari) for the Atari VCS.**

Bushnell, several others of the company's original management departed as well. In the wake of these high-profile departures, the new managers at Atari realigned company focus to favor marketing and advertising and put greater attention on the VCS. Marketing thus began to dictate not only which games would be made, but also when they were to be released. This led to an aggressive period of licensing arcade hits outside of Atari's catalog. The first was an adaption of Nishikado's *Space Invaders* arcade game to the VCS (Figure 5.3). The popularity of the arcade version of *Space Invaders* translated to the home as players bought new VCSs just to play the game at home. While this led to phenomenal short-term profits, it created a number of weaknesses that eventually came back to haunt the company.

Competition in the Home Market
The Emergence of Third-Party Developers

Throughout the second generation, it was common for a single individual to be responsible for all parts of a game's development—the design, programming, graphics, sound, etc. As such, the work of particularly talented individuals translated into great profits for the company. The games created by David Crane, Bob Whitehead, Alan Miller, and Larry Kaplan, for example, consisted of more than half of Atari's profits in 1978. While the company had a good year and the executives received lavish bonuses, its programmers saw no change in compensation and no public credit for their work. When Crane raised these concerns to the company's upper management, they were turned away. Further, in a news article about the company, Atari's new president referred to its VCS programmers as "high strung prima donnas," an off interview quote that was published as part of the story. Disgruntled, Crane, Whitehead, Miller, and Kaplan departed Atari in 1979 and with former Intellivision programmers, founded their own game company, Activision. In 1981, Atari programmers Rob Fulop, Dennis Kolbe, Bob Smith, and others also departed under the same circumstances, founding Imagic. The resentment of these ex-Atari employees was made clear as the instruction booklets for both Activision and Imagic games identified the programmers by name. Activision went a step further and occasionally included the programmer's name on the cartridge label, along with a picture and a personal message that unambiguously established authorship.

These "third party" software developers such as Activision, Imagic, and soon many more, represented a new practice in the game industry as studios created games for hardware they did not own. As a result, both Activision and Imagic became direct competitors to Atari, producing a number of highly innovative and original games for not only the Atari VCS, but also other gaming platforms such as the Intellivision, ColecoVision, and numerous early home computers. The greater variety of game ideas resulted in successful sales and helped keep the VCS in high demand through the early 1980s as competition drove each of the companies to excel. Although Atari brought suits against Activision, the case was thrown out. This effectively provided the legal basis for one company to produce software for another company's product, resulting in a flood of other startups that also wanted to produce games for the VCS. Although Atari's management eventually granted its VCS programmers profit sharing through bonus packages, it had already lost some of its most talented designers and created some of its strongest competitors.

The games produced for the VCS by Activision and Imagic were visually distinctive from those of Atari. Both companies used brighter, more saturated colors for their game worlds and featured some of the most advanced animations for the platform. David Crane's *Grand Prix* (1982, Activision) went beyond any of the previous race games offered on VCS as it included multi-colored vehicles complete with tires that simulated rotation at different speeds. Imagic meanwhile, established the first art department and hired artist Michael Becker as the industry's first videogame art director. This move was prompted by the state of visual quality in many second-generation games as programmers often did not have a background in art. With a dedicated art department, not only did visuals improve, but the process of creating them changed as well. Typically, a programmer laid out images on graph paper, which allowed one to code the coordinates of the individual pixels and their colors into the game. As this labor-intensive method was slow and discouraged refining game visuals, Bob Smith and Rob Fulop created tools that allowed artists to quickly edit pixel art and translate it into computer code. Imagic's Michael Becker first used these tools to create the demon characters for Rob Fulop's *Demon Attack* (1982), which received accolades for its art, animation, and gameplay. Soon after, as games grew in complexity, it became increasingly common to divide the work of making a game between programmers and artists.

GAME AUTHORSHIP AND EASTER EGGS

Throughout the second generation, many programmers hid their names or initials in their games. These *Easter eggs* typically required a great deal of effort by the player to find—effectively a separate game played between programmer and player. The first known occurrence of hidden names appeared on games for the Fairchild Channel F. A collection of demonstration programs for the system known as *Democart* (1977) revealed the name of programmer Michael Glass if a certain combination of the machine's buttons was pressed at the demo's end. *Video Whizball* (1978) displayed the name "Reid-Selth" for its programmer Brad Reid-Selth if the player performed a sequence of actions before starting a new game. The complexity of these unofficial parts of the program grew quickly. Warren Robinett's *Adventure* (1979, Atari) contained a secret room that displayed his name but was only accessible if the player found a one-pixel gray box concealed in a gray wall, then used it to walk through an impassable border. Although executives at Atari and other companies were initially unaware that their programmers were hiding their names, Atari, in particular, decided that Easter eggs like these and others a desirable mystique and sanctioned their creation.

Howard Scott Warshaw of Atari created some of the most elaborate and playful Easter eggs of the era that not only revealed his initials, but also referenced his game career: after collecting seven Reese's Pieces and turning them into Elliot in Warshaw's third game, *E.T.: The Extra-Terrestrial* (1982), the player could revive a dying flower that turned into an animated "Yar" from *Yar's Revenge* (1982). The second time the player performed this task, the flower changed into an "Indy" from *Raiders of the Lost Ark* (1982). A third time revealed the initials "HSW3" in the score area, to signify *E.T.* as Howard Scott Warshaw's third game.

The creator's name or identity as an Easter egg continued beyond the second generation almost as a tradition of the medium. *Mortal Kombat II* (1993, Midway) contained a secret playable fighter named "Noob Saibot," the reverse spelling of the game's main creators, Ed Boon and John Tobias while *Doom II: Hell on Earth* (1994, id Software) used a hidden target in the game's final boss battle—the severed head of its founder John Romero.

Mattel and Coleco Enter the Console Market

Beginning in 1976, toy company Mattel released a number of L.E.D. handheld games based on various sports themes. The following year, the company began developing the Intellivision, a home videogame console designed to compete against Atari's VCS. The popularity of the handheld games, however, and Mattel's reluctance to directly compete against Atari, delayed serious action until the Intellivision was released in 1980. Much like Atari's VCS, the initial Intellivision game catalog concentrated on variety, featuring sports games, with a few gambling, board, and arcade-style games. Mattel's marketing strategy presented the Intellivision as a sophisticated, educational, and family-oriented entertainment system; it was "intelligent television." The campaign also was keen to draw visual comparisons between the Intellivision and VCS using sports games. Since the Intellivision could more easily display a larger number of sprites, it was more able to represent popular sports like football and baseball. The use of well-known journalist George Plimpton as spokesperson further cemented the Intellivision's identity.

By 1982, however, the boom of the Golden Age arcade directed Mattel to pursue more shooting-oriented games. A number of licensed arcade ports produced by rival Coleco also made an appearance on the system at this time. The Intellivision proved a strong competitor to the VCS and inaugurated the first of many "console wars" in home videogames. In reaction to this, Atari rushed production of the VCS's successor, the Atari 5200 Super System, a decision that also would hurt the company. Atari had recognized that arcade games helped sell home units and thus designed the 5200 using the sophisticated hardware from its 400/800 line of home computers (see Chapter 6). Although more powerful, the 5200 struggled to gain traction: it lacked unique game offerings and its poorly designed controllers featured a non-centering joystick that made gameplay feel "sloppy" (Figure 5.7). In addition, much of the built-up anticipation for the Atari 5200 was deflated after Coleco released its sophisticated home system in 1982, the ColecoVision.

Coleco emerged from the market crash of 1977 in financial straits. Although its line of Telstar dedicated consoles, powered by the General Instruments AY-3-8500 "Pong-on-a-chip," had been successful, the flooded market created difficult to absorb financial losses. Coleco's management, however, was undeterred and, like Mattel, produced a number of handheld sports games in the late 1970s. The surge in popularity of arcade games in the early 1980s led Coleco to wisely secure exclusive licenses with a number of Japanese game companies including Nintendo, Namco, Konami, and Sega. Coleco used these licenses to produce a line of miniature arcade cabinets, complete with replicated cabinet art and joysticks (Figure 5.4). Seeing an opportunity to compete with both Atari and Mattel, Coleco used its exclusive licenses to push its 1982 cartridge-based home console, the ColecoVision. In a stroke of masterful marketing, they packaged the ColecoVision with a port of *Donkey Kong*, which, of all second-generation consoles, most closely replicated the images and sound of Shigeru Miyamoto's original arcade game. Coleco's exclusive rights to the home version of many Golden Age greats also allowed it to produce arcade game ports for both the VCS and Intellivision. This earned the company significant sales across all platforms and provided constant opportunities to show the graphical superiority of its own system.

Despite being underpowered compared to its rivals, the VCS had a head start, a well-developed library of ports from Atari's arcade division, a few exclusive licensing deals and robust third-party development. These

FIGURE 5.4   Coleco's Mini Arcade cabinets used VFD technology to create bright colors that other small LED and LCD units could not replicate.

circumstances allowed Atari's VCS console to remain competitive in the early 1980s. Both Mattel and Coleco targeted these great advantages by creating accessories that allowed their systems to play Atari's VCS games. The 1982 "Expansion Module 1" for the ColecoVision and the 1983 "System Changer" for the Intellivision plugged into each console and accepted Atari cartridges. Even Atari released an add-on that allowed its floundering 5200 console to play VCS games, although some models required an upgrade at an official Atari service center first. The introduction of these add-ons resulted in numerous marketing campaigns where each system, aided by the extensive VCS catalog, claimed the ability to play the most games.

Beyond the Arcade

Adding Content to Home Console Games

Arcade games were the single greatest influence on designers of second-generation home console hardware and games, especially so after 1980. Much of this was due to the desire to replicate the proven designs of certain coin-op games. As such, designers of home console games like *K.C. Munchkin!* (1981, Magnavox) and *Astrosmash* (1981, Mattel) strove to create the tension and action of arcade games like *Pac-Man*, *Space Invaders*, and *Asteroids*. The economics that shaped game design in the arcade, however, were not the same as those of the home. Without the need to insert a quarter into the machine, home video games lost the single greatest choice made by the player—whether to play the game again. With replay as a given, games for the home would be played more frequently. Quick deaths and rapid increases in difficulty would not justify the significantly greater cost for those who purchased game cartridges. Designers, thus, needed a way to extend the length of a player's interaction while still employing the qualities that made arcade games enjoyable.

The most common solution to extend play was to allow the player to choose the level of game difficulty. This setting typically governed the number of lives one received, speed of enemies, or other variables that aided or hindered the player's performance. The 1982 version of *Donkey Kong* for the Colecovision, for example, offered a number of skill levels that set the game's countdown timer at higher or lower values, while the difficulty switches for the VCS's version of *Frogger* (1982, Parker Brothers) controlled how soon the game's more difficult enemies appeared.

Another typical approach was a "game select" option that could substantially change the nature of gameplay by altering rules. The *Space Invaders*-inspired, *Alien Invasion* (1981, Fairchild Semiconductor) for the Fairchild Channel F, for instance, featured 10 variations that allowed the player to control the number of shots at a time by both player and aliens. Although seemingly minor, these rule changes resulted in different gameplay experiences. Games on the VCS were particularly notable for their high number of variations. The two-player dueling game *Combat* featured 27 variations spread out between six distinct games with different rules and graphics. One of the more eccentric of these was the "Easy Maze, Billiard Hit, Invisible Tank Pong" variation in which the dueling tanks were only visible at certain times and could only score a hit after a projectile bounced off the maze walls at least once. The Atari VCS's version of *Space Invaders* contained an astonishing 112 variations and included everything from invisible aliens to a cooperative mode that divided the turret's left and right movement between two players. Other variants such as those found in *Video Olympics* and *Basketball* (1978, Atari) featured options for dueling against a human or computer-controlled opponent. Often, the variations were so numerous that manuals listed them in chart form for easy reference. Since programmers needed every byte possible to create a complete game, these minor manipulations were economical solutions to providing more gameplay.

Altering Time in Home Console Games

In addition to creating minor gameplay variations, game designers explored ways to extend the home gaming experience by altering the way time was used. This undercut a central pillar of arcade game design as a majority of postwar electromechanical arcade games such as *K.O. Champ* (Figure 1.11) and many early digital arcade games like *Death Race* (Figure 3.9), gave the player a fixed amount of time for each coin. Additionally, the related rate of increase in game difficulty was also reconsidered. As discussed in Chapters 3 and 4, these systems were designed to limit a player's game time, allowing the machine to acquire more money through replay or new customers. The modification of this fundamental element of arcade games lowered stress on the player and encouraged a more strategic or leisurely pace of play. These modifications allowed the development of new game forms for home consoles; games focused on the exploration of space and the strategic management of resources. Additionally narrative became increasingly important. Critical to their development were the mainframe computer games of the 1960s and 1970s created and modified by amateur computer programmers. Although several home console games still bore a resemblance to popular maze and shooter-type arcade games, they nonetheless led to meaningful distinctions between games for arcades and games for home consoles.

Adventure and Exploration in Console Games

Game designers had considerable freedom to develop games along their own lines despite management and marketing divisions pushing programmers to create games according to arcade conventions. *Adventure* (1979), by Atari programmer Warren Robinett, set a precedent for graphics-based adventure games throughout the second generation and beyond. Robinett wished to re-create Don Woods and William Crowther's 1978 text adventure, *Colossal Cave Adventure* (see Chapter 6). After he encountered the limitations of the VCS, however, Robinett revised the concept and delivered an innovative experience focused on the search for a chalice through dragon-inhabited mazes and torch-lit catacombs. He translated familiar text adventure keyboard commands "GO NORTH," "PICK UP SWORD", and "USE KEY" to the one button Atari joystick: this allowed players to pick up objects by moving over them, to use objects by touching them with other objects, and to drop objects with the push of a button. Without arcade elements such as score, timer, or limited lives, players were free to explore and play at their own pace.

The most novel aspect of *Adventure*, however, was the space. In order to create a feeling that the player had embarked on a journey, the game spanned a set of screens and took the player through different environments: mazes, castles, and catacombs. The catacombs in particular were visually innovative as the player's view consisted of a small circle surrounded by blank space that represented movement by torchlight. Throughout their journey, players needed to revisit certain spaces multiple times to collect items or slay dragons, an unconventional use of space in light of the linear progression through levels of arcade games. To add to the already relatively long game, the player could choose a game variation that placed the objects and dragons in random places throughout the game's world, allowing for a greater degree of replay. These features helped make *Adventure* one of the most successful games of not only the VCS, but of the entire second generation.

The medieval fantasy theme proved to be useful for extending gameplay through exploration, as the pre-industrial setting conjured images of vast natural landscapes with hidden dangers and rewards. The 1982 *Advanced Dungeons & Dragons* (later retitled *Advanced Dungeons & Dragons: Cloudy Mountain Cartridge*), designed by Tom Loughry for Mattel's Intellivision console, used this idea by dividing the game space between two levels: a map-like overworld that represented a landscape of multiple terrains and a subterranean maze of cave passages. The player's task was to find two pieces of a crown guarded by winged dragons in the titular Cloudy Mountain. In order to reach Cloudy Mountain, players needed to make their way through a number of underground passages filled with monsters and, at times, backtrack through previously explored areas to locate crucial items (Figure 5.5).

Loughry felt that players needed to be presented with something new each time they played; that surprise and discovery were the key attributes of an enjoyable game. Randomization, thus, was a core part of *Cloudy Mountain's* design, as each play session yielded a different configuration of the overworld landscape and subterranean caves. Using similar mechanics as the computer game *Rogue* (see Chapter 6), the space of each cave in *Cloudy Mountain* was only revealed by exploration: this resulted in either the surprise of finding a useful item or the shock of seeing a monster. To keep the act of exploration even more full of tension, Loughry programmed the monsters to signal their presence by emitting sounds from off-screen.

Loughry's follow-up adventure game for the Intellivision, *Advanced Dungeons & Dragons: Treasure of Tarmin Cartridge* (1982), proved to be an even greater departure from the arcades. Inspired by a first-person adventure game that Loughry played on a computer mainframe, *Treasure of Tarmin*

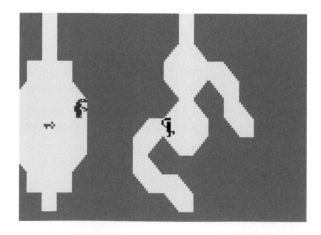

FIGURE 5.5 *Advanced Dungeons & Dragons: Cloudy Mountain Cartridge* (1982, Mattel).

provided a sense of immersion not seen on a home console (Figure 5.6). The player, again tasked with finding treasure, descended through increasingly difficult levels of a labyrinth, gathering weapons and armor of varied quality in preparation for a final confrontation with the maze's minotaur. Randomization again played an important role in the game experience, as each level was assembled from various premade segments and included hidden doors leading to treasure.

One of Loughry's main concerns with a first-person perspective was the ease with which a player could get lost. To help prevent this he incorporated a compass in the interface, a screen-wipe that originated from the left or right edge of the screen when the player turned and, finally, a set of markers on the floor denoting the outside edge of each level. It also incorporated an elegantly designed inventory system, managed by the player and accessed by the Intellivision's unique disk and keypad controller.

The complex game play and process of character development in *Treasure of Tarmin* required a significant time commitment on the part of the player, as the Intellivision was incapable of saving the game's progress. The game's four difficulty settings were measured in the number of levels required to reach the final treasure, an estimated 5 minutes on the easiest setting, to 5 *hours* on the most difficult. The memory resources needed to produce Loughry's two games were significant, which demanded larger cartridges. *Cloudy Mountain* was designed on a 6 kilobyte cartridge at a time when 4 kilobytes was standard, while *Treasure of Tarmin* was even larger at 8 kilobytes.

Exploration-based gameplay appeared in many other home console games of the early 1980s. *Haunted House* (1982, Atari) placed the player in a haunted mansion, searching for pieces of a broken urn. Since the game was comprised of slowly feeling one's way through the dark by way of match light, the game had no timer and awarded the player for using as few matches as

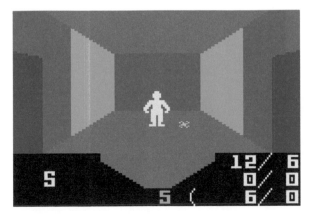

FIGURE 5.6 *Advanced Dungeons & Dragons: Treasure of Tarmin Cartridge* **(1982, Mattel).**

OVERLAYS IN LATER SECOND-GENERATION CONTROLLERS

Beginning with the Intellivision, many consoles featured controllers with a numeric keypad similar to that of a touchtone phone (Figure 5.7). This allowed game designers to program more actions and thus give the player more choices, an approach avoided in the simple to control arcade games of the period. The change of input helped remove one of the barriers to creating games that were better suited for play at home.

A problem with this type of controller design, however, was that any one game might use a different configuration of the buttons, leading to difficulties in controlling the game. To avoid confusion, game developers created overlays that slid into the controllers over the keys. The overlays helped direct the player's attention as unused keys were blocked out and active keys were given meaning with labels and graphics. The Intellivision, Emerson Arcadia 2001, ColecoVision, and Atari 5200 all used this method. Despite being widespread, controller overlays were short lived. Third- and fourth-generation consoles moved away from remotes with keypads and adopted game pads with a simpler button and d-pad setup.

FIGURE 5.7 **Atari 5200 Super System Controllers with overlays for** *Space Invaders* **and** *Soccer***. Each reveals the different input needs of each game.**

possible. Randomized locations of objects, again, played an important part in the game's replayability. Howard Scott Warshaw's *Raiders of the Lost Ark* (1982, Atari) for the VCS, reenacted the film of the same name and put the player on a multi-screen adventure looking for the location of the Ark of the Covenant. The complexity of the game necessitated an inventory system, as multiple items were often required to advance to new sections. Since the VCS joystick had a limited number of inputs, *Raiders of the Lost Ark* experimented with the use of two joysticks—one to control the character, the other to select items from the inventory.

A different approach to action and exploration was used in David Crane's incredible 255 screen game, *Pitfall!* (1982, Activision). *Pitfall!* required the player to move between multiple spaces in search of treasure, often backtracking in order to retrieve an out-of-reach item (Figure 5.8). Crane's design for *Pitfall!* allowed it to remain challenging for new and experienced players without resorting to difficulty settings or game variations. The game had a unique approach to scoring, as collecting treasures increased score but certain dangers, like rolling logs or falling into an underground tunnel, would erode accumulated points. Other dangers like crocodiles, quicksand, and scorpions resulted in an instant loss of a life. The longer one played, the greater the chance that the score would fluctuate, adding another level of challenge to experienced players. Further, he used a timer set at 20 minutes. This feature allowed newer players, who would presumably lose quicker, the opportunity to explore the large game space and see its vast offerings without being required to hurry through it. Once a player mastered the game's early challenges and played longer, the timer became an important consideration and created a new source of tension. The unique combination of elements, coupled with sophisticated graphics that many thought were impossible to display on the VCS, made *Pitfall!* one of the most highly regarded games of the second generation.

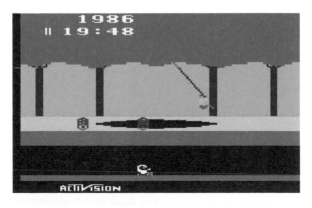

FIGURE 5.8   *Pitfall!* (1982, Activision).

Resource Management Games on Home Consoles

Prior to becoming an Intellivision programmer in 1980, Don Daglow created university mainframe games in the 1970s such as *Star Trek, Dungeon* and others. Additionally, he designed a number of social studies-themed educational games that he used as a middle school teacher. When Mattel's management requested an Intellivision game that differed from arcade-style and sports games, Daglow drew on his background to create *Utopia* (1981, Mattel). The principal gameplay of *Utopia* was centered on managing an island community's happiness by building infrastructure and mitigating the effects of natural disasters. It combined active resource gathering—moving a fishing boat around the screen, with long-term strategic planning—building structures that modified elements such as the rate of currency gain, food produced, and population growth. Like many second-generation games one or two players could play the game, each governing their own island. The game's systems included uncontrollable weather patterns that could help or hinder as well as affordances that created rebellions should the quality of life of the inhabitants drop too low.

Utopia was one of the first "god games," as it allowed an omniscient player to see all and direct all. The Intellivision's keypad controller was well-suited for the gameplay: each button allowed the player to build a different structure, a method of interaction that appeared as a graphical user interface in later simulation and real-time strategy games such as *Sim City* and *Command & Conquer* (see Chapter 6). It was an immediate success and earned praise as a game type that reinforced Intellivision's image as a more sophisticated, "intelligent" console.

A similar management-type game, *Fortune Builder* (1984, Coleco), appeared 3 years later on the ColecoVision (Figure 5.9). One or two players developed land by building infrastructure, residential areas, and commercial spaces while managing a pool of money. The player used a scrolling window to navigate the game space, allowing them to encounter a variety of terrain such as mountains, rivers, and coastlines. Television bulletins occasionally informed the player of severe weather and provided direction for popular and unpopular activities among the city's inhabitants. *Fortune Builder* was not as loosely structured as *Utopia*: players worked toward earning $250,000,000 in a set time limit or raced to reach the goal before their opponent. Like *Utopia*, however, its design was wholly suited for play at home as the game's relatively flat difficulty and longer gameplay time would be unsustainable in an arcade context.

The map-like spaces of these games and others of the second generation like *War Room* (1983, NAP Consumer Electronics) meshed well with the capabilities of the Intellivision and ColecoVision as they utilized *tiling*. As opposed to drawing each pixel and remembering their individual

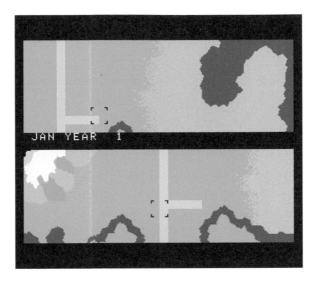

FIGURE 5.9 *Fortune Builder* **(1984, Coleco).**

positions, the tile-based Intellivision and ColecoVision systems created the screen from sets of 8×8 pixel tiles. This reduced the amount of information the processor needed to track and allowed for faster game performance. Additionally, artists could create game visuals faster as tiles could be reused to cover areas quickly. Tiling was particularly apparent in the landscapes of *Fortune Builder* as the mountains and bends in the river were created from the same sets of tiles. Each icon representing improvements on the landscape was also composed of a single tile. Tiling was not exclusive to home consoles as many 2D arcade games such as *Pac-Man*, *Donkey Kong*, and *Gauntlet* also utilized this method of creating graphics. It would also appear in later 2D home consoles of the 1980s and early 1990s such as the Nintendo Entertainment System, Sega Genesis, and others.

Sports Games for the Home

Time of gameplay was also significant in translating sports-based games from the arcades to the home. Atari's coin-op *Football* (1978), for instance, granted the player up to 3 minutes of gameplay per quarter. Players who wished to play longer needed to add additional coins, which broke up the flow of the game or otherwise caused the player to adopt riskier strategies that would result in a quick score. The game length of Bob Whitehead's *Football* (1978, Atari) for the VCS, however, began with five minutes. *Realsports Football* (1982, Atari) simulated a 15 minute game, with later titles adding more time per play. In addition to football, designers recreated most of the major sports in greater detail by including more of the sport's dimensions of play; a trajectory that put sports-based games on the path to simulations.

The North American Console Crash

In 1982 the game industry was riding high and expanding rapidly; projections estimated that the industry would break two billion dollars sometime during the year. Atari, itself, represented the majority of the industry, with arcade games, home consoles, and home computers (see Chapter 6). Atari's competitors also looked vigorous, as analysts predicted a high that would run through 1985. These predictions, however, were based on grossly inflated estimations of worth: the stock of Atari's parent company, Warner Communications was selling at eight times its earnings, while Intellivision producer Mattel was selling at four times its earnings. In addition to a false perspective of the industry's worth, management at many game companies failed to respect the process of game development leading to a number of poor business decisions. The North American crash of 1983 was thus a perfect storm of circumstances occurring within a bubble ready to burst.

Perhaps the main factor that contributed to the crash was the attempt by software developers to cash-in quickly by churning out a high volume of games that were frequently substandard and derivative. Companies large and small, many of which had little to no experience in digital games, attempted to find success in a market that seemed to go only in one direction—up. But, as the major console producers lost control over who could publish content on their systems, consumers were forced to wade through an escalating volume of poorly designed or unimaginative games to find quality.

Two high-profile releases by Atari, *Pac-Man* in the spring of 1982 followed by *E.T.: The Extra-Terrestrial* during the year's holiday season, added to the problems. *Pac-Man* was the most popular arcade game in the United States after its 1980 debut. It spawned copious amounts of merchandise, multiple strategy guides, a Top 40 song, and even a Hanna–Barbera animated series. Expectations, thus, were high when Atari announced the game would be available for the VCS in the early spring of 1982. Atari understood the importance of the game in so far as its ability to generate profit, but it failed to take the steps necessary to produce a quality product.

Rather than being assigned to an experienced programmer, the VCS adaption of *Pac-Man* was put up for grabs and eventually found its way to programmer Tod Frye as his first project. Further, Atari management decided to use cheaper 4 kilobyte cartridges rather than higher capacity 8 kilobyte cartridges, severely limiting the game's scope. Frye's adaption, nonetheless, faithfully recreated the rules and game mechanics of *Pac-Man*, but had little of the game's feel and beloved visuals: the individually colored ghosts of the arcade version were rendered in identical colors that flickered due to the VCS's sprite limitations; the sounds and animations were limited and choppy; it contained none of the cut scenes; and the colorful bonus fruit was

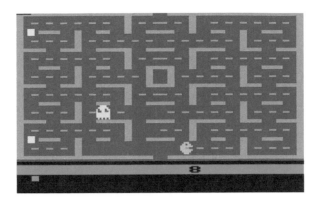

FIGURE 5.10 **The VCS Version of** *Pac-Man* **(1982, Atari).**

replaced with a generic square set of pixels identified as a "vitamin" (Figure 5.10). Since Atari expected sales to be significant, it ordered the creation of approximately 12 million cartridges, a figure that exceeded the estimated number of VCS consoles in the United States by a few million. This decision was based on the assumption that the game itself would sell more consoles, similar to what had happened with the VCS port of *Space Invaders*.

The development of *E.T.: The Extra-Terrestrial*, was similarly compromised by poor business decisions, the most significant mistakes coming from Atari's parent company, Warner Communications. Warner, in an attempt to persuade Steven Spielberg to direct films for Warner Communication's film branch, Warner Studios, agreed to pay Spielberg an exorbitant sum of $21 million dollars for the rights to create an E.T. game. With the deal made, Warner informed executives at Atari that not only must a game based on E.T. be made, but also that it be ready for the 1982 holiday season. Programmer Howard Scott Warshaw had experience producing games, including the acclaimed *Yar's Revenge* (1982, Atari) and *Raiders of the Lost Ark*, but was given just over 5 weeks to take the game from concept to production. Despite this limited time frame, the game was fairly ambitious: an exploration game based on collecting scattered parts of a device randomly distributed through multiple screens in order to "phone home" while avoiding scientists and FBI agents. Each screen allowed E.T. to execute a different power that helped him on his journey. Nonetheless, since development times for most second-generation games typically took a few months, quality testing was skipped and the game shipped in an unpolished state that made it frustrating to play. In particular, the gameplay was disorienting to players as moving from one screen space to another could result in continuously falling into pits. Worse yet, Atari needed to sell a large number of cartridges to recoup the $21 million licensing deal and return a slim profit, leading them to produce 5 million cartridges.

Just as 1982 was a year of intense growth, 1983 and especially 1984 were years of rapid contraction. Although *Pac-Man* and *E.T.: The Extra-Terrestrial* initially made spectacular sales, the gameplay of *E.T.*, in particular, motivated a large number of consumers to return the game. Retailers saw the demand for nearly all console games evaporate and returned their unsold and often unopened merchandise to Atari. Of the 5 million *E.T.: The Extra-Terrestrial* cartridges produced, approximately three and a half million were eventually returned to the company from distributers. Other games were similarly returned. Atari, with a backlog of multiple titles that retailers could not sell, disposed of a majority of the overstock in a Sunnyvale, California landfill. A small portion was sent to a landfill in Alamogordo, New Mexico, where the dumping was sensationalized in local newspapers and national media, growing in scale over time. The end result was a myth that the Alamogordo landfill received *all* 3.5 million unwanted copies of *E.T.* and that the game had single-handedly brought the industry crashing down.

Other Factors

The development and marketing fiasco of *Pac-Man* and *E.T.*, while extremely damaging to Atari, was not in itself sufficient to cause the market crash. The introduction of affordable home computers, like the 1982 Commodore 64, persuaded many consumers to purchase something with an application beyond game playing (see Chapter 6). Consumer confidence was also steadily eroded as many companies over-promised and under delivered. Mattel released the Intellivision II in 1982, which despite its name, was identical to the original Intellivision except for a number of cost-saving elements that lowered the quality of the product but allowed it to play VCS games via the System Changer add-on. Mattel and Coleco both produced other add-ons that turned their consoles into fully functioning home computers; however, Mattel's did not materialize until it was too late and Coleco's "Adam" computer conversion kit did not sell well. Further Coleco had rushed its 1983 Adam computer into production to meet a promised shipping date, half of which were returned as defective.

Fallout of the Crash

As sales of home videogame consoles and cartridges declined, many game producers large and small were forced to shut down. Coleco exited the market completely in 1985. Mattel closed its electronics division in 1984, however investors bought the rights to the machine and continued to release games and units until 1990. Nonetheless, the Intellivision would be seen as a minor player in the upcoming era of the Famicom/Nintendo Entertainment System (see Chapter 7). Warner Communications sold the home console and computer division of Atari in 1984 to help finance the company's value drop and in 1985, the coin-op arcade division was sold as well. Parts of Atari

Inc. bounced between various companies around the world throughout the 1980s and 1990s. It continued to produce home video game consoles through the mid-1990s with the Jaguar, but the brand never regained its earlier status. While home consoles took the brunt of the damage from the crash, arcades in the United States too suffered as an estimated one-fifth closed their doors in 1983. Smaller venues such as bowling alleys and movie theaters, however helped keep arcade games in demand through the 1980s and 1990s.

It is important to keep in mind that the crash of 1983 was confined largely to North America. The console industry in the early 1980s was not as developed in other parts of the world, at times resulting in little indication of anything that could be construed as a "crash." Much of this was due to the greater popularity of home computers in Europe and elsewhere, as they represented a different market and catered to a wider array of gaming preferences. Nonetheless, the fallout created a vacuum that allowed Japanese companies like Nintendo, Sega, and Sony to rekindle the home console market in North America and lead it through much of the contemporary context.

Chapter **6**

Home Computers (1977-1995)

The Microcomputer Revolution

In 1974, computer visionary Ted Nelson wrote the combined books *Computer Lib/Dream Machines*,[*] a counterculture-infused introduction to computers and computer concepts aimed at the general population with the tagline "You can and must understand computers NOW." Nelson's motivation stemmed from his concern with the fundamental misunderstandings of computers by the public and what he saw as narrow-minded computer applications by government and corporate entities. Nelson believed that computers had already remade society by 1974 and would continue to do so at an ever-increasing pace. He saw them as machines capable of empowering humanity and fostering limitless creativity. His book, fighting against restriction, coercion, and "cybercrud," aimed to create a population that was both educated and critical about computer use.

Nelson's book was timely as the mid to late 1970s saw the first "microcomputers." Unlike time-shared terminals connected to minicomputers like the PDP-1 (see Chapter 2), microcomputers were intended for individual use. Technology companies Apple, Commodore, and Tandy (owned by Radio Shack) released the first set of preassembled, mass-produced microcomputers in 1977: the Apple II, Commodore PET, and TRS-80. Coin-op arcade and home console manufacturer, Atari soon followed with the Atari 400 and Atari 800 computers in 1979.

---

[*] Nelson, T. 1974. *Computer Lib: You Can and Must Understand Computers Now.* Chicago: Nelson.

In England, inventor, Clive Sinclair released the affordable ZX80 and ZX81 computers while Acorn Computers created a string of machines including the 1981 BBC Micro. As the price of computer components tumbled in the early 1980s, computers such as the British ZX Spectrum and North American Commodore 64, combined high performance and affordability, helping to place computers in homes throughout the decade.

As the new class of microcomputers was marketed to both businesses and individuals, knowledge of computers was imperative for future political, economic, and cultural development. Universities and elementary schools began teaching how to use computers through educational software, word processors, and even programming languages. Special arrangements between computer manufacturers and schools led to machines like the French TO 7 computer, part of a French educational initiative called "dix mille microordinateurs" (10,000 microcomputers). In England, the British Broadcasting Corporation initiated the BBC Computer Literacy Project, leading not only to the creation of the BBC Micro but also weekly television programs of the 1980s such as *The Computer Programme*, which aimed to educate the population of the British Isles on how to use computers. Although Nelson's prescient *Computer Lib/Dream Machines* predicted the need to "understand computers NOW," it was centered on minicomputers and did not anticipate that the true revolution would come on the wings of the microcomputer (hereafter referred to as simply "computers" to prevent confusion).

Computer Games of the Late 1970s and Early 1980s

The first consumer model computers were marketed primarily on their text-based applications such as programming, organizing payrolls, learning mathematics, and keeping track of inventory. The graphically robust Apple II, for instance, gained its prominence through *VisiCalc* (1979, VisiCorp), the first computer spreadsheet program. Game development was seen by marketing bodies as a secondary function of these machines. Nonetheless the Apple II, ZX Spectrum, Commodore 64, and the Atari 400/800 computers were particularly popular for game development because of their ability to display more complicated graphics and superior sound.

Early games for computers explored various approaches to game design including clones or derivatives of Golden Age arcade games, simulations of card and board games, and the adaption of minicomputer games. As the capabilities of computers were limited in memory and processing power compared to their larger cousins, it was essential for programmers to employ memory-saving tricks, especially for advanced graphics. A common method involved programming in *assembly language,* where the programmer directed the processor's individual actions through abbreviated words and numbers, frequently resulting in unintelligible strings of commands. This contrasted with higher-level languages such as BASIC, which automatically translated clear word commands into multiple actions understandable by the computer. For example, a program that displayed the text "hello world," could be simply executed with one line of code in BASIC, while the same program in assembly language could take upwards of 12 lines of code. Saving a few bytes could result in a game with more appealing visuals or a larger scope, as was the case with *Elite* (see below). The most significant advantage of the tedious assembly language, however, was the greater degree of speed: games written in assembly could outperform those written in BASIC by a wide margin leading to a significant difference in quality.

As opposed to home console games that were sold at established store chains and packaged professionally, marketing for early computer games was informal. Game disks in the United States were commonly packaged in resalable plastic bags with short, photocopied manuals and sold in local stores. This zine-like quality with small runs and local distribution meant that few of the early consumer computer games reached national audiences. In England, retail distribution was hardly an option until the mid-1980s: programmers instead distributed games via mail order, often sent from their home address. Nonetheless, the late 1970s and early 1980s saw the development of three unique genres of commercial computer games: adventure games, role-playing games, and simulation games—all of which were connected to the games produced for minicomputers by hackers in the 1970s (see Chapter 2).

COMPUTERS AND SECOND GENERATION CONSOLES

Early consumer computers shared a number of similarities with second generation consoles. Both contained the same or similar 8-bit processors, both used home televisions for display, and both could even use some of the same game controllers (Figure 6.1). Both types of machines functioned in similar ways as neither was capable of storing information on internal hard drives. Programs, such as games, needed to be loaded into the computer's random access memory (RAM), which temporarily held the information while the machine was running. Computers, such as the TI-99, Atari 400, Atari 800, and Commodore 64, also used cartridges as the standard method of loading programs. Higher capacity 5.25″ floppy disk drives were initially uncommon because of expense and were typically sold separately. Finally, most early computers, like home consoles, featured a *closed architecture* design that did not allow upgrades; the main exception being the ability to add more RAM.

FIGURE 6.1   Challenger Turbo Deluxe Joystick Controller (left) with unconventional pivoting dome and the motion-sensitive Le Stick joystick by Datasoft (right). Both plugged into DE-9 connection ports, which were used, among others, by the Atari VCS, Commodore 64, Atari 400, Atari 800, and many MSX-spec computers.

From Text to Graphic Adventure Games

One of the earliest types of commercialized computer games was interactive fiction. Interactive fiction games used descriptive blocks of text rather than images, to communicate the setting and actions within the game world. Players issued commands by typing words on the keyboard. While the games contained several kinds of play, including turn-based combat, the main focus was on exploration and puzzle solving.

The first interactive fiction game was *Adventure*, or *Colossal Cave Adventure*, created on a university mainframe minicomputer by Will Crowther in 1975 and modified in 1976 by Don Woods. Crowther's game simulated the exploration of Mammoth Cave in Kentucky. It combined elements from his background as a caver with fantasy aspects from the tabletop version of *Dungeons & Dragons* (see Chapter 2). *Adventure* featured puzzles, a combat system and score: players earned points for exploring, collecting treasure, and bringing it back to the surface after descending through the caves. The original game allowed only two-word commands, such as "GO IN" or "OPEN DOOR," due to limitations of the FORTRAN computer language that Crowther used.

Adventure also differed from earlier games like *Spacewar!*, in that it was primarily played via monitor-less teletype terminals connected to a central minicomputer. Players entered commands into a keyboard and waited for the distant computer to process, then sent back the result through long sheets of paper from the terminal's printer. The game became popular on mainframe minicomputers in the late 1970s and spread via the ARPAnet as well as other forms of sharing. Microsoft eventually obtained permission from Crowther and Woods to produce a version of the game as *Microsoft Adventure* (1980), touted as a "complete version of the original."

Adventure's design concept inspired a number of other interactive fiction games, of which *Zork* (1980, Infocom) was one of the most significant. *Zork* began as an effort to top *Adventure* by programmers at MIT's Dynamic Modeling Group consisting of Tim Anderson, Marc Blank, Bruce Daniels, and Dave Lebling; Lebling, as noted in Chapter 2, cocreated an ARPAnet-playable version of *Maze War*. For *Zork*, the group created a setting, puzzles, and creatures using rich descriptive blocks of text. Like *Dungeons & Dragons*, characters had hit points, used different armor types, and engaged in combat with trolls and other fantasy creatures. One of the game's most famous elements was the Grue, an unseen creature that killed players if they lingered too long in dark areas. This added high tension as players had to consider whether to use a limited supply of lantern oil or risk the perils of the darkness.

Zork's most significant improvement over *Adventure* was the design of a text parser that allowed the computer to understand variations of the same command. For example, "GO NORTH" and "WALK NORTH" produced the same result of moving the character. This provided a greater degree of accessibility, as it reduced the need to hunt for the correct command to accomplish the action. Further, the range of commands could be more complex than two words, allowing the game to have a variety of interactions and puzzles; objects could be used in conjunction with the environment through phrases such as "TIE ROPE TO RAILING," further expanding the immersive capabilities.

Members of the original *Zork* group incorporated in 1979 as Infocom, a company initially dedicated to developing productivity software for computers. In the meantime, *Zork* spread through the ARPAnet and became a favorite on mainframe minicomputers where, like *Adventure*, it was played via terminal and printouts. The members of Infocom, seeing an opportunity in computer games, worked to bring *Zork* into the commercial context. The central hurdle in this adaption was the game's size as it was one megabyte or approximately 1000 kilobytes, well beyond the maximum 48 kilobytes of RAM on even the highest performance Apple II computers. The solution involved more efficient compression methods as well as cutting large amounts out of the original game. *Zork*'s initial commercial release in 1980, was followed by *Zork II* (1981) and *Zork III* (1982), each containing elements cut from the original.

Infocom initially used a publisher for its games, but after a string of problems, decided to self-publish its software. The company built a reputation on its interactive fiction games, releasing more than 20 throughout the 1980s, despite the computer game industry's growing emphasis on graphics. Infocom ran an aggressively anti-graphics ad campaign in the mid-1980s, expounding on the merits and depth of using one's imagination rather than relying on the computer display. The company also gained fame for its inclusion of "feelies," small tangible items directly related to the game. The feelies for Infocom's *The Hitchhiker's Guide to the Galaxy* (1984), for example, included papers representing "Destruction Orders for Your Home and Planet," an empty bag representing "Microscopic Space Fleet," and a "Don't Panic" button, among other items.

Although Infocom resisted graphics, other adventure game companies made graphics a central part of their games, feeling that text-only games were wasteful and did not take full advantage of a computer's capabilities. On-Line Systems, founded by husband and wife team Ken and Roberta Williams, began its line of adventure games with the *Hi-Res Adventure* series. Inspired by Crowther and Woods' *Adventure*, Roberta Williams designed *Mystery House* (1980, On-Line Systems), a game that closely followed the design conventions of *Adventure*: players read text descriptions of the scene and used two-word commands to solve a murder mystery. Roberta Williams' game was, however, a major departure from formula: it used simple line drawings to visually represent the player's view of the game spaces (Figure 6.2). This combination of text and image helped compensate for the shortcomings of each mode of presentation; images reduced the

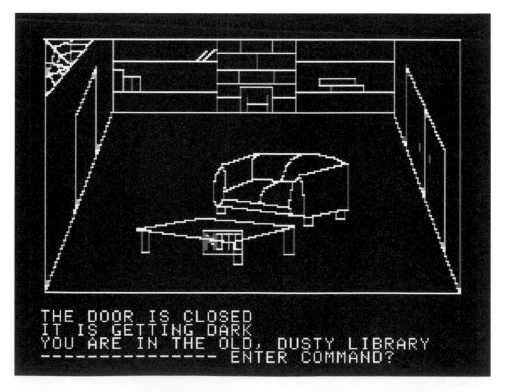

FIGURE 6.2   Hi-Res Adventure #1: *Mystery House* **(1980, On-Line Systems).**

need for lengthy text descriptions, while words clearly identified the visually ambiguous objects in the rooms. Visuals also offered clues to the solution of puzzles rather than explicitly communicating them via text. As the sophistication of visuals in graphics-based adventure games grew, the player's need to be sensitive to subtle cues also became greater.

The second of the *Hi-Res Adventure* games, *The Wizard and the Princess* (1980, On-Line Systems), combined text entry with images, but did so with full color graphics, a setup used in subsequent Hi-Res Adventure games through 1983. The color capabilities of early home computers were limited to a specific palette: game artists compensated for this by creating greater visual subtlety through employing *optical color mixing*, an technique that relied on the human eye's ability to blend different colors placed closely together. A regular pattern of red placed in a field of white, created pink; black pixels in a field of blue created navy blue. A number of computer games from all genres of the early 1980s used this approach, particularly those featuring large images on the screen.

On-Line Systems, renamed Sierra Online in 1982, initiated a major turning point for the burgeoning adventure game genre with Roberta Williams' fairytale-inspired *King's Quest* (1984, Sierra Online). The game was the result of a collaborative effort between IBM and Sierra Online to help demonstrate the color graphic capabilities of the ill-fated IBM PCjr home computer. Each of the game's 80 single screen spaces were represented in vivid blocks of multiple pure colors rather than the mixed colors used in other adventure games. The impressive graphics of *King's Quest*, however, required conscious use of computer resources as storing each of the game's 80 game spaces would have used too much disk space. The game, instead, relied on vectors to draw the outlines of objects, which were then filled in. The effect of outlining, then filling, was seen each time the player moved to a new space. Although it was slower to draw the graphics this way, it allowed the game to have a larger world.

The gameplay of *King's Quest* was also significant as players directed an avatar through various animated screens using a joystick or arrow keys. This imparted a sense of depth, as the game's protagonist, Sir Grahame, could move vertically and horizontally in the game space, walking in front of or behind objects such as rocks, trees, and walls. *King's Quest* retained text commands for opening doors and picking up objects. This provided a different experience, as the position of the character on the screen became an essential consideration for the execution of actions. For example, players needed to move Sir Grahame in front of a door before typing the "OPEN DOOR" command. The combination of controlling the character and using typed commands remained consistent through subsequent sequels until *King's Quest V: Absence Makes the Heart Go Yonder!* (1990, Sierra Online), which adopted the icon-driven, point-and-click interface.

Early Computer Role-Playing Games

The late 1970s and early 1980s saw the beginnings of commercialized CRPGs, a genre that became a staple of computer gaming in the mid to late 1980s. As opposed to text adventures, which replicated the story-telling aspects of the tabletop *Dungeons & Dragons*, CRPGs featured robust systems for simulated combat with monsters or other foes. This led to the same "hack-and-slash" style of gameplay seen in the *Dungeons & Dragons*-inspired PLATO network games of the 1970s (see Chapter 2). Although more combat intensive, early CRPGs moved at a more methodical pace akin to a board game rather than the comparative hyper-speed of their contemporary arcade games.

Gameplay, like tabletop RPGs, followed a prescribed order: creation of a character or party of characters, purchase of equipment and supplies, descent into a dungeon and combat with monsters. Often the games incorporated a first-person perspective with simple graphics representing rectangular hallways. Players plodding through the spaces created maps on graph paper, as computer resources were limited. So universal was this form of gameplay, that CRPGs became synonymous with the term "dungeon crawl." Gameplay frequently culminated in a battle with a dragon, evil wizard, or other powerful enemy, a pattern long established by several earlier games on PLATO. Two early-1980s games proved particularly successful and influential on later releases: *Wizardry: Proving Grounds of the Mad Overlord* (1981, SRI Tech) and Richard Garriott's *Ultima* (1982).

Wizardry: Proving Grounds of the Mad Overlord was designed by Robert Woodhead and Andrew Greenberg for the Apple II computer. The game attempted to reproduce the PLATO network's multiplayer, party-based games like *Oubliette,* but in a single player format. *Wizardry,* unlike other early CRPGs, allowed players to manage a party of six characters instead of a single character as they embarked on a quest to retrieve an amulet from a 10-level dungeon. Like a character sheet from the tabletop version of *Dungeons & Dragons* or the many dungeon-based PLATO games, the initial version of *Wizardry* displayed a large amount of information all at once to the player: various key commands for actions, active spells, the name and status of each party member, and a simple line drawing rendered in perspective that represented the dungeon hallways. *Wizardry* became one of the most popular CRPGs, despite its graphic simplicity and extreme difficulty, spawning an entire franchise that remained strong throughout the 1980s. It was particularly influential in Japan and was one of the games that helped shape the basis for Japanese role-playing games (JRPGs) (see Chapter 7).

In the late 1970s, high school student Richard Garriott taught himself computer programming by creating games inspired by Tolkien's *Lord of the Rings* novels and tabletop role-playing games. After gaining proficiency with programming and game design, Garriott then self-published one of his test games, *Akalabeth: World of Doom* (1980), while still in high school. Although sold at local computer shops, the game gained the attention of software publisher California Pacific, which promptly licensed and distributed *Akalebeth* nationally.

Garriott's first game as a professional was *Ultima* (1981), which featured many refined concepts explored in his earlier noncommercial games. *Ultima*'s story was a postmodern mash-up that blended medieval fantasy with science fiction as players used a time machine to graduate from leather armor and axes to vacuum suits and blasters in order to confront and defeat the game's final evil wizard. The game world featured a variety of environments: vast natural landscapes, towns, and subterranean dungeons that encouraged players to explore.

Ultima used a map-like overworld with icons to represent the various cities and dungeons in a continuous shifting of perspectives (Figure 6.3)—an element similarly employed the following year in Tom Loughry's *Advanced Dungeons & Dragons: Cloudy Mountain Cartridge* for the Intellivision (see Chapter 5). Players that moved over the city icon from the turn-based overworld map abruptly transitioned into a large populated game space where the player could purchase supplies or talk with certain inhabitants. Walking over a dungeon icon in the overworld map, meanwhile, changed the view to a first-person labyrinth where players hunted for treasure and looked for secret doors much like *Wizardry* and other dungeon-based games on PLATO. Combat against enemies such as bats, necromancers, orcs, and knights, like the rest of the game, followed a turn-based procession of action. Similar to contemporary text adventures, contextual information about the environment, the results of combat and dialog between characters were communicated through a text box. Following the closure of Garriot's publisher and a brief stint with Sierra Online, Garriott formed Origin Systems in 1983. With

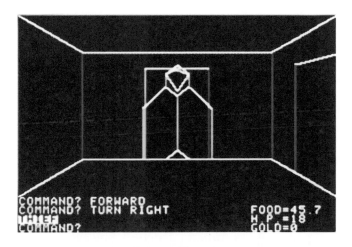

FIGURE 6.3 *Ultima* **(1982, Origin Systems).**

Origin Systems, Garriott was able to exercise greater creative control over the direction of his work.

From his first game through *Ultima III: Exodus,* Garriott remained the sole programmer, designer, and artist of his games. As the Ultima series became more popular, however, it was necessary not only to expand the game development team, but also to explore new narrative and gameplay themes. *Ultima IV: Quest of the Avatar* (1985, Origin Systems), departed from the typical hack-and-slash, dungeon crawl style of gameplay that had dominated CRPGs as it took place in a world where the monstrous forces of evil had already been vanquished. Gameplay, instead, revolved around developing eight personal virtues in a game where the main enemy was internal. Although combat against small antagonists remained a part of the game, objectionable player actions that eroded the social fabric of the game world such as lying, stealing, or cheating other characters limited one's ability to embody the virtues, providing an innovative form of consequences for choices. Once the player had developed their character through virtuous acts such as helping others, the player ventured into the Great Stygian Abyss in search of the Codex of Ultimate Wisdom and returning it to the surface.

Other Directions in CRPGs

First-person dungeon crawling games were not the only CRPGs to emerge from earlier games on minicomputers. *Rogue* was a turn-based minicomputer game developed by Michael Toy, Glen Wichman, and Ken Arnold in the early 1980s. Inspired by *Adventure*, *Rogue* retained the latter's use of text to describe the contents of rooms as well as the results of player actions. The game, however, featured none of the former's puzzle solving and instead emphasized "hack-and-slash" gameplay against monsters. The game space was constructed from ASCII characters with the player represented as an "@" symbol, while each of the game's 26 monsters corresponded to a different letter of the alphabet. Players of *Rogue,* as in the many computer games inspired by *Dungeons & Dragons*, gathered gold, gained levels, collected powerful items, and fought increasingly dangerous monsters. The game's most distinctive element, however, was its ability to randomly generate each of the dungeon layouts. This feature was created in response to the limited replayability of text adventures like *Adventure* and *Zork*, as puzzle solutions and maze layouts remained identical in subsequent playthroughs.

Rogue was eventually released as a commercial game for the IBM PC in 1984, where it retained the use of its iconic text-based visuals; later versions ported to other computer platforms throughout the 1980s, however, featured more representational graphics. Thanks to its randomly generated dungeon layouts, *Rogue* was a popular computer game and spawned a subgenre of "roguelike" games. Its commercial debut, however, was not successful due to rampant software piracy, which forced its developer out of business.

FIGURE 6.4 Computer games such as *Star Control* **(Toys for Bob, Inc., 1990) requested a special phrase upon startup that was generated from a three-ply code wheel.**

This issue plagued many computer games of the time, leading developers to utilize cypher-based copy protection measures in the late 1980s and early 1990s such as game manuals, special black and red reference cards that were difficult to photocopy as well as code wheels (Figure 6.4).

Flight and Vehicle Simulations on Computers

Flight Simulator (1979, subLOGIC) began as a 1975 thesis project by Bruce Artwick while at the University of Illinois Urbana-Champaign. Heavily based on the earlier PLATO flight simulators, *Airace* and *Airfight*, Artwick attempted to prove that consumer grade computers were capable of computing real-time simulated flight. Adapting his thesis project to the commercial context, Artwick founded the software company, subLOGIC with Stu Moment in 1978 and eventually produced a version for the Apple II and TRS-80. Consisting of 36 square miles of space rendered in wireframe visuals, players engaged in free flight over airports, bridges, and mountains (Figure 6.5). *Flight Simulator*, however, included a "British Ace" mode of play that allowed users to engage in World War I-style dogfights with computer-controlled enemies, as well as perform bombing runs of the enemy's airbase and fuel depot. Players earned points for enemies shot down and the amount of damage done to fuel depots.

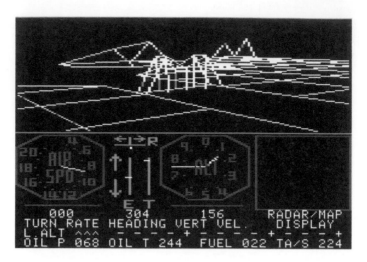

FIGURE 6.5 *Flight Simulator* **(1979, subLOGIC).**

The commercial release of *Flight Simulator* was highly successful and gained the attention of Microsoft, who, after licensing the game, began producing its long series of *Microsoft Flight Simulator* games in 1982. Each subsequent release increased the level of graphical realism as well as the size of the game world. The series became notable for its use of separately sold add-on cities and planes that presaged the popularity of downloadable content (DLC) for games in the contemporary context.

Although later versions of *Flight Simulator* did not contain the combat elements of the original, several other early computer games made flight and combat a central part of gameplay. Atari's *Star Raiders* (1979) for the Atari 400/800 computer drew inspiration from the space combat sequences of Star Wars: players flew through a simple star field in the blackness of space, fought enemy spacecraft, and jumped between sections of the galaxy through hyperspace. In addition to its action gameplay, the game contained the strategic element of deciding which areas of the galaxy to defend. Invading forces that destroyed star bases severely hampered the player's ability to repair and resupply for the hyperspace jumps, thus complicating the gameplay. The popularity of *Star Raiders*, like many combat-focused flight simulation games, extended beyond computers to home consoles as the game was eventually ported to Atari's VCS and 5200 consoles in 1982.

Flight and vehicle simulators played an important role in establishing the reputation of Lucasfilm Games (later renamed LucasArts) as an innovator in computer game technologies and design. An offshoot of Lucasfilm Ltd., the film studio headed by *Star Wars* director George Lucas, Lucasfilm Games grew out of the company's special effects-based computer division. The group, formed in 1982, was led by veteran programmer and game

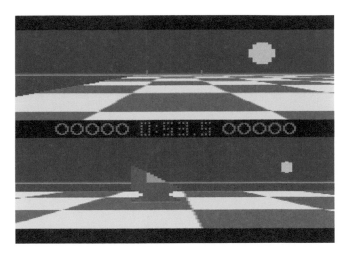

FIGURE 6.6 *BallBlazer*™ **(1984, Lucasfilm Games). (Courtesy of Lucasfilm Ltd. LCC©.)**

designer Peter Langston, who had cocreated a turn-based minicomputer game, *Empire* (1971) while at Harvard University.[*]

Aided by an initial partnership with Atari, the new studio released its first games, *Ballblazer* and *Rescue on Fractalus!* in 1984 for the Atari 400/800 computers. *Ballblazer* combined elements of ball and paddle games with a first-person vehicle simulation as opposing players attempted to carry and launch a ball through moving goal posts to score points. Because of the emphasis on movement and competition, the game's visuals needed to clearly and economically communicate the illusion of perspective and the sensation of movement. *Ballblazer*, thus, represented its game space as a simple checkerboard pattern of alternating colors (Figure 6.6). To better communicate the smooth sensation of movement, it incorporated the technique of *anti-aliasing*, which reduced the appearance of hard, jagged edges on the checker boarded playfield. In addition, distant objects appeared to dip below or rise above the horizon line, suggesting a curved playing surface. *Ballblazer* was also notable for its procedurally generated soundtrack that combined a number of smaller "riffs" into a different musical composition each time the game was played.

The other launch title of the Lucasfilm games group was *Rescue on Fractalus!*, a combat-focused flight simulator that involved picking up downed space pilots and destroying enemy laser guns and ships (Figure 6.7). Rather than wireframe graphics or an outer space setting, *Rescue on Fractalus!* took place in a complex mountainous environment that was

---

[*] Not to be confused with John Daleske's 1973 *Star Trek*-themed, *Empire*, for PLATO (see Chapter 2).

FIGURE 6.7 *Rescue on Fractalus™* **(1984, Lucasfilm Games). (Courtesy of Lucasfilm Ltd. LLC©.)**

based on the work of Loren Carpenter of the Lucasfilm Computer Division. Previously, Carpenter had created the computer-generated terrain for the "Genesis effect" sequence from the film *Star Trek II: The Wrath of Khan* (1982) by using fractal geometry.

Fractal geometry allowed computers to create more natural looking terrain than that created by hand. It could be produced by simple sets of repeating, ruled patterns that represented an efficient use of computer resources. After David Fox of the Lucasfilm games group approached him with an idea for a game, Carpenter was able to significantly simplify the fractal-generated terrain process, allowing it to run on a consumer grade computer. Fox then crafted the remaining game around the landscape. *Rescue on Fractalus!* followed many elements of flight simulators through its control scheme composed of individual flight commands for adjusting thrust, landing, turning off the ship's systems, opening the air lock, and activating the boosters to return to the mother ship. Similar versions of the fractal technology developed for *Rescue on Fractalus!* were also used in other games from the studio, *The Eidolon* (1985) and *Koronis Rift* (1985), both of which presented the game space from a first-person perspective.

In England, meanwhile, the innovations of the space-based flight simulator *Elite* (1984, Acornsoft Limited) catapulted the British computer game industry to international prominence. David Braben and Ian Bell of Jesus College, Cambridge began development of *Elite* as a demonstration of 3D graphics on the BBC Micro. Refining the technical aspects further, the two worked toward a game that replicated the expansive fictional worlds of Star Trek and Star Wars. It also drew on elements such as the space station docking sequence from Stanley Kubrick's 1969 film, *2001: A Space Odyssey*. With a playable demonstration of the game completed, the two were able to secure

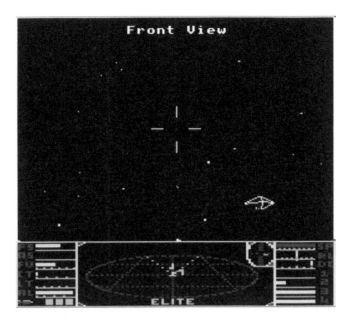

FIGURE 6.8   *Elite* **(1984, Acornsoft Limited).**

Elite's publication through Acornsoft, the software development division for the BBC microcomputer (Figure 6.8).

Elite had one of the largest game worlds created on any platform of the day: 2500 planets with alien races spread across eight galaxies. Players were encouraged to explore the vastness of the game space by buying and selling commodities at different docks across distant alien markets. Those looking for fast money could trade in illegal cargo; however, they risked running afoul of authorities and becoming wanted felons. In addition to management and cargo hauling, the player could collect bounty on space pirates and attack other cargo ships, also a felony, providing elements of action through 3D dogfights in space. The length of play of *Elite* extended well beyond what was typical of the many arcade-derived games for computers: a single game could be played for weeks as the player attempted to reach "elite" status through accumulating more than 6000 kills before succumbing to pirates, the authorities, or both.

The size, complexity, and nonlinear nature of *Elite*'s game world and the ability to play everything from hero to villain, made it one of the earliest commercial instances of *open world* sandbox gameplay. These features, in addition to the ability to customize the capabilities of the player's ship, were all the more impressive as *Elite* ran on the BBC microcomputer which had only 18 kilobytes of usable memory at the time. The marvel of this seemingly endless game was accomplished by Braben and Bell's mastery of *assembly language*, which saved space and improved performance of the 3D objects.

Visuals and Action-Adventure Games for Computers

Detailed graphics became an increasingly important part of computer games as larger capacity 5.25″ floppy disks and new models of computers with better visual capabilities—the Commodore 64, ZX Spectrum, and more powerful versions of the Apple II—arrived on the market. This, seen across all genres, was illustrated by the differences between the *Hi-Res Adventure* titles and *King's Quest*. Visual richness was also seen in a number of original action-adventure games that combined puzzle solving with faster play reminiscent of arcade games. For example, Silas Warner's World War II espionage game, *Beyond Castle Wolfenstein* (1984, Muse Software) featured characters wearing German-style military outfits, a contrast to the stick figure visuals of Warner's previous *Escape from Castle Wolfenstein* (1981, Muse). English developer, Ultimate Play the Game (later known as Rare), built a reputation on smooth animation, detailed graphics, and responsive controls in the mid-1980s through its isometric Filmation game engine, which made its debut in Tim and Chris Stamper's *Knight Lore* (1984).

As visual detail became a greater selling point for games in the mid-1980s, programmers often struggled to produce appealing art and smooth animations. Some, however, like programmer Jordan Mechner, were able to overcome deficiencies by employing innovative techniques. *Rotoscoping* was an animation method developed by Max Fleischer in the mid-1910s. In it, individual frames of video were traced on paper. This allowed an animator to produce life-like movement without the need to work out each individual frame. Mechner, inspired by his film history classes at Yale in the early 1980s, used the technique in two action-adventure computer games, *Karateka* (1984) and *Prince of Persia* (1989). Both also used the cinematic conventions of classic film to provide narrative structure to their games.

Mechner's *Karateka* drew from the samurai epics of Japanese director Akira Kurosawa to produce an action game set in feudal Japan. For the game's visuals, he shot film footage of his family and their karate instructor, which was then traced onto graph paper and then coded into the game pixel by pixel. The game's plot centered on rescuing the protagonist's kidnapped girlfriend from an evil warlord. *Karateka* began with an introductory narrative segment that revealed the game's story without using words. It showed the cruelty of the warlord, the anguish of the woman's plight, and entrance of the hero; distinct musical themes accompanied each character and helped communicate individual personalities. Gameplay entailed increasingly difficult martial art fights that required players to consider different attacks and counter attacks against a single opponent in a slightly choppy side-scrolling game space (Figure 6.9).

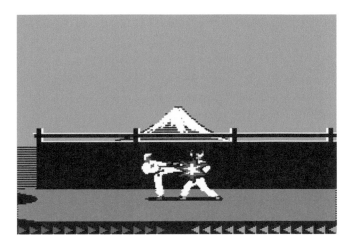

FIGURE 6.9 *Karateka* **(1984).**

Prince of Persia, even more ambitious in the design of its gameplay, also used rotoscoping and dialog-less cut scenes to communicate the story. Its Arabian Nights-themed narrative told of the player's unjust imprisonment after a coup by the sultan's advisor, Jaffar. When Jaffar's advancements on the sultan's daughter are refused, he gives her an hour to live unless she marries him. This narrative element structured the gameplay as the player was given 1 hour to escape the maze-like dungeon of pits, falling platforms, spike traps, and sword-wielding enemies. Narrative elements also extended to the game's action, which included drama-filled sword fights rotoscoped from actors Errol Flynn and Basil Rathbone in the 1938 film, *The Adventures of Robin Hood*. Mechner's cinematic approach to game creation also extended to the interface as it was virtually nonexistent; the only visible element was a set of simple, unobtrusive triangles at the bottom of the screen representing health.

The Mouse and Computer Games of the Later 1980s and 1990s

The mid to late 1980s saw the introduction of a new generation of 16 and 32 bit computers designed with more robust multimedia capabilities. They were responsible for accelerating the revolution in graphic design, video production, animation, and other creative areas, fundamentally transforming their professional practices. Although platforms like the Apple II, ZX Spectrum, and Commodore 64 continued to be popular throughout the decade for creating and playing games, developers rushed to take advantage of higher resolutions and new forms of interaction available through the Apple Macintosh, the Atari ST, and Commodore Amiga. Since the new computers produced higher screen resolutions, specially designed computer monitors became essential, phasing out the living room television as a computer display. As the capabilities of home computers grew, the demand for larger storage capacity grew as well: the size of programs and files made hard drives another essential component. Relative to floppy disks, hard drives accessed information quicker and eliminated the need to swap disks in the middle of gameplay.

The most significant changes for computers and game design came with Apple's Macintosh. Announced through an iconic commercial that referenced George Orwell's novel *1984*, the Macintosh was presented as a tool of freedom for a population "held captive" by constraints of other companies' computers. Designed for use by the broader population, the Macintosh was made to be approachable through its pairing of a mouse and graphic user interface (GUI). Using the mouse to issue instructions introduced a spatial dimension to computer interactions that eliminated the need to memorize a large number of text commands. Users could process information visually through commands in pull down boxes grouped by common themes or through icons and buttons that paired familiar office items with computer functions. The Macintosh, however, was not the first commercial instance of a GUI and mouse combination, as seen on the Xerox Star of 1981 and the Visi On GUI of 1983, but it was a watershed moment that signaled the beginning of the GUI's popularization. The following year Microsoft launched its first version of Windows, while GUIs also appeared on the Atari ST and Commodore Amiga computers. For games, mouse-driven interactions and icons became the heart of a number of new design concepts, which changed existing genres and aided in the creation of new ones.

Later Role-Playing Games

Since the majority of CRPGs featured a plethora of systems that tracked hit points, experience points, weapon damage, spells, inventory, food, and more, the games tended to feature information-dense interfaces spread out across multiple different screens. Players typically toggled these interfaces through keyboard shortcuts that added to the already significant number of regular keyboard commands. *Dungeon Master* (1987, FTL Games) was one of the first CRPGs to use the mouse to move between different information screens. The player was able to check inventory, character stats, equip weapons, and change the marching orders of party members in the first-person dungeon crawler, using boxes with character names and icons. Movement, spell casting, weapon attacks, and picking up items from the ground also could be executed with the mouse, creating a more seamless approach to interaction.

The game was also significant for its departure from the systems of the tabletop *Dungeons & Dragons* that had shaped the CRPG genre. *Dungeon Master* was played in real time, rather than in turn-based movement and combat, meaning that careful consideration and board game-like strategy was replaced with a need to react and make decisions quickly. Spell casting in *Dungeon Master* was brought about by building spells from sets of symbols powered from a pool of mana points, instead of the *Dungeons & Dragons* system of limited spells cast per level, per day. Another notable departure was that characters in *Dungeon Master* increased their skills through practice, much like the earlier *Moria* on PLATO. This allowed characters to uniquely develop according to each player's individual play style rather than as a fixed progression of gaining levels. These elements, plus the game's large windowed, first-person perspective, made *Dungeon Master* an immersive experience that garnered multiple awards and served as inspiration for a number of later CRPGs.

By the early 1990s, nearly all CRPGs were designed for mouse input. Icon-based interfaces, particularly beneficial for CRPGs, helped simplify the complex text-based control schemes. The Amiga and Atari ST versions of several games published by Strategic Simulations Inc. such as *Phantasie* (1987), *Demon's Winter* (1988), and *Eye of the Beholder* (1990, Westwood Associates), along with *Wizardry VI: Bane of the Cosmic Forge* (1990, Sir-Tech Software, Inc.) and Richard Garriot's *Ultima VI: The False Prophet* (1990, Origin Systems), all featured redesigned interfaces that promoted efficient management of the game information. Mouse-based interfaces for CRPGs remained the basis for interaction through the 1990s and early 2000s despite great diversification in design and gameplay.

Developing the Point-and-Click Adventure

In the mid to late 1980s, Lucasfilm Games began working in the graphic adventure genre with *Labyrinth: The Computer Game* (1986), based on the 1986 fantasy film *Labyrinth*. The player had 13 hours to defeat the game's antagonist, Jareth (based on David Bowie's character from the film) who was located in a castle at the center of the labyrinth. Like the conventions of interactive fiction and graphic adventure games, the player gathered items and used them to solve puzzles in order to progress. Unlike *Zork* and *King's Quest*, however, *Labyrinth: The Computer Game* did not employ typed text commands, but used two boxes; one containing a list of verbs such as "open" or "talk" and the other, nouns, such as "door" or "Jareth." The design of this interface with pre-written text prevented the often frustrating message of "I don't understand," which was a common response for mistyped words or words outside of an adventure game's vocabulary.

The interaction via menus of text in *Labyrinth: The Computer Game* was further refined in Lucasfilm Game's *Maniac Mansion* (1987), themed as a parody of B-horror films. From a group of six teenagers, the player selected a pair of companions to aid in a quest to rescue the main character's girlfriend from a mad scientist's mansion. Through Lucasfilm Games' playful humor and animated cut scenes, the player solved puzzles by collecting and manipulating objects in the game space. Some puzzles were only solvable by certain characters, adding variety to the gameplay and allowing players to experience the game differently based on their character choices.

Originally designed for a single button joystick on the Commodore 64, the game's interface allowed players to pair a bank of verbs with objects in the game space by selecting them (Figure 6.10). Selecting "open" and then moving the mouse over the graphic depiction of the door, for instance, directed the player's character to open a door. This method of interaction governed the performance of actions, talking to people or examining objects, in a similar manner. The following year, the game was ported to the IBM PC, where it allowed players to use either the keyboard arrow keys or the mouse, allowing point-and-click interactions. Although mice were not standard equipment at the time, point-and-click gameplay was revolutionary for the adventure game genre.

In order to speed up the game's creation and provide an efficient way to interpret the commands, programmer Chip Morningstar aided designer Ron Gilbert by developing the Script Utility Manager for Maniac Mansion, otherwise known as SCUMM. For Lucasfilm Games, the SCUMM engine proved to be remarkably versatile. It and its many revisions powered

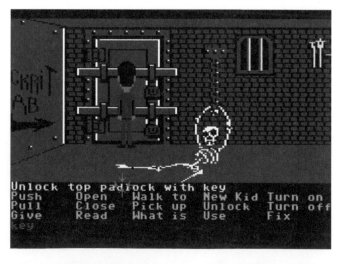

FIGURE 6.10 Original Commodore 64 version of *Maniac Mansion*™ (1987, Lucasfilm Games). (Courtesy of Lucasfilm Ltd. LLC©.)

much-admired games, such as *Zak McKracken and the Alien Mindbenders* (1988), the pirate adventure *The Secret of Monkey Island* (1990) and later, the motorcycle adventure game, *Full Throttle* (1995).

As mice became more common, the interfaces of adventure games moved away from words and depended entirely on icons. One of Lucasfilm Games' more unique point-and-click adventures was Brian Moriarty's *Loom* (1990). Set in a fantasy world with mystical craft guilds, players guided a young weaver, Bobbin Threadbare, on a journey to protect the world from forces of chaos. The basic setting and motivation were typical of many adventure games, but the interface and game design were not. *Loom*, unlike the bank of text commands used in *Maniac Mansion* and other Lucasfilm games of the period, used a musical note interface to cast spells by clicking a series of notes (Figure 6.11). The spell effects ranged from simple commands that opened doors, to the ability to spin straw into gold. Throughout the story, players learned an increasing number of spells and versatile ways to apply them, including playing the notes backward for a reverse effect. For the sake of immersion in the narrative Moriarty omitted or modified, many expected "game-like" elements from *Loom*. These changes included removing the potential for player death, eliminating the need to collect and combine objects located in disparate locations, and cutting difficult puzzles that served as roadblocks to progression. *Loom*, thus, was designed to be completed.

Loom's success represented the growing presence of a diverse, but underserved population of players less interested in the arcade-like, challenge-based gameplay that dominated the popular market. *Loom*'s more casual-oriented design provided an alternative approach that was explored by other games of the period, like *Myst* (see Chapter 8), and continued through games like *The Sims* (see Chapter 9) as well as later independent games based on narrative exploration (see Chapter 10).

FIGURE 6.11 *Loom*™ **(1990, Lucasfilm Games). (Courtesy of Lucasfilm Ltd. LLC©.)**

Infocom and Sierra Online also developed adventure games for mouse interaction. An early mouse implementation was used in *Beyond Zork: The Coconut of Quendor* (1987, Infocom) created by Brian Moriarty prior to his employment at Lucasfilm Games. The combination adventure/role-playing game, although entirely text based, drew a simple map of lines and rectangles as the player explored the game space. The player, on certain computer platforms, could click the map with a mouse to ascend or descend into new spaces. Steve Meretzky's text-based *Zork Zero* (1988, Infocom), featured an interface bordered in color and used graphic puzzles, as well as the option to navigate via mouse. *Return to Zork* (Activision), had by 1993, completely adopted mouse and icon-based gameplay as well as graphics that represented the world, using an immersive first-person perspective much like dungeon crawling CRPGs.

At Sierra On-Line, Roberta Williams' third-person, *King's Quest V: Absence Makes the Heart Go Yonder!* (1990) completely abandoned the use of text and focused solely on mouse input through icons that moved the character and interacted with the game world. Subsequent games by all three major producers of adventure games, as well as those produced by other companies, continued strong into the 1990s, as many began to move away from pixel art and toward film and computer-generated 3D imagery (see Chapter 8).

THE RISE AND DOMINANCE OF THE IBM COMPATIBLE PC

The consumer computer market from the early 1990s onward coalesced around Apple's Macintosh line of computers and the IBM PC, despite a bevy of new computers in the later 1980s. Apple's computers had a long lineage of supporting the creation and play of computer games, but the IBM PC was still largely seen as a machine for business purposes as initial models featured little to none of the multimedia capabilities of other computers. However, the IBM PC featured an *open architecture* design that gave users the ability to upgrade not only memory, as seen in many other computers, but also the individual components of the hardware, such as processor and motherboard. "IBM compatible" computers sold by companies like Compaq, Gateway, Dell, and Hewlett-Packard replicated this design feature throughout the 1980s and 1990s.

The *open architecture* design, significant market penetration in the business world, and familiarity with IBM compatible PCs, offered an opportunity to expand into games. A number of technology companies in the late 1980s, such as Creative Technology Limited and ATI Technologies, began to develop powerful sound and graphics cards that brought the PC superior multimedia capabilities. With third-party hardware development, the PC quickly rose to prominence, eclipsed competing computers, and became the standard for computer gaming that has remained largely unchallenged (Figure 6.12).

FIGURE 6.12   Interior of an IBM compatible PC from the mid-1990s showing the *open architecture* **concept.**

Management and Strategy Games in the Late 1980s and Early 1990s

Don Daglow's 1981 *Utopia* for Intellivision (see Chapter 5) represented one of the first "god games," wherein omniscient players developed an island nation and managed its population, using an overlay on a 12-button keypad. In the late 1980s, several strategy and management games on home computers not only expanded the gameplay of the early concept, but also effectively digitized the keypad overlay in the form of a GUI using pull down menus driven by the mouse.

In 1984, game designer and model builder Will Wright created one of his first commercial games, *Raid on Bungeling Bay*. The game consisted of a top-down arcade-like shoot 'em up in which the player shot down enemy planes and bombed enemy factories, using a helicopter. While the game was successful and received a port to the Famicom/NES as well as Japanese MSX-spec computers, Wright found more pleasure in arranging the placement of buildings, roads, and other features in the game's level editor. This activity led Wright to investigate systems related to civic engineering and city planning, as well as the work by British mathematician John Conway and his *Life* systems dynamics simulation program from 1970. In the interim, Wright cofounded game company Maxis with Jeff Braun, eventually resulting in the creation of *SimCity* (1989, Maxis).

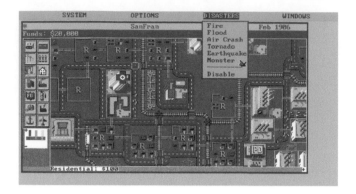

FIGURE 6.13 The original DOS version of *SimCity* **(1989, Maxis). (Courtesy of Electronic Arts.)**

In *SimCity*, the player received resources in the form of tax dollars, space to build, and a number of construction options that ranged from residences to airports (Figure 6.13). Little, however, directed the player toward a specific type of play, as *SimCity* was not designed with an end goal. Players could build a variety of cities as they interacted with the game's many systems, including taxes, crime, pollution, traffic congestion, and population. The game was also built around mouse interaction and featured an icon-based interface inspired by the GUI of the Apple Macintosh's *MacPaint* art program.

In addition to *SimCity*, Sid Meier's *Civilization* (1991, MicroProse) represented another major innovation in management game design from the period. MicroProse, cofounded by Sid Meier and Bill Stealey in 1982, built a reputation on realistic, military-themed, flight simulators, such as *F-15 Strike Eagle* (1984) and *F-19 Stealth Fighter* (1987), the latter utilizing simple 3D polygons. Meier, by the turn of the decade, however, wanted to explore other game ideas. After partnering with Bruce Shelley, a former Avalon Hill board-game designer, the pair created the business simulation game, *Sid Meier's Railroad Tycoon* (1990, MicroProse), a game that drew from Francis Tresham's 1974 railroad building board game called *1829*.

The success of *Railroad Tycoon* pushed Meier and Shelley to continue looking beyond military flight simulations and into strategy-based management games. Inspiration came from the city-building gameplay of Will Wright's *SimCity*, the board game *Risk*, *Railroad Tycoon*, and other sources. The end result was *Civilization*, a game where players nurtured a fledgling nation over thousands of years, from prehistory through the space age. The turn-based game allowed players to set building projects, found cities, set government types, trade, and go to war with neighboring nations. Although more structured than *SimCity*, the game allowed significant freedom of play and featured three distinctive victory conditions centered on building, conquering, and surviving.

One of the most important design features of the game was its *technology tree*, a series of branching technological developments that allowed players to advance their civilization from pottery making to space flight. With each newly discovered technology, players could create new types of buildings and units along with other types of advances. The ability to choose one's path through the technology tree, along with random map generation at the beginning of each new game, allowed for a high degree of replayability.

Synthesis and Development of the RTS Game

The more casual gameplay of *SimCity* and *Civilization* proved popular, but not all game developers were satisfied with the open-ended goals of *SimCity* and the methodical turn-based gameplay of *Civilization*. Westwood Studios (formerly Westwood Associates) applied its experience in real-time action and the simplification of game interfaces, seen in its earlier CRPG *Eye of the Beholder,* to the creation of the strategy game, *Dune II: The Building of a Dynasty* (1992, Westwood Studios). *Dune II*, based on Frank Herbert's 1965 science-fiction novel *Dune* and its 1984 film adaption, pitted dynasties from the fictional Dune universe against each other in a battle to control spice production on the desert planet Arrakis.

The design of *Dune II*'s core gameplay was reminiscent of elements from Will Wright's *SimCity* and Sid Meier's *Civilization*; the player placed individual structures in the game space while directing the movements of military units. Like the technology tree of *Civilization*, the creation of certain buildings gave the player the ability to produce new units as well as additional structures. The game interface, too, featured a windowed view of the game world surrounded by a frame of buttons and mouse-driven icons. *Dune II* set itself apart from these earlier strategy games, however, by pressuring the player to make simultaneous decisions about managing resources, building structures, producing units, and fighting the enemy in real-time. This accelerated, strategy-based gameplay became known as *real time strategy* (*RTS*). Although earlier games such as *The Ancient Art of War* (1984, Everyware), *Carrier Command* (1988, Realtime Games Software Ltd.), *Herzog Zwi* (1988, Technosoft Co. Ltd.), and *Populous* (1989, Bullfrog) contained several of these elements, Westwood's game created the basis from which the majority of others would follow.

Westwood Studios followed the success of *Dune II* with *Command and Conquer* (1995), a semi-futuristic RTS that mixed real-life military units with science-fiction elements (Figure 6.14). More so than *Dune II*, the armies of *Command & Conquer* showed greater asymmetry: units differed in cost, health, range, speed, and damage, elements that required constant evaluation in the game's skirmishes. *Command & Conquer* also refined the

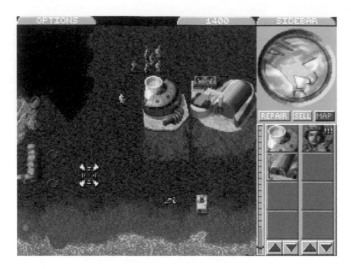

FIGURE 6.14 *Command and Conquer* **(1995, Westwood Studios). (Courtesy of Electronic Arts.)**

interface and further streamlined the interactions, increasing the speed and flow of gameplay. Movement and attack orders could be issued to unlimited units via simple mouse clicks in the game space without clicking action icons. In addition, the player's view of the battlefield scrolled effortlessly in eight directions by positioning the mouse at the screen's edge. The game used the larger storage capabilities of the CD-ROM to present the narrative through full motion video segments that combined live actors with computer-generated 3D backdrops, a setup used by other games of the early to mid-1990s (see Chapter 8).

While Westwood Studios based its RTSs on ideas of realism enhanced by a sense of techno-science fiction, the early RTSs of Blizzard Entertainment (formerly Silicon & Synapse) drew from medieval fantasy themes, particularly those from the tabletop war game, *Warhammer: The Game of Fantasy Battles* (1983, Games Workshop). Blizzard's inaugural RTS, *Warcraft: Orcs and Humans* (1994), was created out of a desire to add competitive multiplayer gameplay to the basic design of *Dune II*.

In *Warcraft: Orcs and Humans*, like *Dune II*, players built bases, gathered resources and directed armies of units, each with different strengths and weaknesses. The game differed from *Dune II*'s build/expand/fight setup, however, by introducing greater variety in the missions and integrating the game's original mythology into the gameplay. For example, the Orc campaign's mission, "The Dead Mines," did not feature base-building gameplay and instead gave the player a limited number of units to move through a dungeon-like environment in search of the Orc war chief's daughter. The game's sequel *Warcraft II: Tides of Darkness* (1995, Blizzard Entertainment), like *Command & Conquer*, similarly utilized an asymmetric approach to each side's units and added further variety to the mission types.

Following Westwood and Blizzard Entertainment, other studios provided unique forms and variations on the evolving RTS genre. *Z* (The Bitmap Brothers, 1996) eliminated the base-building component and focused on capturing enemy territory with armies of gun-crazed, beer-drinking robots. *Total Annihilation* (Cavedog Entertainment, 1997) used well-designed artificial intelligence and innovative specialized units rendered in three-dimensions. *Age of Empires* (1997, Ensemble Studios) brought a historical approach to the RTS, akin to *Civilization*, as players advanced through epochs of time.

Westwood continued to release new titles and expansions in the Command & Conquer franchise, with the alternate history-theme *Command & Conquer: Red Alert* (1996, Westwood Studios), which made Internet-based, multiplayer game play a central feature. Blizzard's *StarCraft* (1998), however, proved to be a standout in the genre as its asymmetric design was ideal for competitive multiplayer gameplay (Figure 6.15). The game featured three distinct factions, each with different buildings and systems, while every individual unit's strength was countered by an opponent unit's abilities. The user interface made the most pertinent information available at a glance through floating overlays displaying resources and unit health. The game space also functioned differently through the use of an isometric perspective allowing for the tactical use of height that granted increased vision and weapon range. These elements created the potential for a dynamic tug of war, where a well-orchestrated counter move could suddenly alter the momentum of a battle; features that helped establish professional e-sports game leagues.

FIGURE 6.15 *StarCraft* **(Blizzard Entertainment, 1998).**

StarCraft was also more visually complex than many of its RTS predecessors. The main parts of the user interface were moved from their traditional position on the sides of the screen to the bottom, changing the proportions of the game space from square to rectangle and giving an overall cinematic impression. Instead of pixel art, the units consisted of *pre-rendered* sprites created from 3D models, the same technique used to create the characters of *Killer Instinct* (1994, Rare), *Donkey Kong Country* (1994, Rare), and Blizzard's own roguelike *Diablo* (1996).

The combination of 2D and 3D elements affecting the visuals and gameplay of *StarCraft* and other games of the period connects to a larger discussion on the transition to 3D in the 1990s. As discussed in Chapter 8, the occasionally awkward mixture of 2D and 3D across different genres was fueled by a desire for visual and spatial realism as developers desired state-of-the-art fully 3D characters and environments without losing the visual fidelity offered by the tradition of pixel art. Chapter 9, meanwhile, discusses the successful implementation of fully 3D visuals and spaces in the late 1990s as well as within contemporary game design.

Chapter 7

Japan, 2D Game Design and the Rebirth of Consoles (1983-1995)

Japanese Games and Game Companies in the Early 1980s

Japanese arcade and console manufacturers experienced tremendous growth throughout the 1980s relative to the contracting North American market. Arcade games continued to be in demand throughout the 1980s as Japan's concentrated population was able to sustain dedicated game centers. The heavy reliance on train stations created spaces where large segments of the population spent time waiting, an ideal setup for arcade games. Japanese arcade manufacturers continued to push new game concepts and technologies, defining the post-Golden Age arcade, as well as shaping the console market. Japan's home console market was relatively undeveloped until the simultaneous release of Nintendo and Sega's first cartridge-based units in 1983. The aggressive expansion that followed reached a fevered pitch in the late 1980s and early 1990s as the war for dominance among Japanese console manufacturers took place on an international level, with the virtually vacant and highly profitable market of the United States serving as the main battlefield. This struggle helped fuel a continual need for high quality games, produced by a host of third-party developers in Japan and eventually, the United States; a situation that reignited the console industry in North America and established a pattern of Japanese dominance in home video games that largely persists today.

2D Game Design Trends after the Golden Age Arcade

Arcade games, by the mid-1980s, could no longer rely solely on their novelty for success. Second-generation home consoles and home computers brought many of the hits of the Golden Age, albeit in imperfect form, to the masses. Further, as more games were created for the home with longer play and more complex rules and interactions, arcade games needed new ways to stay enticing. Since arcade games relied on both sight and sound to attract customers to the cabinet, attention focused on aesthetic features.

The widespread adoption of 16-bit processors allowed attract modes to grow in complexity: short narrative segments of still or minimally animated images and text, flashed between the demonstration of gameplay, high score board, and large colorful title graphics. Game worlds transitioned from black backgrounds that represented the voids of outer space or other abstract locations, to more colorful and recognizable places, like cities, forests, and building interiors. In-game narrative segments introduced characters and provided context for actions between stages. Games featured a wider array of sounds including digitized voices, recognizable sound effects, and game music that recalled the synthesized 1980s musical genres of synthpop and techno. Even minor elements, such as the sound effect acknowledging coin deposit, were also enhanced with voices and musical jingles.

Pseudo-3D in Games

Arcade game designers who desired to simulate the feeling of movement through space at high speeds, increasingly relied on *pseudo-3D* visuals in the mid to late 1980s. Pseudo-3D games depended on the use of depth cues, such as imagery created in one-point perspective and changes in the scale of objects, to create the illusion of 3D space. This technique, seen as early as 1975 in *Interceptor* (Taito) by Tomohiro Nishikado and appearing in racing games *Night Driver* (1976, Atari) and *Pole Position* (1982, Namco), saw widespread use in the post-Golden Age arcade as 16-bit processors could smoothly manipulate the size of game sprites.

One of the industry's most prolific game designers, Yu Suzuki of Sega, made the most significant advancements in pseudo-3D hardware and game design of the period. Suzuki's first major project was *Hang On* (1985, Sega), a motorcycle racing game that featured detailed images and a fluid sense of motion. *Hang On*'s impressive performance was based on a development by Suzuki's team known as the "Super Scaler." The Super Scaler consisted of advanced hardware technologies that could quickly and smoothly change the size of thousands of 2D sprites per second, producing the sense of motion. This development became the heart of many of Sega's most popular simulation-based games of the 1980s, all of which Suzuki had a hand in creating: *Space Harrier* (1985), *Outrun* (1986), and *Afterburner* (1987). The games themselves largely followed previously established conventions of game design. More importantly, however, they led Suzuki down a path to fully 3D game worlds explored in arcade games (see Chapter 8) and refined on home consoles in the 1990s (see Chapter 9).

Side-Scrolling Action and the Beat 'em Up

The appearance of a new type of game in the mid-1980s combined the character driven, sideways perspective of titles like *Donkey Kong* and *Burger Time* with concepts from scrolling shoot-'em-ups like *Zaxxon* (1982, Sega) and *Defender*. These side-scrolling action games such as *The Legend of Kage* (1984, Taito), *Rolling Thunder* (1986, Namco), and *Shinobi* (1987, Sega) featured large-sized sprites that represented human characters in colorful, scrolling environments. The core gameplay of these games consisted of fighting against large groups of weak enemies using punches, kicks, bullets, swords, and even occasional "ninja magic." Like Golden Age shoot-'em-ups, the games employed the "one hit death" rule for both player and enemies, making gameplay continuously tense. The games also contained various enemy types, each with distinctive patterns of behavior, which allowed designers to adjust the difficulty by modifying the number, type, and combination of enemies encountered at one time. These elements, plus intuitive gameplay influenced by high-concept action films of the 1980s, made side-scrolling action games ideal for the coin-operated arcade.

A more defined type of action game, known as the "beat 'em up," emerged from this loose pool of game concepts as well. The first fully-developed beat 'em up was *Nekketsu Kouha Kunio-kun* (1986, Technōs Japan). *Nekketsu Kouha Kunio-kun*, westernized as *Renegade*, was designed by Yoshihisa Kishimoto and centered on fighting multiple opponents with kicks and punches in a scrolling arena-like space. While scrolling had been employed in earlier action games, most notably *Kung Fu Master* (1984, Irem), *Nekketsu Kouha Kunio-kun* gave both the player and enemies a greater amount of health. The health system allowed Kishimoto to create gameplay centered on "knock-down-drag-out" fights, as seen in the 1973 Bruce Lee film, *Enter the Dragon*, as well as the altercations Kishimoto himself frequently experienced as a youth. Players needed to hit enemies multiple times, "beating them up," in order to defeat them. The combat system of *Nekketsu Kouha Kunio-kun* was highly developed relative to other side-scrolling games as players could punch, kick, grab, charge, throw, and hit enemies fallen on the ground. This created the opportunity for multiple strategies of play. Once the area was mostly cleared of enemies, a tougher "boss" character joined the fight, requiring the player to adopt a new strategy in order to progress to the next level.

Kishimoto desired gameplay that could lead to situations in which enemies surrounded the player. Although earlier games like *Robotron 2084* surrounded the player with hostile robots, it did so by an awkward mix of perspectives in which characters were represented in profile, but moved up and down the screen as if they were viewed from above. *Nekketsu Kouha Kunio-kun* instead featured an isometric game space populated with sprites rendered in a three-quarter perspective. The use of this perspective combined with separate buttons for punching and kicking, however, necessitated an extra button dedicated to "jump." The result was a three-button control scheme that was quickly adopted by others beat-'em-up games of the late 1980s and early 1990s.

Kishimoto's follow-up game built on *Nekketsu Kouha Kunio-kun*'s combat systems and featured long, side-scrolling levels instead of short, bounded arenas. The most significant change, however, was the ability for two players to play simultaneously, a feature well suited to the public spaces of arcades. The game's title, *Double Dragon* (1987, Technōs Japan), was derived from the two player simultaneous gameplay and its inspiration from the film, *Enter the Dragon* (Figure 7.1). While Kishimoto's previous game was successful, *Double Dragon* and its sequels created a worldwide sensation that inspired other beat 'em ups such as *Golden Axe* (1989, Sega) and *Final Fight* (1989, Capcom).

Following the convention set by *Double Dragon*, beat 'em ups of the late 1980s and 1990s increased the number of simultaneous players by expanding the pool of playable characters and the number of joysticks. Japanese companies, Capcom and Konami, created beat 'em ups based on licensed

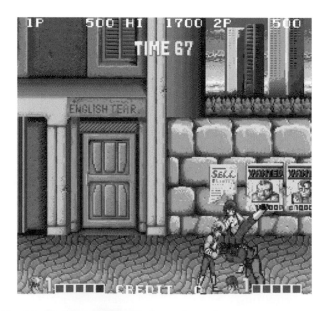

FIGURE 7.1 *Double Dragon* **(1987, Technōs Japan).**

FIGURE 7.2 *The Simpsons Arcade Game* **(1991, Konami) with four sets of controls allowing players to play as the entire Simpson family. (Courtesy of Arcadia, McLean, IL, www.vintagevideogames.com)**

animation and comic book characters, such as *Teenage Mutant Ninja Turtles* (1989, Konami), *The Uncanny X-Men* (1992, Konami), and *Alien vs. Predator* (1994, Capcom) (Figure 7.2). In the mid-1990s, Sega achieved a certain degree of success in translating the 2D beat-'em-up formula to full 3D with *Die Hard Arcade* (1996). The genre's overall repetitive gameplay of punching and kicking, nonetheless, wore thin with players and the side-scrolling beat-'em-up disappeared from arcades by the end of the 1990s as home consoles provided more novel forms of games.

The Head-to-Head Fighting Game

The emergence of head-to-head fighting games in the 1980s represented the culmination of arcade competition and spectatorship begun in the late 1800s. In 1984, game designer Takashi Nishiyama of Irem created the side-scrolling action game *Kung-Fu Master*. In it, players punched and kicked their way through a series of long lincar stages full of adversaries and bosses.

The game was distinctive for using a bar to represent player health, as well as the health of the boss character, a feature that was appropriated in later beat-'em-up design. Nishiyama, despite the game's success, left Irem and joined Capcom where he was tasked with creating a side-scrolling action game that could compete against his own *Kung-Fu Master*. Rather than a game based on attacking multiple opponents, Nishiyama's *Street Fighter* (1987, Capcom), like the earlier *Yie Ar Kung-Fu* (1985, Konami), effectively consisted of a sequence of 10 increasingly difficult boss fights that took place in a much smaller game space. This form of gameplay allowed for dramatic ebb and flow of combat as multiple punches and kicks were exchanged between the fighters, each trying to deplete the other's health bar. As a competitive arcade game, score played a key role in providing a measure of player performance. Each landed punch, kick, and other technique added to the player's point total. Victorious players received points for the amount of match time and health remaining, encouraging quick but careful fights, while mini games based on board breaking and other demonstrations of skill awarded bonus points between sets of rounds.

Street Fighter distinguished itself in a number of ways that laid the foundation for subsequent head-to-head fighting games. The game's sprites were large and multicolored thanks to the increased capabilities of post-Golden Age arcade hardware. Characters were furnished with more personality, providing background stories and other biographical details. The design itself was more complex: attacks were distinguished not only by punches and kicks (as in *Yie Ar Kung-Fu*) but also by relative strength, promoting a strategic form of play. Any attack could be more or less advantageous depending on the opponent and their actions, effectively making the game a more complex version of rock, paper, and scissors.

The game's design concept was supported by a previously unheard of six-button layout that allowed players to precisely control their fighter's actions.[*] In addition, players were able to execute physics-defying super moves that caused an overwhelming amount of damage and could quickly decimate an opponent. Although these moves were grossly unbalanced in a game that allowed competition against the machine and other players, this game mechanic could only be triggered by a secret combination of button and joystick movements; a privileged form of knowledge known only to the best "street fighters."

Street Fighter was followed by other head-to-head fighting games like *Violence Fight* (1989, Taito) and *Pit-Fighter* (1990, Atari Games). These and other head-to-head fighting games of the late 1980s and early 1990s provided compelling gameplay, but few could match the popularity of *Street*

---

[*] A deluxe version of the cabinet was also created which consisted of two pressure sensitive controllers. The design was dropped, however, as players damaged both the machine and themselves with the force of their strikes.

Fighter II: The World Warrior (1991, Capcom) (Figure 7.3). *Street Fighter II*, more so than its predecessor, was designed for competitive head-to-head tournament play. This feature, like the beat-'em-up's growing number of simultaneous players, took advantage of the arcade's social aspects by providing a novel form of competitive play and spectatorship that home consoles were unable to completely replicate. *Street Fighter II*'s large cast of playable characters, each with meaningful differences in speed, strength, reach, and special abilities, created exciting and varied gameplay and led to intense debate among fans about which characters had the greatest overall advantages. The unbalanced amount of damage caused by special abilities in the first game was toned down relative to its predecessor, as super moves became an integral part of the regular gameplay. Skilled players became

FIGURE 7.3 North American cabinet for *Street Fighter II: Champion Edition* (Capcom, 1991), which differed from the original release by allowing players to compete as the game's "boss" characters. (Courtesy of Arcadia, McLean, IL, www. vintagevideogames.com)

notable for their ability to string together combinations of attacks, which could quickly finish an unwary opponent. While this was originally a programming flaw that was assumed to be unexploitable by players, it nonetheless became a widely used approach that grew into a staple design feature in later games of the franchise.

Western Responses to the Head-to-Head Fighting Game

Many Japanese developers closely followed the design and pixel art aesthetic of *Street Fighter II*, as seen in the Fatal Fury, Art of Fighting, and King of Fighters game series.* American developer Midway and British developer Rare, however, each sought to represent the genre in more visually distinctive ways. *Mortal Kombat* (1992, Midway), designed by Ed Boon and John Tobais, contained essential elements of the head-to-head fighting genre: distinctive characters, secret special moves, bonus stages, and a multiple button layout. The game's most distinctive aspect, however, was its theme and visuals: a postmodern pastiche of criminal underworlds, Hollywood fame, magic spells, Japanese gods, and ninjas. These elements were met with a heavy emphasis on the graphic depiction of violence. Characters spurted blood when hit, and a unique game mechanic allowed the winner to kill the losing character in a particularly brutal manner. The character Sub Zero, for example, pulled the head with attached spine off opponents and held it up for display; an act made all the more intense by the game's use of digitized images of real actors rather than pixel art.

The "fatality" game mechanic illustrated the ultimate form of social competition and game spectatorship and created an enduring mystique among players. It was immediately used in subsequent head-to-head fighting games such as *Time Killers* (1992, Incredible Technologies) and *Eternal Champions* (1993, Sega). *Mortal Kombat*, however, garnered a large following through its secret content, which included the special moves and fatalities as well as unique fights with hidden characters, all of which fueled wild but unfounded speculation about the extent of the game's hidden content.

British game developer Rare, added to the fighting game boom with *Killer Instinct* (1994), which also inherited the genre's rapidly evolving conventions, such as distinctive characters, multiple button layouts, blood, and finishing moves performed at the end of the match. Rather than using pixel art or digitized actors, the characters of *Killer Instinct* were created through a process called *pre-rendering*. Pre-rendering was a common way to balance the desire for high quality 3D imagery with the limitations of consumer computing power. In pre-rendering artists constructed highly detailed 3D models that

---

* Many of these games were overseen by Takashi Nishiyama after leaving Capcom for rival developer SNK.

were turned into a series of animated 2D sprites. This allowed the visuals to maintain the 3D look while requiring a fraction of the processing power to animate the individual frames. It was seen in Rare's Super Nintendo platformer, *Donkey Kong Country* (1994, Rare), as well as numerous other games throughout the 1990s such as *Oddworld: Abe's Oddysee* (1997, Oddworld Inhabitants), and Blizzard Entertainment's *Diablo* (1996) and *Starcraft* (1998). For *Killer Instinct*, in particular, it allowed gameplay to respond quickly to user input, a must for competitive fighting games.

The distinctive element of *Killer Instinct*'s design, however, focused on combining individual special attacks to create chains of combinations. This design concept required a different approach to the control scheme as forcing the player to use a complex set of commands for each special attack was not viable—especially since combinations could build up in excess of 50 individual hits. Instead, *Killer Instinct* allowed the player to execute a simple combination of multiple techniques with a few button and joystick inputs; combinations that could then be extended with further input from the player. To create a sense of balance between players who had increasingly become dependent on trapping opponents in a seemingly never-ending sequence of combinations, *Killer Instinct* featured a "combo breaker." This mechanic would interrupt an opponent's chain of attacks if timed properly and could create an opportunity to counter with a supercharged combination of one's own. Thus, the longer a player strung together combinations, the more chances they gave an opponent to counter and potentially turn the momentum of the match. The growing popularity of 3D fighting games (see Chapter 8) throughout the 1990s and the ability to play them on increasingly sophisticated home consoles (see Chapter 9), like the beat 'em up, led to the decline of 2D fighting games in North America and with it, the disappearance of dedicated arcades.

Japanese Companies Transition to the Home

Nintendo had produced home video games since the late 1970s with its various color TV game dedicated consoles (see Chapter 3), however, it wanted a more sophisticated unit that could play its hit arcade games. Starting in 1981, Nintendo engineer Masayuki Uemura, began experimenting with a cartridge-based console capable of reproducing *Donkey Kong*. Meanwhile Nintendo considered licensing and producing software for the ColecoVision in Japan. The fees proposed by Coleco, however, caused Nintendo to balk and fully support Uemura's engineering efforts. Nintendo's decision was fortunate as the 1983 crash hit North America and caused Coleco to abandon the market.

The console that emerged from Uemura was dubbed the Family Computer, or Famicom (Figure 7.4). Although the Famicom was designed for *Donkey*

FIGURE 7.4   Nintendo's Famicom Console and Controllers. (Photo by Evan Amos.)

Kong, it exceeded the arcade game's technical abilities by including the ability to smoothly scroll from one screen to the next. This uncommon but forward thinking technical feature for a home console would become one of the Famicom's greatest assets.* Like consoles and several arcade games, the Famicom used tile-based graphics that filled the screen using blocks of 8 × 8 pixels. Early games for the Famicom saved memory resources by repeating tiles as often as possible and commonly led to brick and block patterns used to construct game worlds.

The importance of the Famicom was related, in part, to its well-designed controller. The iconic plus-shaped directional pad, or "D-pad," was based on the controls of Nintendo's *Donkey Kong* Game & Watch LCD handheld. Prior to the *Donkey Kong* Game & Watch, the handhelds used simple one or two-button inputs; however, since *Donkey Kong* was designed as a series of horizontal and vertical movements, these capabilities were translated into the efficient, plus-shaped control pad. It would appear in some form in nearly every console controller produced since. This control scheme was ideally suited for 2D game design as it allowed the player intuitive movement through space from either a top-down or sideways perspective. The "A" and "B" buttons, meanwhile, created a consistency with the majority of two-button arcade games.

There were also ergonomic benefits. The controller sat comfortably in the user's hands as both index fingers supported it equally, while it was held in place by the thumbs. The controller's design took advantage of the fine motor skills of the fingers, rather than the larger, less accurate motions of the wrist needed for the VCS joystick. The move away from the 12-button numerical keypad, as on the Intellivision, ColecoVision, and Atari 5200, made interaction with the game more intuitive and reduced the amount of time needed to find the correct button. Without the need for overlays to guide a player's decisions concerning which button to press, players could

---

* The earlier Atari 8-bit and Commodore 64 computers as well as the ColecoVision also had built-in scrolling capabilities. Also, Shigeru Miyamoto originally desired scrolling level transitions in *Donkey Kong*, but they could not be implemented because of hardware limitations in 1981.

concentrate almost exclusively on the screen. Aided by this unique combination of hardware and controller, the Famicom encouraged the production of fast, responsive 2D games that successfully captured the essence of arcade gameplay for the home.

Although, the initial batch of processors turned out to be faulty causing a recall of the units, the Famicom was met with tremendous success in Japan, selling three million units between its 1983 launch and 1984. Nintendo's goal, however, was the United States. After a proposed deal with Atari to license the Famicom fell through (just prior to the beginning of Atari's woes), Nintendo decided to market the system to the United States directly, a move which required a number of adjustments to the Famicom. It featured a new American-style form factor created by industrial designer, Lance Barr, which fit with contemporary home electronics trends. It was also rebranded as the NES, complete with light gun and toy robot. Nintendo's main problem with breaking into the American market, however, was convincing retailers to stock another videogame console after the weight of nine major console releases between 1977 and 1983 helped flood the market. Nintendo was finally able to win over American retailers by guaranteeing that any unsold consoles would receive a complete refund. After a mediocre, but encouraging series of test market launches in 1985 and early 1986, the NES was launched nationwide in the fall of 1986.

Stabilizing and Controlling the Console Market

It was clear from the beginning that Nintendo intended to assert total control over the home console market through strict procedures in dealing with third-party developers. A company that produced games for Nintendo's console was limited to a maximum number of five games per year. In addition, Nintendo insisted on exclusivity and extracted a high licensing fee. Its control also extended to the ability to override or censor anything it found objectionable in the game content, in the interest of protecting the company's image, particularly its American branch, Nintendo of America. With three million consoles sold in the first year of the NES's American launch and six million the year after in a market that was supposedly "dead," developers were eager to create games for the system.

In order to eliminate the threat from counterfeit or unlicensed games, the American and European version of the NES was designed with a lockout chip, a safeguard that prevented the system from starting if an unlicensed cartridge failed an authentication by the system. Competitors eventually found a way to circumvent this early form of digital rights management (DRM), but, along with Nintendo's licensing policy, it allowed the company to more easily manage its image and build a reputation on high quality games. These actions allowed Nintendo to achieve a near monopoly on the home console market by the late 1980s, with an estimated share of greater than 90% in both Japan and the United States.

Establishing Nintendo's Franchises

The Famicom's 1983 launch titles and early offerings were heavily tilted toward the arcade, with ports of *Donkey Kong, Donkey Kong Jr.*, and *Popeye* closely followed by *Mario Bros., Galaxian, Pac-Man, Xevious, Space Invaders*, and many other Golden Age Japanese arcade games. In the mid-1980s, however, Nintendo and its designers began to transition away from an arcade-centric mindset to one focused on developing games better suited for extended play sessions in the home; much of which was achieved through finding and adopting a different approach to level design.

Leading Nintendo's transition was the industrial designer turned game designer, Shigeru Miyamoto and newcomer Takashi Tezuka, also a traditionally educated designer. Miyamoto and Tezuka's main achievements for the Famicom/NES centered on refining familiar coin-op game elements and creating novel level design that resulted in a depth of gameplay rarely seen on prior consoles. Their evolving design sensibilities and a range of technological enhancements to the Famicom, allowed the team to create some of Nintendo's, and the game industry's most lauded games.

Miyamoto and Tezuka's first Famicom game was *Devil World* (1984, Nintendo), a dot-gobbling, fireball shooting, maze game featuring devils, crucifixes, and bibles that only saw release in Japan and Europe; Nintendo of America objected to the overt use of religious symbolism. Little separated *Devil World* from an arcade game, as the game endlessly repeated two mazes and a bonus stage until the player ran out of lives. Nonetheless, it took advantage of the Famicom's ability to scroll in the game space. In the months following *Devil World*, Miyamoto designed the stunt motorcycle racing game, *Excitebike* (1984), which featured a game engine capable of more smoothly scrolling between the string of individual screens that made up the game levels. The illusion of movement from left to right at high speeds was crucial for the game's racing theme. However, with the exception of a track editor that allowed players to create and play customized levels, *Excitebike* was still effectively an arcade racing game designed for short bursts of play.

Super Mario Bros.

The tipping point for Miyamoto and Tezuka's design of console-based games was their next project, *Super Mario Bros.* (1985, Nintendo) (Figure 7.5), a game with an incalculable impact on the game industry that remains strongly influential today. *Super Mario Bros.* centered on Mario's quest to free the kidnapped princess of the Mushroom Kingdom from the clutches of the Koopa Clan, a ruthless band of turtle-like creatures led by Bowser.

FIGURE 7.5 *Super Mario Bros* **(1985, Nintendo).**

Although platforming elements of running and jumping had existed prior to *Super Mario Bros.*, the game cemented a number of unique concepts that struck a balance between fast arcade-like action and longer durations of play suited for the home. It also helped rekindle the North American console market and served as one of the first gaming experiences of a new generation of players who would eventually become designers themselves.

The initial design idea for *Super Mario Bros.* involved controlling a large-scale character in space. Many arcade games, like *Donkey Kong*, contained all of the action in a single screen, requiring small characters in order to maximize the play space. An increase in a character's scale (made possible by assembling multiple small tiles together), however, required a larger play space than could be displayed on the screen. This led to the game's signature expansive world of colorful environments representing land, sea, and air. To make gameplay feel continuous through large spaces, *Super Mario Bros.* utilized the fast scrolling game engine developed for *Excitebike*. It allowed Mario to smoothly accelerate to a run rather than move at a constant speed, as in earlier games like *Donkey Kong* and *Mario Bros.* The result was a 32 level experience that cohesively combined bonus challenges, multiple strategy boss fights, hidden objects, and secret areas. These elements encouraged the player to experiment, discover, and explore the bounds of play within the game space, a signature aspect of Miyamoto's design philosophy.

Adding to its sheer scale, *Super Mario Bros.* featured well-designed interactions between its individual mechanics, enemy behaviors, and level design that created intuitive and compelling gameplay. Power-up mechanics, central to the game, increased the player's abilities in the game world. Although many games of the time included power-ups (*Pac-Man*, *Galaga*, and *Devil World*), *Super Mario Bros.* gave the player a wider range with the ability to break blocks, throw fireballs, or temporarily become invulnerable. These skills, gained and lost during gameplay, created a dynamic ebb and flow that required the player to continually adjust and change strategies. Principally important among the game mechanics was the jump, which deviated significantly from the straight vertical or preset arcs of *Pitfall!*, *Pac-Land*, and even Miyamoto's earlier arcade games. Players could adjust their position slightly left or right in midair, allowing for subtle and precise redirection. Further, the player could control the height of the jump based on an intuitive notion that the longer the player pressed the jump button, the higher Mario would jump. While a previous game, *Ice Climber* (1985, Nintendo), for the Famicom/NES allowed a slight left or right alteration of the player's jump mid-air, it was not nearly as developed as that of *Super Mario Bros.*

With such an uncommonly high degree of control over Mario's movement, the game needed to teach the player the subtlety of the mechanic before increasing the challenge. Early in the first level, for example, the player encountered a set of three green pipes, each progressively higher, and containing zero, one, and two Goomba enemies. This set of obstacles required mastery of the jump mechanic before the player could progress. A small jump, created by a quick tap of the button, sufficed for the first pipe but not for the second or third, which required a longer press. The Goombas between the pipes were moving targets that required the player to adjust the trajectory of the jump in order to land on or avoid them. A player who failed at either action would die, but since this occurred at the game's beginning, the player could quickly try again without losing ground. A later level, World 6-1, featured stair-like structures arranged in different configurations that led to bottomless pits. Although these structures required careful timing and accuracy of jumps to ascend, the player would have become skilled enough to pass them easily. A cloud-riding enemy called Lakitu, however, complicated this task by repeatedly dropping the un-stompable, spike-shelled, "Spiny" character into the game space, reducing player maneuverability.

The Legend of Zelda

At the same time that Miyamoto and Tezuka designed *Super Mario Bros.*, the team was also creating *The Legend of Zelda*, which released the following year in 1986 (Figure 7.6). *The Legend of Zelda* used a similar narrative form to *Super Mario Bros.*: it centered on a lone hero, Link, who attempted to rescue the Princess Zelda from the evil Ganon, while uniting the disparate pieces of the magical Triforce of Wisdom. While Miyamoto and Tezuka drew elements from the Japanese localizations of CRPGs *Ultima II* and *The Black Onyx*, *The Legend of Zelda* featured none of the RPG genre's signature experience points or character stats. Players instead explored the unfamiliar landscape in search of items that would grant them access to closed areas and eventually complete the game's goal. A raft, for example, allowed the

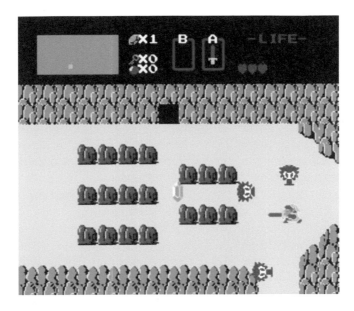

FIGURE 7.6   *The Legend of Zelda* **(1986, Nintendo).**

player access to islands while a power bracelet granted the ability to move large rocks and access new spaces. This experience of unpacking elements of the game space was also found in the side-scrolling shooting platformer, *Metroid* (1986, Nintendo), which used new weapon powers to open previously encountered doors.

Rather than a gentle introduction to gameplay as seen in *Super Mario Bros.*, players of *The Legend of Zelda* were placed in a 128-screen overworld without the means to attack. Those who ventured into one of the three available starting pathways confronted enemies they could not fight, leading to a quick and helpless death. Further, while players were aware that they needed to find pieces of the Triforce, they were given no indication of where to begin, as the massive *open world* game space did not suggest any particular path. While these were common elements among computer-based adventure and role-playing games, they were unconventional for console games. This prompted Nintendo to include directions in the game's manual for obtaining the sword and reaching the first two dungeons.

Super Mario Bros. and *The Legend of Zelda* were followed by sequels that deviated significantly from their predecessors. *Super Mario Bros. 2* (1986, Nintendo), utilized game mechanics and level design that often intentionally misled the player, deviating from Miyamoto's encouragement-based approach to platformers. For instance, early in the beginning level, the player encountered a poison mushroom that closely resembled the power-up mushroom but would instantly kill the player when touched. Although the game was intended to create a greater challenge for those who had completed *Super Mario Bros.*, Nintendo considered the game too difficult for

FROM CARTRIDGES TO DISKS, TO CARTRIDGES AGAIN

Super Mario Bros. was originally to be the last cartridge-based game for the Famicom, as Nintendo planned to switch to floppy disk-based games played on the Famicom Disk System (FDS) add-on. The FDS increased the Famicom's base-available memory, sound capabilities, and offered larger storage for games—attractive qualities for game designers, who were at increasing odds with the limitations of Nintendo's early cartridges. The FDS helped Japanese designers break from conventions of arcade games by encouraging larger, more ambitious game levels with the potential for multiple hours of content. *The Legend of Zelda* and *Metroid* exemplified this with content that players would not likely complete in a single sitting. As the FDS had the ability to write data like a personal computer, these large leveled games allowed players to save their progress on the game disk.

The increased capacity and enhancements brought by the FDS were invaluable help that allowed developers to move into new territory, but it was never released outside of Japan; issues with the inability to control piracy and counterfeiting plagued the add-on, making a worldwide release ill-advised. This created a problem for the international versions of *The Legend of Zelda* and *Metroid* as players needed a way to continue their progress. Nintendo's initial solution was to give players a password on death that could start a new game with certain items—a solution used in the 1987 North American release of *Metroid*. This was unsatisfactory, however, as the player needed to input a 24 character code via the D-pad, after every death. The North American release of *The Legend of Zelda* was different as it included a battery-powered memory chip inside the cartridge that mimicked the FDS's data writing capabilities. The battery-backup save-game was used for numerous North American game releases thereafter, including *Dragon Warrior* and *Final Fantasy*. Nintendo eventually dropped support for the FDS entirely and opted to upgrade the contents of the cartridges with more memory as well as *bank switching* capabilities (see Chapter 5). This created a noticeable difference in visual quality and game content between early Famicom/NES games versus those produced later in the console's lifecycle.

international release. Instead, the North American version of *Super Mario Bros. 2* (1988) used the setting and mechanics of the Arabian Nights-themed *Yume Kōjō: Doki Doki Panic* (1987, Nintendo) and replaced the character sprites with those inspired by *Super Mario Bros.*.* *Zelda II: The Adventure of Link* (1987, Nintendo), was a similar departure, as the top-down perspective was replaced with a side-scrolling action game that utilized experience points, random encounters, and an overworld map similar to *Dragon Quest* and other Japanese RPGs (see below).

---

* The original Japanese version of *Super Mario Bros 2*, however, did eventually make its way out of Japan and was titled, *Super Mario Bros: The Lost Levels* as part of a four game compilation, *Super Mario All-Stars* (1993, Nintendo) for the Super Famicom/Super Nintendo Entertainment System (SNES).

Although both sequels were commercially successful, Nintendo embraced a more conservative approach to subsequent games in these key franchises. *Super Mario Bros. 3* (1988, Nintendo) sported more than 90 levels and spaces with a game world alive with interaction; it featured new power-ups, an inventory system, several mini games, and wandering mini bosses brought together by an overworld map laid out like a board game. It allowed players the choice to experience everything offered by the game world or to take the shortest route to a final showdown with one of seven "Koopaling" bosses. Despite its unparalleled grand experience, the game returned to the accessible essence and feel of the original. It made the learning curve more forgiving through level design that helped the player learn the game's new mechanics and included a more frequent placement of extra lives near the game's beginning. *The Legend of Zelda: A Link to the Past* (1991, Nintendo) for Nintendo's "next-gen" Super Famicom/SNES (discussed below) similarly returned to its inaugural roots. In all, this experience helped to solidify the design philosophy at Nintendo for the remainder of the 2D era and provide a starting point for its first 3D games in the mid-1990s (see Chapter 9).

Computer Games and the JRPG on the Famicom/NES

As discussed in Chapter 6, the home computer industry saw rapid expansion throughout the 1980s and gave rise to a number of distinct forms of gameplay and game interfaces. Many computer game developers, aware of the mass appeal of the Famicom/NES, also created games for the console. This allowed Nintendo's players access to a wider variety of game types than what had typically been developed for consoles. Although the Famicom/NES was not as technologically robust as home computers like the Amiga, it nonetheless, featured ports of point-and-click adventure games (*Maniac Mansion* and *King's Quest*), vehicle simulators (*Silent Service* and *F-15 Strike Eagle* by MicroProse), and RPGs (*Wizardry: Proving Grounds of the Mad Overlord* and *The Black Onyx*), ports which often saw release on the Famicom years before the NES. In addition to adapting specific computer titles, general design concepts also flowed from computer games to Nintendo's console with games like *The Goonies II* (1987, Konami) and *Friday the 13th* (1989, Pack in Video) which combined the action of platforming gameplay with adventure-based, first-person exploration. Both, like *The Legend of Zelda* and computer adventure games relied on the player's willingness to explore the bounds of the game world and its various interactions to make progress.

Important in the exchange between computers and the Famicom/NES, were the concepts that led to *Dragon Quest* (1986, Churnsoft), the game that created the framework for subsequent JRPGs. Japan had few computer

RPGs until the mid-1980s with *The Black Onyx* and localizations of the Ultima franchise, and even then, they were appreciated by only a small subsection of Japan's gaming population. Yuji Hori, a developer associated with software publisher Enix, was an avid fan of Western RPGs, however, he felt the genre's unfamiliar game mechanics and number management created a significant barrier for new Japanese players. Thus, Hori along with programmer Koichi Nakamura, looked to create a form of RPG more simplified in its systems, eventually resulting in the Famicom game, *Dragon Quest*.

In *Dragon Quest* (titled *Dragon Warrior* in the United States), the player wandered through a map-like overworld of natural landscapes with icons representing towns, caves, and dungeons. Like the Ultima games, once the player moved over one of the map icons, the perspective abruptly changed to a full-scale representation of the space, complete with non-player characters (NPCs), stores, and treasure chests where appropriate. In the overworld map, the player fought enemies in turn-based random encounters, gathered gold and gained experience points—all staple elements of early CRPGs. Hori's design for *Dragon Quest*, however, simplified the standard RPG formula: it reduced the character's attributes to two (strength and agility), compressed the myriad classes/professions into a single character, awarded the majority of experience points in simple low numbers, and replaced spell levels with a pool of magic points that were spent on spell cast. Leveling increased all character stats and attributes and provided a clear indication of character progression rather than changes in hit points and number modifiers common in Western RPGs.

One of the game's most distinctive elements was its manner of interaction. *Dragon Quest* adopted the interface from the Hori's earlier Famicom port of the graphic adventure, *The Portopia Serial Murder Case* (1985, Churnsoft), which consisted of selecting predetermined commands from a series of menus using the Famicom's d-pad. These changes to the formula for RPGs, aided by a series of articles in manga magazines explaining the concepts of the gameplay, as well as character artwork by famed manga artist Akira Toriyama, helped propel *Dragon Quest* to success among Japan's Famicom player base.

Dragon Quest's popularity led other Japanese developers to create RPGs as well. *Final Fantasy* (1987, Square) used the same basic systems, overworld map, and Famicom friendly interface of *Dragon Quest*, but added a more tactical element to combat: players used a party of characters, composed of multiple classes and abilities, to fight mixed parties of enemies. Player choice in managing the fight, in addition to the exploration and fulfillment of the main quest, thus became a central element of the game. The JRPGs by Enix and Square resulted in a long line of sequels that inspired other developers and franchises. The North

American localization of these initial JRPGs and others created a small, but devoted fan base that grew stronger after the 1997 North American release of *Final Fantasy VII* (Square) and the 1998 Game Boy release of *Pokémon* (1996, Game Freak).

Sega Joins the Console Market

Nintendo supercharged the home console market in Japan and reawakened the desire of North American retailers, however, the Famicom/NES was not the only 8-bit Japanese console of the period. The SG-1000 by Sega, launched the same day as the Famicom but paled in comparison as seen in the choppy scrolling and undesirable flickering sprites of games such as the shoot-'em-up *Orguss* (1984, Sega) and port of arcade platformer, *Wonder Boy* (1986, Sega). An updated version of the console, the SG-1000 Mark II was released shortly thereafter, in 1984.

While commercially unsuccessful in the Japanese market, Sega was undeterred and decided to compete with Nintendo head-on, by designing a system to exceed the Famicom's capabilities. The SG-1000 Mark III, internationally known as the "Master System," was designed, like most previous consoles, to replicate the performance of arcade machines at home. The unit's ability to smoothly scroll the screen and scale the size of sprites allowed Sega to port its *pseudo-3D* and action platformer arcade games in an attempt to help drive console sales. With Yu Suzuki's *Hang-On* as a pack-in launch title, followed by ports of other Sega games, such as *Afterburner*, *Altered Beast*, *Outrun*, and *Space Harrier*, the SG-1000 Mark III/Master System performed better than its predecessors but was inconsistent in different regions, leading to tepid third-party support. The console was virtually locked out in Japan and North America by Nintendo's monopoly created by its exclusive licensing agreements and several years' headstart. Despite this, Sega was able to produce a few successful original titles for its console such as JRPG *Phantasy Star* (1987, Sega). In Europe the Master System was more popular, as Nintendo had been unable to control the market as in Japan and the United States. The Master System encountered virtually no competition in Brazil, allowing it and the later Mega Drive/Genesis to capture the market and continue to produce demand for games through the 1990s.

16-Bit Consoles, Marketing, and Game Design

Nintendo's dominance of 8-bit consoles made all previous attempts to compete virtually impossible. The success of the Famicom/NES, however, made Nintendo slow to accept change in an industry becoming more dependent on rapid advancements in technology. Falling prices of 16-bit processors in the late 1980s made their inclusion in a new generation of consoles cost effective and allowed Nintendo's competitors to leapfrog and outperform the 8-bit Famicom/NES. This inaugurated new set of "console wars," this time between Japanese companies, as Sega, Nintendo, and newcomer NEC, aggressively vied for market share.

The framework of intense competition drove many underlying game design decisions as a "next-gen" version of a game within a popular genre could either retain customer loyalty or lure them from a competitor. This was particularly true of Nintendo's Super Famicom/SNES as its exclusive relationship with developers allowed for "super" versions of titles in various franchises, such as Adventure Island, Bomberman, Castlevania, Double Dragon, Mega Man, Metroid, and Punch-Out!!, many of which were highly lauded by game critics for their refinements. In these and other cases, game graphics received a vast amount of attention, as marketing relied on a player's ability to instantly judge a game, fairly or unfairly, based on its visual detail. Vivid colors brought characters and objects to life, while environments composed of multilayered, parallaxing backgrounds contributed to the period's distinctive and much-loved visuals leading to a Golden Age for pixel art.

New Contenders

In 1987 computer manufacturer NEC and software developer Hudson Soft released the PC Engine in Japan, inaugurating the fourth generation of home consoles. Although the unit used an 8-bit processor at its core, it was capable of 16-bit visuals, which brought high-fidelity ports of arcade games to the home. These advanced visual capabilities were the central feature of the console's advertising efforts as the console was renamed the Turbo Grafix-16 for its 1989 North American launch. The PC Engine was able to temporarily overturn Nintendo's dominance in Japan before settling for a second place position, however, its performance in the United States was abysmal, as Sega's new 16-bit console quickly captured a sizeable portion of the next-gen market.

The form factor of Sega's 16-bit Mega Drive/Genesis console stood in stark contrast to the toy-like aesthetic of the Famicom. It projected an overall impression of maturity and high-tech futurism as its asymmetric layout of vents, buttons, and switches bore a resemblance to high-end audio mixing equipment, while the characters "16-BIT" were conspicuously embossed in gold on the console's top (Figure 7.7). Sega, continuing the quest to capitalize on its arcade catalog, based the Mega Drive/Genesis console on its System16 arcade board, used for *Shinobi*, *Altered Beast*, and *Golden Axe* among others. With this, the gap between post-Golden Age arcade games and console games significantly narrowed, allowing the console to faithfully reproduce popular arcade games more accurately than the PC Engine/

FIGURE 7.7   Japanese release of Sega's Mega Drive and controller, marketed as the "Genesis" in the United States. (Photo by Evan Amos.)

Turbo Grafix-16. The design of the controller for the Mega Drive/Genesis was also heavily influenced by Sega's arcade games: its 8-directional game pad followed the standard 8-directional arcade joystick while its three buttons allowed the console to reproduce the typical "attack/jump/special weapon" control scheme of Sega arcade games like *Altered Beast*, *ESWAT Cyber Police*, *Shinobi*, and *Golden Axe*. In addition, the rounded edges and small projections at the ends of the controller provided a greater degree of ergonomic comfort relative to the rectangular game pad by Nintendo.

New Platformers for New Consoles and Intensified Competition

Replicating the performance of arcade machines was a compelling feature of the new consoles, but ports of arcade games alone did not suffice in a game market rapidly transitioning away from arcades and into new territory. In particular, Sega's initial lineup of unmodified arcade ports was criticized as being light on content. Both NEC and Sega included arcade-like action platformers with shooting or other combat-focused mechanics, but neither system initially had a viable Mario-style platformer with compelling game design and a mascot capable of siphoning Nintendo's fans away.

The first direct challenge to Mario was the PC Engine/Turbo Grafix-16 platformer, *Bonk's Adventure* (1989, Red Company/Atlus). *Bonk's Adventure* was a brightly colored, light-hearted, prehistoric-themed game, starring "Bonk" a child-like caveman with a colossal head that "bonked" enemies. The game used many design elements from *Super Mario Bros.*—a smooth scrolling game space, an ebb and flow of power-ups, hidden rooms, boss fights, and a highly controllable jump mechanic. The game spanned different environments and created the feeling of embarking on a journey. Although it was released on multiple game platforms (including the Famicom/NES) and led to a number of sequels, it was unable to significantly impact the game market, as Nintendo had already produced more elaborate and refined platformers like *Super Mario Bros. 3*.

FIGURE 7.8 *Sonic the Hedgehog* **(1991, Sonic Team).**

Sega was more successful with its platformer, *Sonic the Hedgehog* (1991, Sonic Team). Both the game and the character, Sonic, were intended to promote the technical power of Sega's Mega Drive/Genesis console by focusing on speed (Figure 7.8). The game's concept was based on a particular design problem with the platformer genre: players needed to traverse a linear sequence of levels in order to make progress. This structure, inherited from arcade games, gradually grew in difficulty with each level (as discussed above in relation to *Super Mario Bros.*). Skilled players, however, were still required to play through the beginning levels in order to get to the later, more difficult content.

Nintendo's Shigeru Miyamoto addressed this problem by creating level-skipping warp zones in the Super Mario Bros. games. Sega programmer, Yuji Naka, however, wanted to make his love of fast moving objects into a fun experience by creating a game that allowed skilled players to complete early stages in extremely fast time before getting to the game's later content. This concept was reinforced by Naoto Oshima's design of a feisty, anthropomorphic, blue hedgehog that sported a spiky hairstyle and wore bright red running shoes. In the final game, Sonic ran through roller coaster loops, rolled into a ball, and shot through serpentine tubes at almost dizzying high speeds. The game's brightly colored zones featured highly animated objects and parallaxed backgrounds that made Sonic's world one of constant motion. Although still a linear experience of running from left to right, the level design of *Sonic the Hedgehog* was more open, with each stage often featuring multiple pathways to the end goal. Since the game's timer counted up and not down, players were free to either cruise through the level as fast as possible, like a race, or meticulously explore the entirety of the game space, looking for the collectable golden rings or power-ups.

Sonic the Hedgehog propelled Sega to its first major home console success and provided the first real threat to Nintendo in the North American market, especially after the game was bundled with new systems. Sega also went on the offensive against the monopoly of Nintendo with a confrontational North American marketing campaign, unified by the catchphrase "Genesis does what Nintendon't." The Genesis' offerings included games that not only pushed the boundaries of represented violence, such as an uncensored version of *Mortal Kombat* and the fighting game *Eternal Champions* (1993, Sega), but also games with celebrity sports personalities of the early 1990s such as Joe Montana, Arnold Palmer, and Pat Reilly in addition to "King of Pop," Michael Jackson.

Nintendo, meanwhile, launched its 16-bit Super Famicom/SNES in Japan in 1990 along with its new platformer, *Super Mario World* (1990, Nintendo), produced by Shigeru Miyamoto and directed by Takashi Tezuka. *Super Mario World*, like its predecessor *Super Mario Bros. 3*, was essentially a retelling of the original *Super Mario Bros.* with a number of added mechanics in the form of power-ups, enemies, and environmental objects. Like *Super Mario Bros.*, it was designed to subtly teach the game's basic behaviors before testing players with challenging content. As a backup, it also included optional text boxes explaining the game mechanics; a feature found in many of Nintendo's subsequent Mario games. A notable feature was its break from the sense of linearity as the activation of a switch or object in one level often required the player to revisit already completed levels in order to progress to new or secret areas. This Zelda-like design feature encouraged players to investigate game spaces in total and provided a new objective in an otherwise familiar level, thereby efficiently increasing the game's content; a concept that was central to the later fully 3D *Super Mario 64* (1996, Nintendo).

Nintendo's reputation as a provider of quality platformer game design was further enhanced with two titles, created later in the Super Famicom/SNES's life cycle, *Donkey Kong Country* (1994, Rare) and *Super Mario World 2: Yoshi's Island* (1995, Nintendo). Each game closely followed the form of the earlier *Super Mario World*, but signaled a maturing of design for 2D platformers at a time when 3D-based gameplay was becoming increasingly common. Each game also provided a significant visual departure from the 16-bit era's pixel art graphics as *Donkey Kong Country* utilized pre-rendered visuals while *Super Mario World 2: Yoshi's Island* featured graphics resembling a series of hand-drawn 2D layers—a deliberate pushback by Miyamoto against the encroaching visual realism in games (see Chapter 8).

While 2D platformers were synonymous with Nintendo, the Super Famicom/SNES was designed with capabilities that foreshadowed the coming wave of 3D-based gameplay. Key was the *mode 7* background layer graphics setting, which could rotate and scale a background layer, producing the effect of smoothly moving through space in a *pseudo-3D* perspective.

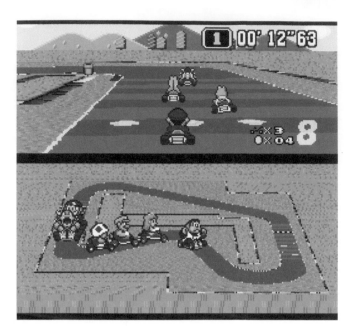

FIGURE 7.9 *Super Mario Kart* **(1992, Nintendo).**

This effect was used to create racing and flying gameplay as in *F-Zero* (1990, Nintendo), *Pilotwings* (1990, Nintendo), *Super Mario Kart* (1992, Nintendo) (Figure 7.9), *Top Gear* (1992, Gremlin Graphics), and *Super Star Wars* (1992, Sculptured Software/LucasArts).

The competition between Nintendo, Sega, and NEC occurred in a complex time of change for digital games and digital culture. Compact disc-based games and hypermedia applications that combined image, sound, text, and video with nonlinear access exploded into the marketplace and brought with it a new experience of media for consumers. 3D graphics appeared in more sophisticated forms than simple wireframes on home computers. Finally, virtual reality made its first commercial debut, sparking the imagination of the public and raising expectations for the future. All of these developments in the late 1980s and early 1990s made an impression on the highly competitive home console market, as Nintendo, Sega, and NEC looked to enhance the capabilities of their products in a rapidly changing environment. This set of topics and their impact on games across the industry will be more fully explored in Chapter 8, as a new visual and spatial realism came to dominate the design of digital games in the early to mid-1990s.

Early 3D and the Multimedia Boom (1989-1996)

Two Paths to Realism: Multimedia Imagery and Real-Time 3D

The late 1980s and mid-1990s saw a revolution in multimedia. The computer industry standardized the format for inexpensive, high-capacity CD-ROMs, sparking massive interest among application developers. Programs such as *Compton's MultiMedia Encyclopedia* (1989) and *The New Grolier Multimedia Encyclopedia* (1992) brought text, image, sound, and video together, which allowed new ways to present, access, and understand information. Films such as *Terminator 2: Judgment Day* (1991), *Jurassic Park* (1993), and *Toy Story* (1995) represented important milestones in 3D, computer-generated imagery. Finally, virtual reality made its public debut to high expectations.

Many games of the period used the above advances to bring a greater sense of visual realism to gameplay that was generally expressed in one of two ways. The first focused on photo-realism, which was attained through using a mix of digitized images, full motion video, and pre-rendered 3D imagery. This was prominent in adventure games as well as a number of interactive movies that featured more complexity than the laser disc games of the Golden Age arcade (see Chapter 4). The second approach focused on spatial realism and was achieved through the real-time calculation of 3D filled polygons, a visual improvement over earlier 3D wireframes. Real-time 3D graphics in the late 1980s and early 1990s, however, were computationally intensive and lacked detail. This resulted in a significant reliance on 2D imagery to supplement the limited 3D forms as seen in a number of the period's computer games.

The emphasis on greater visual fidelity, however, also generated controversy as a new generation of game designers looked to create works that subverted established game conventions through explicit expressions of violent imagery; a development that coincided with a similar trend in some comics and animation. The sudden appearance of more realistic representations of violence, and darker, more intense visuals intended for older players, caught the public by surprise. The controversy that developed led to the creation of a rating system for games much like that of the film industry that remains in place today.

CD-ROMs and Photo-Realism

Interactive Film and Games

The proliferation of multimedia technologies in the late 1980s and 1990s briefly reignited interest in laser disc arcade games as well as created a market for CD-ROM interactive film games at home. While few of these games represented innovations in design, they provided the highest degree of realistic imagery of the time as they were filmed like movies and often utilized a first-person perspective. Developer American Laser Games, whose founder, Robert Grabe designed police training simulators, created a number of live-action gun games such as the wild-west-themed, *Mad Dog McCree* (1990) and the police action drama, *Crime Patrol* (1993). While the games were designed like other gun games with players using a light gun to shoot on-screen characters within a short window of time before the characters shot the player, they emphasized narrative in a way that exceeded many gun games of the 1980s (Figure 8.1). The sequel to the arcade laser disc classic *Dragon's Lair*, was finally released in 1991 with *Dragon's Lair II: Time Warp* (Leland Corporation), which continued the story of Dirk the Daring and was played almost identically to its 1983 predecessor. Sega's arcade division went farther than its competitors and produced a curious set of hologram-based cabinets that used a concave mirror to create games that appeared to float in space. This visually innovative concept was used in two games: *Time Traveler* (1991, Sega) featuring a time-traveling cowboy who avoided dangers through properly timed button and joystick movements, and *Holosseum* (1992, Sega), a 2D pixel art head-to-head fighting game intended to compete with *Street Fighter II*.

The late 1980s to early 1990s also saw the emergence of CD-ROM-based consoles that brought many arcade laser disc games to the home and supported a plethora of other games with multimedia elements. Unlike the market for cartridge-based home consoles, which was dominated by Nintendo

FIGURE 8.1   The 1993 DOS version of *Maddog McCree* for IBM PCs (pictured above) featured video that was highly compressed, resulting in a pixelated appearance common among CD-ROM games of the time. (Courtesy of Digital Leisure Inc./Her Interactive.)

and Sega, the early market for CD-ROM consoles was highly fragmented. All three of the major Japanese players in the "console wars" developed CD-based add-on modules for their 16-bit systems, however, due to a falling out between Nintendo and its CD development partner Sony, only the 1989 TurboGrafx-CD and 1991 Sega CD saw commercial release. New Western competitors quickly joined the market with the 1991 Philips CD-i and 1993 Panasonic 3DO; all of which took place while CD-ROMs became a standard feature of home computers. Because of the wide variety in CD-based consoles and games, third-party software was often released on multiple platforms.

Game developers struggled at times to adapt existing game types to a new mode of video presentation. Nintendo licensed its Mario and Link characters for a series of CD-i platformer games featuring fully animated cut scenes with *Hotel Mario* (1994, Philips Fantasy Factory), *Link: The Faces of Evil* (1993, Animation Magic), and *Zelda: The Wand of Gamelon* (1993, Animation Magic). Although visually consistent with Nintendo's iconography, the games played slow relative to expectations as the CD-i was not designed to replicate the same arcade-like performance specs and responsiveness of Nintendo's hardware. In addition, the notoriously poor quality of the games' animated sequences detracted from the overall experience.

Other games experimented with CD media in different ways. *Supreme Warrior* (1994, Digital Pictures) attempted to meld the action of a cinematic kung fu fight, the immersion of a first-person perspective, and gameplay of a head-to-head fighting game by having the player throw strikes and blocks against segments of video-recorded enemies. *Slam City with Scottie Pippen* (1994, Digital Pictures) similarly used the premise of reacting in time, but applied it to a series of one-on-one street basketball matches. Despite these attempts to enhance well-known game types and create unique approaches to immersion, the relatively slow speed of early CD-ROMs coupled with the segmented structure of the video clips created noticeable pauses and jumps in gameplay. This, in addition to titles designed by developers with little to no experience in games, made many genres initially unsuitable for CD-based games.

Puzzle Games in the Era of Multimedia

The types of games that did excel, however, typically had a slower pace of gameplay and often centered on themes of investigation requiring the player to solve puzzles. Games like *Voyeur* (Philips P.O.V. Entertainment Group), first appearing on the CD-i in 1993, followed the basic design format of a point-and-click adventure, with static images full of "hot spots." As suggested by the game's title, *Voyeur* contained a number of mature narrative themes dealing with sexual situations, which added intrigue but also caused it to carry a warning label about its content. The game's concept, similar to Alfred Hitchcock's 1954 thriller *Rear Window*, centered on the player watching the various rooms of a corrupt businessman's mansion from a building across the street. The goal was to gather incriminating evidence that would ruin the businessman's chances of becoming President of the United States. Gameplay focused on a large still image of the mansion's exterior like a map where the player could click on different windows to either investigate the objects in an empty computer-generated room or "video record" the mansion's inhabitants by watching actors play out scenes. This structure not only offered an opportunity to showcase the game's multimedia visuals but also helped mitigate the relatively slow rate of data transfer from CD-ROMs of the early 1990s by limiting the main interactive portions of the game to static, non-video images.

The 7th Guest (1993, Trilobyte), designed by Rob Landeros and Graeme Devine, centered on the player navigating a pre-rendered haunted mansion filled with logic puzzles presented from an immersive first-person perspective (Figures 8.2 and 8.3). The game's story that framed the puzzles was communicated through short video sequences of live actors captured in front of a blue screen. To enhance the immersive quality of the game, the interface was minimal as the main interactions were executed by a context-sensitive cursor that changed from a navigation to investigation tool depending on its placement on the screen. The game was also

FIGURE 8.2   A ghostly apparition retreats down a hallway in *The 7th Guest* (1993, Trilobyte). (Courtesy of Rob Landeros.)

innovative for its sophisticated video compression technology created by Graeme Devine, an impressive feat, as no off-the-shelf options were available at the time.

Of all the multimedia puzzle games produced in the early 1990s, however, *Myst* (1993, Cyan Worlds) proved to be the most popular (Figure 8.4). Drawing on their knowledge gained from creating interactive children's stories, brothers Rand and Robyn Miller designed *Myst* for an older, nongame playing audience. As such, accessibility was one of the major design concerns. Unlike the predominant conventions of arcade, home console, and

FIGURE 8.3   A cake-based puzzle in *The 7th Guest* (1993, Trilobyte). (Courtesy of Rob Landeros.)

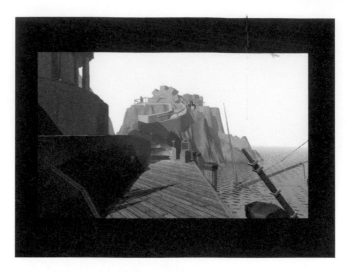

FIGURE 8.4 *Myst* **(1993, Cyan Worlds). (Myst is Copyright 2013 Cyan Worlds, Inc. All Rights reserved. Used with Permission.)**

earlier puzzle/adventure games, *Myst* eliminated player death and the ability to become stuck due to a "wrong" decision. This allowed players unfamiliar with digital games to enjoy the immersive first-person game world without the stress of limited lives or timers. Progress was hindered only by the player's inability to solve the game's puzzles.

Myst's story and gameplay revolved around piecing together the conflicting account of events surrounding the disappearance of a wizard-like character Atrus as given by Atrus' two sons. Imprisoned in magic books, each son communicated to the player through fragmented video clips gained from solving the game's various puzzles and exploring different time periods or "ages" of the game's island. Narrative, ambiance, and immersion took precedent as every interaction was designed to feel like a natural extension of the game's world and not overly "game-like." Aiding this was one of the most visually rich environments of the period. Each of the game's 2500 still images showcased the surreal island in fully textured 3D graphics; distant hills and trees were rendered in atmospheric haze, while close surfaces resembled industrial metal platforms, smooth marble columns, and wooden plank bridges. Environmental sounds—waves lapping on the island's shores, wind blowing across mountaintops—supported the highly detailed visuals while an atmospheric soundtrack by Robyn Miller played in the background. This immersive ambiance, made possible by the high storage capacity of CDs as well as design choices that allowed free exploration of the game space, drew players into the game world as few other games of the time could, launching a wave of puzzle games featuring highly detailed visuals.

Other games of the period included *Night Trap* (1992, Digital Pictures), a campy horror-themed game in which the player attempted to protect a

**CONTROVERSY AND THE FORMATION OF
THE ENTERTAINMENT SOFTWARE RATING BOARD**

Night Trap, however, was more notable for its relationship to a 1993 joint Senate Judiciary and Government Affairs Committee hearing on the marketing of violent video games in the United States. The hearings focused almost exclusively on games for the home that utilized digitized images of human beings, rather than those created with traditional pixel art, with particular emphasis on *Night Trap*, *Mortal Kombat*, and the gun game *Lethal Enforcers* (1992, Konami). After a number of testimonies by psychologists and other researchers, many of whom made dubious and exaggerated claims about the content of the games, the hearing resulted in a request for a ratings system that would allow consumers to understand the appropriateness of a particular game. However, since the home game industry of the early 1990s was highly fragmented between console, home computer, and third-party developers, various publishers created their own rating systems. Eventually, the industry joined behind the ratings system proposed by the newly formed Entertainment Software Rating Board (ESRB) leading to a new sense of unity among game developers.

slumber party of women against a group of vampire-like beings. The game consisted of watching video feeds from different rooms of a house and properly timing the activation of traps to save the women. Players who failed to activate the trap saw the vampiric beings capture and drain the victim's blood using an exaggerated drilling device, after which the player was scolded for failing to properly act.

Real-Time 3D and Spatial Realism

Early Commercialized Virtual Reality

Although not as visually accurate as film-based games, virtual reality (VR) of the late 1980s and mid-1990s attempted to create a sense of true presence in digital spaces using a variety of control devices and display technologies. Researchers in government and commercial technology labs had laid the groundwork for virtual reality with technologies such as head-mounted displays (HMDs), input devices for virtual spaces, and haptic feedback. These advances, from the late 1960s onward, saw application in scientific visualization and allowed researchers to explore and manipulate data in new ways.

Virtual reality, however, was unavailable to the public until the late 1980s, when a number of high profile commercial products entered the market. The first major company to develop virtual reality products was

VPL Research, founded in 1984 by Jaron Lanier. Lanier was a former member of Atari's Sunnyvale Research Lab, which focused on radical and experimental advancements in interactive and entertainment technologies. He combined his interest in music and programming to produce the unconventional game, *Moondust* (1983, Creative Software) for the Commodore 64 computer. In *Moondust,* the player attempted to "smear" or "smudge" prismatic pixels over a target while simultaneously controlling an astronaut and six spaceships. The spaceships left psychedelic color trails and changed the tones of the game's ambient soundtrack. The success of this game, despite its unusual nature, allowed Lanier to leave the Atari Lab and launch VPL Research.

VPL Research became most famous for the DataGlove, a fiber optic-wired glove capable of accurately recording a user's hand position in a completely computerized environment while taking input from finger movement. Designed by Tom Zimmerman initially out of a desire to play air guitar, the glove became an icon of virtual reality as users could "see" a representation of their hand in virtual space when wearing an HMD. The combined expense of the glove and accompanying equipment, however, generally limited its use to scientists and other virtual reality developers.

Seeing an opportunity to capitalize on the growing awareness of virtual reality among the public and its application to digital games, VPL and Abrams/Gentile Entertainment collaborated with former Intellivision producer Mattel to create an affordable consumer-grade version of the Data Glove in 1989. The controller, marketed as the Power Glove and built for the Nintendo Entertainment System (NES), was intended to allow the user to control games using primarily hand and finger motions as well as a bank of programmable buttons (Figure 8.5). Of the two games designed explicitly for the Power Glove, *Super Glove Ball* (1990, Rare) came closest to creating an experience akin to the more complicated virtual reality simulations at VPL. Effectively a combination of the sport of squash and *Breakout, Super Glove Ball* tasked the player with swatting or grabbing a bouncing ball with the Power Glove to break tiled blocks on the walls, ceiling, and floor of a

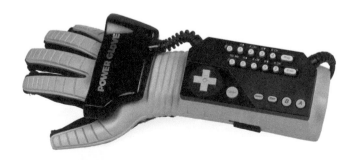

FIGURE 8.5   Mattel's Power Glove controller. (Photo by Evan Amos.)

room presented in perspective. The setup allowed the player to think in three dimensions, as physical movement forward and backward could be represented in the game space. Despite an appealing advertising campaign with taglines like "now you and the game are one" and "everything else is child's play," the Power Glove failed to deliver the experience of virtual reality desired by the public as it was notoriously inaccurate and more often than not, impeded the player's performance.

Nintendo, still interested in virtual reality, developed and launched the Virtual Boy in 1995 (Figure 8.6). Like other HMDs, the Virtual Boy used stereoscopic imagery to trick the brain into seeing a 3D space. Games for the Virtual Boy primarily consisted of animated sprites positioned at nearer or farther distances from the viewer, making superficial use of the stereoscopic depth. Nonetheless, the unit did prove to have true 3D capabilities as seen in *Red Alarm* (1995, T&E Soft), which was similar to *Star Fox* (discussed below). However, since the Virtual Boy used cartridges with a small memory capacity and a relatively slow processor, *Red Alarm* consisted of wireframe models without hidden line removal, creating a confusing experience when flying through the game's tunnel-like spaces. In addition to the lack of support from third-party software developers, the unit's harsh monochromatic red

FIGURE 8.6 Nintendo's Virtual Boy featured a controller with two directional pads, a design that potentially allowed players control along the *x*, *y*, and *z* axis.

images created by a bank of red light-emitting diode (LEDs), a cost-saving decision, frequently led to eyestrain and headaches if played for long periods of time. Due to low sales despite a price drop, Nintendo quickly discontinued the Virtual Boy in Japan after only 4 months on the market, while the North American version was pulled after 6.5 months.

In addition to the home market, a few companies created specialized VR arcade machines in the early 1990s. Virtuality (originally W Industries) was founded in 1987 by British VR pioneer Jon Waldern and became known worldwide for its VR arcade units. One of its early units consisted of a "pod" featuring a waist high ring that allowed the player to stand and prevented them from falling. A large HMD and a handle-shaped controller allowed players to duel against each other in games like *Dactyl Nightmare* (1991), a first-person shooter that took place in a world of untextured 3D polygons. *Dactyl Nightmare* was one of the public's first experiences with immersive virtual reality as it was prominently displayed in large amusement centers. The game space consisted of four platforms with simple architectural elements connected to a central low platform. This level design required players to run upstairs and look around the environment, emphasizing the dimensionality of the space. Each player used the controller to aim and fire a slow-moving projectile at their opponent, the object being to score as many points as possible in the few minutes of game time. As an additional thrill, bright green pterodactyls encircled the playfield and randomly swooped down to pick up battling players. The pterodactyls then flew high above the game space and dropped the players to their death. This free fall experience proved too thrilling for some players as it led to a sense of vertigo and in severe cases, physical illness. The company also produced a number of other games and unit styles that included a sit-down cockpit for vehicle-based simulations like racing or flying. Virtuality was not alone in bringing VR to arcades. *Virtual Combat* (1993) produced by VR8 Inc. was a tank-based game in which an HMD was mounted on an arm above the game cabinet. The game and its company, however, were short lived. The arcade environment, in both cases, proved less than ideal for virtual reality due to the greater expense incurred by the player, the relatively short play time, and the physiological reactions of the experience.

By the late 1990s, it was apparent that virtual reality was far from the promise hyped by innovators, news programs, and tech enthusiasts. Rather than realistic, all-immersive, and interactive cyberworlds, the public saw monochromatic 3D shapes haphazardly controlled by clumsy, inaccurate devices. Highly anticipated peripherals failed to appear as both the Sega VR and Atari Jaguar VR HMDs were canceled before reaching production. The public scaled back its expectations and progressively saw virtual reality as a marketing gimmick. Major VR companies folded: virtual reality giant and DataGlove creator VPL Technologies effectively went out of business

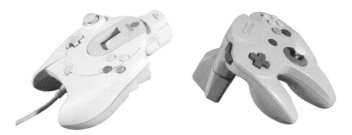

FIGURE 8.7 Early haptic feedback add-ons for the Sega Dreamcast and Nintendo 64.

in 1992, while *Dactyl Nightmare* producer Virtuality remained unprofitable through 1995 despite investment interest.

Devices like the Power Glove and Virtual Boy, based on legitimate virtual reality technologies, illustrated the central problem with VR in the 1990s: affordability came at the cost of performance and quality of experience. The most advanced and accurate scientific VR equipment sold for thousands of dollars. VPL's DataGlove and its sensors, for instance, could be purchased for $8,800 while the equipment to run it cost more than $75,000 at the time. The Power Glove, an affordable $89, simply could not duplicate the same abilities as the fiber optic Data Glove. In addition, consumer model HMDs were particularly lackluster in performance as they often caused headaches and nausea due to issues with image processing and display latency. All of these elements arrested the momentum of virtual reality in the early 1990s.

Large-scale interest in stereoscopic HMDs did not resurface until the second decade of the 2000s, but one virtual reality technology did find its way into the mainstream. The user's inability to "feel" the virtual world resulted in significant investigation into *haptic feedback*, or touch-based interfaces, among early VR pioneers. This allowed for easier and more meaningful ways to interact with virtual spaces. In an attempt to create more immersive game experiences, haptic feedback in the form of vibration increasingly became a standard feature for game controllers starting in the late 1990s. Sony's Japanese version of the 1997 Dual Analog controller for the PlayStation, the 1997 Rumble Pack add-on for the Nintendo 64, and the 1998 Jump Pack for the Sega Dreamcast created another dimension of immersion as explosions, jolts, and other impact-related gaming events could be felt by the player (Figure 8.7). This feature, initially an unusual upgrade, became standard on nearly all console game controllers within a few years.

Simulators in Arcades Spawn a 3D Revolution

For some designers, the use of 3D imagery and spaces was a logical path of progression as certain genres more easily lent themselves to the use of 3D game spaces than others.

Racing games strove to simulate the sensation of movement through space since the earliest period of the digital arcade; this objective remained unchanged in the late 1980s to early 1990s as developers created arcade-based racing games that used 3D polygons with high screen refresh rates. Japanese developer Namco, with a history of popular racing games such as *Pole Position*, offered one of the earliest visions of 3D racing with the 1988 Formula 1-themed, *Winning Run*. The hardware was designed to process 60,000 polygons per second in order to create a believable experience of driving at 300 km/hour. Using haptic feedback, *Winning Run* furthered the sensation of movement with a large cockpit-like cabinet that tilted, bumped, and swayed according to the player's input. Atari Games, the spun off coin-op division of the old Atari company, produced two notable coin-op 3D driving games, *Hard Drivin'* (1989) and *Race Drivin'* (1990). These games, while not as fast as *Winning Run*, provided the sensation of driving on rollercoaster-like racetracks and featured a steering wheel that shook and provided resistance. The race to produce faster hardware for simulators continued to make leaps with Yu Suzuki's Formula 1 racing game, *Virtua Racing* (1992, Sega), capable of computing 180,000 polygons per second. Its successor, *Daytona USA* (1993, Sega), surpassed this with 300,000 polygons per second; performance, in both cases, that resulted from a partnership between Sega and the aerospace company that would eventually become defense contractor, Lockheed Martin.

The hardware developed for racing games powered a new generation of arcade games that brought 3D gameplay to other genres. The arcade system boards designed for and descended from Namco's *Winning Run* and Sega's *Virtua Racing*, appeared in the *rail shooter* games *Solvalou* (1991 Namco), *Galaxian 3: Project Dragoon* (1994, Namco), *Virtua Cop* (1994, Sega), *Time Crisis* (1995, Namco), and *House of the Dead* (1997, Sega). Rail shooters automatically moved players through space on a predetermined and fixed path like being on a rollercoaster. This concept, when combined with traditional gun game gameplay resulted in an experience featuring enemies that popped on and off the screen, sending a barrage of damage at the player and creating an incentive to shoot as fast as possible. The concept of rail shooters was not unique to the early 1990s as earlier games such as Atari's first-person, vector-based *Star Wars* (1983), as well as gun games like the 2D horizontal-scrolling *Operation Wolf* (1987, Taito) employed the same concept. The new simulator-based hardware, however, allowed for rapid changes in camera angles and a feeling of cinematic intensity, particularly exploited in the gun games, *Time Crisis* and *House of the Dead*.

Sega's arcade system board for *Virtua Racing* was also used to bring the 2D-based head-to-head fighting game into the 3D era with *Virtua Fighter* (1993). Directed by Yu Suzuki, *Virtua Fighter*'s roots in simulation technology were apparent not only in its more realistic representation of space but also in its attitude toward game design. Unlike *Street Fighter II* and *Mortal Kombat*, which utilized fantasy fireballs and other projectile-based super moves, button and joystick combinations in *Virtua Fighter* triggered characters to execute punches or kicks grounded in relatively more realistic martial arts techniques. This forced the player to rely less on devastating power moves and made gameplay more tactical as the consideration of distance, speed, and reach of attacks required greater attention. Even the aesthetic exclamation point at the end of a match reflected a grounding in realism as *Virtua Fighter* took a cue from televised sports with the use of an instant replay of the match's final moments, connecting the game to the experience of physical competition.

New 3D head-to-head fighting games, grounded in a similar sense of spatial realism, quickly followed. *Tekken* (1994, Namco), designed by *Virtua Fighter*'s departed main designer Seiichi Ishii, utilized a unique "limb-based" control scheme where each button corresponded to the movement of the right or left arm or leg while *Dead or Alive* (1996, Team Ninja) included a system that allowed players with proper timing to counter and reverse the attack of opponents. As the 3D head-to-head fighting game developed further, combatants were granted more freedom to move through the game space, which further altered gameplay strategies. This drew an increasing distinction between 3D head-to-head fighting games and their 2D cousins. Other changes included new approaches to animation as sophisticated motion capture technology recorded the movements of actors through sensors. First employed in *Virtua Fighter 2* (1994, Sega), motion capture from actors delivered more accurate and fluid animations for game characters. By the beginning of the 2000s, this became a commonly used method of creating animation for games of all genres.

Adapting Home Consoles to a 3D Context

The proliferation of 3D-based games in the early 1990s pushed console manufacturers Nintendo and Sega to design hardware upgrades and add-ons for the Super Famicom/Super Nintendo Entertainment System (SNES) and Mega Drive/Genesis consoles in order to remain competitive in a rapidly changing game landscape. Nintendo's *Star Fox* (1993), an action-oriented game directed by Shigeru Miyamoto, involved flying a spaceship with limited control of movement along planet surfaces and through asteroid fields while shooting at enemies (Figure 8.8). The most distinguishing feature of the game was its use of untextured 3D polygons to create the player's ship, as well as enemies.

The visuals for *Star Fox* were made possible by the addition of a 3D graphics processor in every cartridge dubbed the "Super FX" chip. The chip, created by British computer game developer Argonaut Software, played a prominent role in Nintendo's marketing as it received its own logo that was

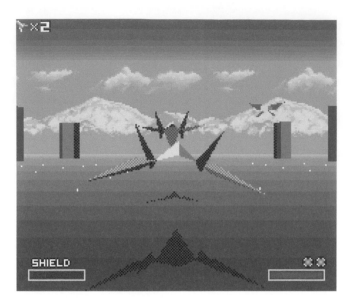

FIGURE 8.8 *Starfox* **(1993, Nintendo).**

used in commercials and emblazoned on cartridge boxes. The Super FX chip and its successor, the Super FX2, were used primarily in racing and simulator-based games, but also included a 1995 port of id Software's first-person shooter, *Doom* (see below) and the visually distinctive 2D platformer, *Super Mario World 2: Yoshi's Island* (1995). For all of the effort, however, the chip appeared in only eight games as Nintendo began working toward a new, fully 3D console.

Adding more advanced chips to cartridges worked briefly for Nintendo, but Sega's desire to leapfrog its competitor made this approach too expensive and impractical. Instead, the company developed a mushroom-shaped add-on that attached to the cartridge slot of the Mega Drive/Genesis. Released in 1994 as the 32X in the United States, Mega 32X in Europe, and Super 32X in Japan, the unit provided an upgrade to sound and graphics that gave the Genesis the ability to process tens of thousands of texture-mapped polygons per second. This upgrade brought Sega's 3D arcade games, *Virtua Racing* and *Virtua Fighter* to the home, in addition to other arcade head-to-head fighting games. First-person shooters, *Metal Head* (1995, Sega) and a port of id Software's *Doom* (see below), also showcased the unit's immersive 3D capabilities.

Unlike Nintendo's Super FX chip, the 32X was not a commercial success and within 2 years, it was discontinued. The largest problem stemmed from a rift in Sega's development teams: the American branch developed and supported the 32X, while the company's Japanese branch gave priority to the "next-gen" CD-based, 3D-capable, Saturn console. Further, the Saturn was pushed into production ahead of schedule resulting in a tight window that saw the North American launch date of the 32X precede the launch of the Saturn by only 6 months, and in Japan, by 12 days. Consumers passed on what was perceived as a mere incremental upgrade. With sales low, support for the 32X by third-party developers steadily eroded in 1995 and completely evaporated by 1996.

Combining 2D Images with Real-Time 3D in PC Games

As discussed in Chapter 6, home computers of the 1980s built a solid reputation on simulation and role-playing games. Computer game developers of the early 1990s, continuing these traditions, enhanced this gameplay by combining more action-oriented elements with immersive real-time 3D worlds. Due to technological constraints, however, several real-time 3D games of the period still relied heavily on 2D imagery for its superior visual detail and clarity.

Alone in the Dark (1992), by French developer Infogrames featured 3D characters investigating a possessed mansion. The game's horror theme was reinforced through a number of fixed camera positions that presented the space from odd angles, which often hid dangers. Since creating solid geometry walls and texture-mapping the mansion's interiors would have taxed the home computers of the early 1990s too much, the 3D space was instead constructed out of simple wire frames. The simple space was then overlaid with a 2D image that matched the particular perspective of the camera angle. This allowed the game to have richly detailed environments that reinforced the atmosphere of a haunted mansion, yet created a sense of embodiment in space; all of which were used to elicit a sense of fear in the player.

Simulation and ideas of virtual reality were key components in the development of early first-person shooters. An ambitious example of this new type of game was Bethesda's *The Terminator* (1991). The game, based on the 1984 science fiction film of the same name, was another early example of *open world* game design translated into 3D, as the game space consisted of nearly 60 square miles based on the city of Los Angeles. The game, according to the manual, was conceived as a simulation of the film, which allowed the player to "rewrite the movie every time you play." The game's range of systems and behaviors was impressive: buildings opened and closed according to set schedules in real time; cars with manual or automatic transmission could be driven as well as refueled; and certain items purchased or stolen from stores could be used in combination with each other for different effects.

The gameplay was based on urgency as the player assumed the role of the terminator character or the soldier from the future, Kyle Reese, in a race to be the first to either eliminate or protect the film's central character, Sarah Connor. After searching the large gamespace for weapons and supplies, driving vehicles, and dealing with the consequences of actions like stealing, the gameplay culminated in an often frantic gun battle between the player and computer controlled opponent. The game also allowed two players to link their computers together and battle across the virtual city, a form of gameplay that would become one of the defining elements of the first-person shooter. Although the game used solid-colored, 3D shapes to represent the outdoor environments of the city and its inhabitants, store interiors were represented as highly detailed 2D images. This combination of 2D and 3D was necessary as items like bandages, ammunition, and other small objects would have been impossible to discern visually with the low detail of the 3D models.

The dungeon crawling role-playing game (RPG), *Ultima Underworld: The Stygian Abyss* (1992, Blue Sky Productions), combined elements and systems of the well-developed computer role-playing game (CRPG) genre with the concept of a flight simulator. The resulting game space featured texture-mapped walls, floors, and ceilings that became progressively darker with distance. Using a first-person perspective, players could freely look up and down as well as jump over pits and traverse angled floors as they fought monsters, leveled up characters, and collected items. Detailed 2D sprites representing enemies, items, and environmental decorations scaled in distance from the player much like the sprite scaling in Yu Suzuki's *Hang-On* and *Space Harrier*. The departure from the typical grid-based CRPG and freedom to look in any direction at any angle from a first-person perspective, added an extra level of tension, as combat situations required more movement in tight dungeon corridors.

Despite relying heavily on less computationally intensive 2D elements, *Alone in the Dark*, *The Terminator*, and *Ultima Underworld*, unfortunately moved at slower, less responsive rates due to the complexity of 3D forms. Further, the intricate game systems and multitudes of keyboard commands governing minute actions slowed the pace of gameplay. The 3D first-person shooter games developed by id Software (written in lowercase) and others inspired by id, however, addressed these issues by distilling gameplay into a few essential actions while utilizing new game technologies to speedup performance.

The Influence of id Software

Id Software, founded in 1991, initially consisted of John Carmack, John Romero, Adrian Carmack (no relation to John Carmack), Tom Hall, and Jay Wilbur. The programmers, artists, and designers of id, prior to the company's official formation, created 2D maze games like John Carmack's *Catacomb* (1990, SoftDisk) and platformers like Tom Hall's *Commander Keen in "Invasion of the Vorticons"* (1990, Apogee Software). These games, although 2D, provided the foundational traits for id's first-person shooters. John Carmack's *Catacomb* was a fast-paced maze game similar to the arcade game, *Gauntlet* (1985, Atari Games). It consisted of increasingly difficult levels where the player gathered treasure, collected keys to unlock doors, discovered secret areas, and fought against monsters. Carmack's game placed emphasis on the shooting mechanics by offering the player a variety of shots:

a fast single shot, a slow, more powerful charged shot, a steam of rapid-fire shots, or a halo-like circle that expanded from the player's position. Navigation of maze-like spaces, discovering secrets, and choosing between multiple offensive capabilities became archetypical design elements for id's later games.

Tom Hall's *Commander Keen in "Invasion of the Vorticons"* was a computer-based platformer that emphasized exploration and discovery by using design elements from console games like *Super Mario Bros 3*, as well as John Romero's earlier *Dangerous Dave* games from 1988. One of the game's standout elements was a complex approach to level design, as open blocks of space required the player to explore the entirety of each level before progressing. A smooth scrolling game engine aided the free feeling of exploration, an important technical achievement made possible by John Carmack. While platformer games were common on home computers, many loaded a single screen at a time, which created a discontinuous feeling of space, or scrolled in a jarring and choppy way. *Commander Keen*, with its effortless movement and engaging gameplay signaled a new direction for computer games in general, while the concept of smoothly moving through space became the major focus of id.

SHAREWARE AND COMPUTER GAMES

The *Commander Keen* series and many other action-oriented computer games were distributed via a form of viral marketing called *shareware*, which served as an alternative to mail order or retail methods. With shareware, a piece of software was released under a license that made it free to distribute on disk, online bulletin board services, or any other means. Users of shareware who liked the software would then send money to the developer in an "honor" system. This radical concept originated in the early 1980s and was most successfully implemented in application-based software.

Games distributed as shareware in the late 1980s were typically divided into three or more episodes. Each consisted of 8 to 10 levels that allowed a developer to release the first episode free and receive payment from those wanting to play the remainder of the game. The shareware version of a game could comprise up to one-third of the game's total content, but the most enticing elements of gameplay were reserved for the game's final episodes. As the advertisement of digital computer games was typically limited to computer magazines, this word-of-mouth marketing depended on passionate players to aid sales. Shorter demos of gameplay replaced shareware episodes by the late 1990s, as content became more expensive and more labor intensive to produce. This, in addition to cross-platform releases of games and the adoption of game structures tied to a cohesive narrative rather than episodic divisions, helped end the use of shareware for computer games.

Id developed the form and technology of the first person shooter (FPS) across three titles, *Hovertank 3D* (1991), *Catacomb 3-D: The Descent* (1991), and *Wolfenstein 3D* (1992) before culminating in *Doom* (1993). Id distilled their games into a few essential actions and optimized the way the software computed the 3D space, rather than making it bigger like *The Terminator* or more geometrically complex like *Ultima Underworld*. The games thus delivered fast and frantic, arcade-like gameplay from a first-person perspective. This was made possible by a series of efficient game engines by John Carmack, the later of which were inspired by *Ultima Underworld*'s use of texture mapping.

Like *Ultima Underworld*, Carmack's engine scaled 2D sprites in a 3D game space, but was able to run faster because of the use of *raycasting*. Raycasting involved the projection of a cone of rays from the player's position on a 2D map. Walls caught within the radius of the cone were rendered in a 3D perspective and displayed as the player's first-person view. Thus, the computer only calculated as much as what the player could see, saving processor resources and facilitating smooth gameplay. The maze-like setting for these games also avoided the problems inherent in early 3D outdoor spaces like *The Terminator*, as the player's view could be more easily controlled with a number of well-placed walls, removing the need to render far off objects.

Id's early work in first-person shooters led to *Doom*, a standout example in the quest to make computer games faster, as well as a major milestone in the pursuit of spatial realism. Similar to id's earlier games, *Doom* placed the player in a hostile environment, fighting off enemies. Its streamlined game design eliminated earlier elements like score and bonus treasure in favor of a greatly expanded set of shooting mechanics represented by eight distinct weapons. In addition to sharpening its focus, *Doom* defined the free-for-all "deathmatch" style of the multiplayer game, made possible by increasingly available home networking technology (Figure 8.9).

FIGURE 8.9 *Doom* **(1993, id Software).**

The game's art, inspired by the darkly surreal illustrations of H.R. Giger, matched the gameplay of battling demons and zombie-like enemies in spaces with flickering lights, pits of toxic waste, and unsettling textures. The generic maze-based levels of id's earlier games were replaced with a more realistic treatment of space as hallways, staircases, windows, and elevators granted access to new areas. Frequently spaces suddenly opened and lights shut off unexpectedly which contributed to the overall horror theme of the game. The digitization of stop-motion animation models, designed by Adrian, Carmack, and Gregor Punchatz, created some of the monsters of *Doom* that further enhanced the visuals. Digitized and pixel art images were mapped to 2D sprites with each frame of a character's animation created from eight angles to simulate dimensionality in 3D environments.

THE INTERNET, MODDING, AND FIRST-PERSON SHOOTERS

Game mods are unofficial modifications, created by players, which change the behavior, appearance, or functionality of games. The practice of modding, an integral part of computer gaming since *Spacewar!*, gained mass appeal after the release of *Doom*. Prior to *Doom*, a mod typically involved hunting through files and lines of code to replace or overwrite a segment of game data. This was time consuming and often made changes difficult to reverse. *Doom* was designed to be "mod friendly," as game assets, like maps and art, were separated from the engine in WAD files ("Where's All the Data"). This allowed easy modification with little fear of damaging the core functionality of the game.

Many player-created mods affected minor portions of gameplay, like substituting the 1990s children's TV character Barney, the purple dinosaur, for the bosses in *Doom* or creating a new weapon type. Other mods, called *total conversions*, were more ambitious as they replaced nearly everything from the original game leading to an entirely new experience—turning *Doom* into a first-person shooter based on the 1986 film *Aliens*, for example. Other FPSs like *Duke Nukem 3D* and the later *Unreal* (1998, Epic Games) went further and released the game's development tools to the public, enabling modders to potentially create content at a highly polished level.

The Internet was essential to mods as it served as a medium of communication for modding communities and allowed ideas to spread. Development tools often came with limited support or without instructions prompting modding communities to create "how to" guides as well as programs that made modification easier. The Internet also served as a channel of distribution as web rings and personal web pages hosted the files and allowed the public to learn and experiment with creating 3D spaces and game assets. As discussed in Chapters 9 and 10, the work of some amateur modders would lead to professional careers, as user-generated content became a hotbed of creativity and innovation in the 2000s.

The team also digitized first-person perspectives of real world objects, such as the game's iconic shotgun, which was based on a toy.

In response to the overwhelming success of *Doom* and its sequel *Doom II: Hell on Earth* (1994), numerous "Doom clones" appeared on the game market that behaved like id's product and collectively helped conventionalize first-person shooter design. A contributing factor to this conventionalization was that id licensed its game engines to other game developers. Any developer, for a licensing fee, could use and modify the code in order to build and sell games. The practice introduced a fundamental change in game development: companies could focus their efforts on delivering higher quality visuals and unique tweaks using proven technology, rather than creating a game engine on its own. Major first-person shooters such as Raven Software's *Heretic* (1994), *Hexen: Beyond Heretic* (1995), Apogee's *Rise of the Triad* (1994), and Rogue Entertainment's *Strife* (1996) all used the underlying technology of id's game engines.

Id was not the only company that created game engines and licensed them to other developers. The Build engine, designed by Ken Silverman, was capable of complex level design and special effects that surpassed the *Doom* engine but still relied on 2D sprites in a 3D space. Silverman's Build engine powered a number of first-person shooters including *Duke Nukem 3D* (1996, 3D Realms), *Blood* (1997, Monolith), and *Shadow Warrior* (1997, 3D Realms), as well as nine other published games, making it a widely used 2D sprite, 3D space game engine in the 1990s.

The Triumph of Real-Time 3D in Games

The rapid evolution of game technologies in the mid to late 1990s greatly improved the range of application and level of detail allowed in real-time 3D games. Developers eagerly took advantage of these new capabilities by creating games in full 3D without the reliance on 2D images. This created one of the game industry's largest shifts. As real-time 3D flourished, interest in using film in games for both gameplay and narrative purposes faded, largely disappearing by the turn of the millennium. Rising production costs, the growing number of CDs required to play higher resolution video, and the lack of dynamic gameplay all contributed to the decline of filmed sequences. Nonetheless, live-action video provided a model that guided game development into the contemporary context. It served as a bridge between largely text-driven narrative forms of earlier games and the *scripted sequences*, *quick time events*, and *setpieces* that came to dominate the contemporary context, subjects discussed in detail in Chapter 9.

Contemporary Game Design (1996–Present)

New Hardware for Real-Time 3D Gaming

The momentum behind real-time, polygon-based 3D games began as a jog in the early 1990s (see Chapter 8) and became a sprint by the decade's end. New hardware upgrades for IBM compatible computers changed the fundamental nature of PC gaming, taking it from its methodical, turn-based roots and transforming it into a preeminent platform for fast-paced 3D games. Intel's 1993 Pentium processor, a much faster chip relative to the earlier 386 and 486 processors, made much of this transition possible, as it was better designed for calculating complex 3D images. The Pentium and its successor, the Pentium II, became standard requirements for 3D computer games of the mid to late 1990s. The demand for peak performance also led to a market for consumer model 3D-accelerated graphics cards, which made certain 3D games run faster. Although 3D-accelerated graphics cards were initially a luxury for enthusiasts, they became a required component for gaming by the early 2000s.

The hardware for home consoles, too, was changing. Between 1994 and 1996, Sega, Sony, and Nintendo each released a new "fifth-generation" home console. Sony's entrance into the home console market with the 1994 PlayStation proved to be a disruptive event for both Nintendo and Sega. Developers, long loyal to the two gaming giants, became interested in Sony's platform after seeing its 3D capabilities, which provided sufficient power for games, and its large storage capacity CDs that allowed the use of video without special add-ons (see Chapter 8). The cartridges for the 1996 Nintendo 64, though able to load game data faster than CDs, paled in terms of storage capacity and required developers to resort to a number of tricks to provide the desired game experience. Sega meanwhile, attempted to compete in the 3D-focused fifth generation with its 1995 CD-based Saturn console. The unit's performance, however, was lackluster. An unusual hardware design made it difficult for game developers to take full advantage of 3D applications, which further exacerbated Sega's problems in the console market. With the leading hardware and software developers firmly committed to 3D visuals delivered in real time, interest in 2D games began to rapidly evaporate.

3D Game Design in the Late 1990s
Platforming and Adventure Games in Full 3D

Character-based action games, such as 2D platformers, became staples of the game industry as they helped build brand identity (see Chapter 7). The prospect of "upgrading" these 2D games into full 3D was enticing for both developers and players; however, it posed problems related to views of the game space, level design, and the fundamental movement-based gameplay. Although a number of developers in the late 1980s and early 1990s experimented with gameplay from 3D or pseudo-3D perspectives, the first major set of fully 3D character-based action games was Nintendo's *Super Mario 64* (1996), Naughty Dog's *Crash Bandicoot* (1996), and Core Design's *Tomb Raider* (1996). These titles helped lay the groundwork for subsequent 3D games as they required their developers to rethink inherited assumptions and develop new design solutions.

Nintendo's *Super Mario 64*, overseen by Shigeru Miyamoto, not only translated the essence of its 2D predecessors, but also took advantage of the new possibilities offered by 3D space. *Super Mario 64* featured many of the traditional Mario game elements such as distinctive game worlds, collecting coins, and discovering hidden areas, but did so with a unique sense of looseness that inspired playful exploration. Arcade-influenced design concepts, intended to promote a fast turnaround of players and encourage repeat play—timed levels, the accumulation of score, one hit death—were completely removed. Players, instead, were invited to experience the simple pleasure of unhindered movement through 3D space: Mario could walk, run, jump, slide, flip, climb, swim, ricochet off surfaces, and even fly through the air (Figure 9.1).

These athletic interactions were supported by multi-tiered game levels that maximized their space by containing up to six different objectives that were completed over several visits. These objectives ranged from defeating a boss character to winning a race against a computer-controlled opponent. Coin collecting, ever a staple of the franchise, became an excuse to explore

FIGURE 9.1 *Super Mario 64* **(1996, Nintendo).**

every 3D nook and cranny in detail and helped make the game spaces feel alive as players always had something to do. Each completed objective yielded a special star currency that was used to unlock more of the game's levels. Although previous games like *Super Mario World* allowed players to repeat levels in order to attain different rewards, repeating levels was essential for *Super Mario 64*, as the game contained 15 main levels; a number that on the surface was significantly lower than the franchise's preceding 2D games. Reusing the levels for alternative objectives, thus, helped maximize the gameplay and familiarize the player with the 3D spaces.

The game's large range of movement options in 3D space required that *Super Mario 64* have a different type of controller, one capable of reading greater nuance. The Nintendo 64's unique three-pronged controller (Figure 8.7) was developed in tandem with *Super Mario 64* and met the game's input needs. Although it featured several new buttons, the central analog stick was the most important for input. The traditional directional pad measured a discrete number of states that were either "on" or "off." The analog stick, in contrast, allowed nearly an infinite number of states, creating a remarkable degree of precision for moving in 3D environments. In *Super Mario 64*, this meant Mario's movement became even more intuitive. Pushing the stick slightly in any direction made Mario walk; pushing it all the way accelerated him to a run.

Even with analog control, the typical Mario-based gameplay of jumping on enemies to defeat them was more difficult to execute in a 3D environment—especially for those unfamiliar with 3D gameplay. The player was thus given more spatially friendly attacks: the ability to slide into or punch and kick enemies while a set of "hit points" permitted players to misjudge distances or run into the enemy multiple times before losing a life. Since these actions in *Super Mario 64* required a high degree of spatial awareness, the game included a system that allowed players to dynamically switch between three distinct camera modes: following Mario, fixed in place, or orbiting around Mario by using the directional arrows of the controller. Although far from the first instance of player controlled cameras in 3D space, this consideration became a major point of investigation for subsequent games and had ramifications for the design of future controllers as well.

Crash Bandicoot, by American developer, Naughty Dog, was released on Sony's PlayStation a few months after *Super Mario 64* and represented a more literal translation of 2D platformer gameplay to a 3D console. The game introduced the animal character Crash, a spastic bandicoot that became Sony's answer to Mario and Sonic. Like Nintendo's platformer games, the player guided the character through themed levels, collecting objects and discovering secret places in an attempt to rescue Crash's bandicoot girlfriend. Levels in *Crash Bandicoot*, unlike the open architectural spaces of *Super Mario 64*, limited lateral player movement and closely resembled the long, linear levels of 2D platformers. Certain game spaces even shifted the non-controllable camera from the predominant behind the character view to a more familiar horizontal, side scrolling perspective. These decisions stemmed from a concern for the player's ability to adapt to 3D spaces, as well as finding ways to acquaint players with the game's orange marsupial mascot. The limitation of player movement enabled Naughty Dog to add more detail to the environment, which, along with unique and sophisticated programming techniques, resulted in the game's lush, jungle setting.

Tomb Raider, by English developer Core Design represented another early approach to fully 3D games and game spaces. The game focused on adventure and exploration, as the game's character, archaeologist Lara Croft, avoided traps and searched for treasure in locations ranging from Peru to the lost city of Atlantis. Like *Super Mario 64*, *Tomb Raider* featured a range of acrobatic moves that allowed the player to jump, flip, climb, and cling to ledges. These techniques were used to solve the game's "3D spatial puzzles" which usually required properly timed jumps, followed by a sequence of other moves to reach keys or other items that allowed the player to progress. *Tomb Raider*, in addition to platforming gameplay, took advantage of its 3D space by including numerous combat segments that involved shooting enemies and dodging in multiple directions. The design of the 3D levels in *Tomb Raider* struck a balance between elements of *Super Mario 64* and *Crash Bandicoot:* they contained a variety of vertical heights and explorable spaces, but typically followed the form of branching linear paths.

Game spaces and control schemes evolved rapidly throughout the remainder of the decade and into the 2000s, as developers became increasingly ambitious with a better understanding of the nature of 3D gameplay and the capabilities of 3D hardware. One standout example was Nintendo's *The Legend of Zelda: Ocarina of Time* (1998). Nintendo's *Ocarina of Time*, developed by many of the core creators of *Super Mario 64*, expanded on the 3D platformer's open, but individual, game levels. Players of *Ocarina of Time*, like the previous 2D Zelda games, crisscrossed an interconnected game world, descended into dungeons, fought enemies, and collected objects that granted further access to new spaces. As the franchise was heavily reliant on swordplay, the game's developers created an innovative way of performing accurate attacks in 3D space called the "Z-targeting" system.* The Z-targeting system allowed the player to lock the game camera and orbit around a single enemy. This allowed players the ability to dodge as well as providing the opportunity to design new types of encounters. Variants of the Z-targeting system were widely adopted after *Ocarina of Time* and appeared in games ranging from the first-person shooter adaption of Metroid, *Metroid Prime* (2002, Retro Studios), to the unforgiving third-person, action role-playing game *Dark Souls* (2011, From Software).

First Person in Full 3D

The effects of full 3D graphics were not as dramatic on first-person shooters because they were already partially in 3D (see Chapter 8). They and their technologies were, nonetheless, a major source of the industry's rapid adoption of 3D graphics and gameplay. *Descent* (1995, Parallax Software) was an early example of adapting ideas of the first-person shooter to fully 3D graphics. The gameplay took place in outer space mining colonies overrun by malfunctioning robots. Since the player had 360° freedom to move and turn in any direction in zero gravity space, the design of the robot enemies required using 3D polygons as creating 2D sprites to represent each possible angle would have been inefficient and unconvincing. The game levels took advantage of the ability to fly in any direction as they included sets of turns and loops that would not have been used in standard horizontal-based first-person shooters. The novelty of *Descent*'s gameplay, originating in its 360° control, led to a set of sequels, *Descent II* (1996, Parallax Software) and *Descent III* (1999, Outrage Entertainment), as well as the Descent-like *Forsaken* (1998, Probe Entertainment).

One of the biggest impacts on fully 3D first-person shooters was id Software's *Quake* (1996), which used 3D polygons to create spaces, objects, and enemies. The *Quake* engine, as in id's earlier games, efficiently processed 3D elements and allowed the game to run at the desired speed. Part of

---

* So called because it was activated by the "z" trigger on the Nintendo 64 controller.

the game's efficiency stemmed from the highly compressed color palette of browns and grays. Without a wide range of colors, the game could more easily recreate fully 3D environments, however, it also led to criticism of *Quake*'s "muddy" visuals. Although the original version of the game did not support a 3D graphics card, id created a hardware-accelerated version of *Quake* called *GLQuake* in 1997 which enhanced the game's colors and smoothed out the textures in addition to granting a boost in performance. For *Quake*'s highly dedicated and competitive multiplayer deathmatch communities, the performance boost afforded by 3D graphics cards in a game based on quick reactions potentially meant the difference between winning and losing, effectively making the cards an essential component for gameplay.

Despite the breakthrough engine technology, little in terms of gameplay and level design separated *Quake* from partially 3D games like *Doom*. The game, like its predecessor, emphasized the horizontal plane as the player used the standard first-person shooter control scheme based entirely on the keyboard for movement and actions. While *Quake* included commands to look up and down, they were not easily triggered through their default key bindings and were infrequently needed despite the fully 3D game space.

First-person shooters after *Quake,* adjusted rapidly to the new possibilities of fully 3D gameplay. Spatially, games began to include more vertical elements in the level design, as well as hazards that originated above and below the player. As game spaces evolved in later fully 3D first-person shooters such as *Quake II* (1997, id Software), *Hexen II* (1997, Raven Software), and *Unreal* (1998, Epic Games), control schemes shifted away from a reliance on the keyboard's arrow keys. In place of arrow keys, players used the keyboard's WASD keys to move on the ground and used the mouse to change the angle and direction of the view. This provided greater precision and allowed the player to quickly react to changes in the surrounding space.

One of the most coherent and seamless uses of 3D space in first-person shooters was Valve Corporation's *Half-Life* (1998). Built using a heavily modified version of the *Quake* engine, *Half-Life* intertwined narrative and gameplay in ways seldom seen at the time. The game was set in a sprawling, underground research complex devoted to all types of scientific inquiry. After an accident during a physics experiment opened an interdimensional rift to a hostile alien planet, the player as a surviving scientist, attempted to escape from the depths of the sprawling research facility and halt the ensuing alien invasion. Much of the game consisted of navigating maze-like spaces, gathering weapons, avoiding hazards, and shooting, as in other first-person shooters. *Half-Life*, however, took full advantage of the possibilities offered by a completely 3D game world. Instead of cut scenes or text boxes, the game's narrative unfolded in space around the player, creating a continuous experience. Characters, friendly and hostile, acted out scenes and spoke dialog that provided information about the game world. Events, such as the dramatic entrance of a helicopter, helped build tension, while the collapse of a ceiling punctuated gameplay. In all cases, the player remained in control.

Half-Life accomplished its narrative feats through a heavy reliance on *scripted sequences*, preset behaviors of the environment or characters triggered by the player's presence. This contrasted with the roaming monsters and static levels of earlier games, as scripted sequences allowed developers to ensure that certain segments of gameplay played out identically each time. Scripted sequences, in addition to relaying the game's narrative, guided the player toward goals that would be difficult to communicate without breaking immersion. *Half-Life* also featured numerous spatial-oriented puzzles that utilized the 3D space to a higher degree than its predecessors. Some puzzles centered on activating objects, such as a rocket booster, by triggering a specific sequence of scattered inputs; others required the player to assemble a makeshift platform of crates to bypass electrified water.

MULTIPLAYER-ONLY FPSs

The focus on Internet connectivity and deathmatch modes of gameplay in the late 1990s led to the creation of a special subset of multiplayer-only, first-person shooter games. *Quake III: Arena* (1999, id) and *Unreal Tournament* (1999, Epic Games), along with *Half-Life* mods, turned into stand-alone games, *Team Fortress Classic* (1999) and *Counter Strike* (2000), featured specially designed game spaces for multiple players that avoided the narrow, linear hallways typical of single player games (Figure 9.2). They often featured unique types of multiplayer game modes such as "capture the flag" or "king of the hill" in addition to the traditional free for all deathmatch. Modding communities were particularly important for these games, as amateur designers created new maps and other gameplay features based on the immediate needs of the community, which ultimately helped contribute to the games' longevity.

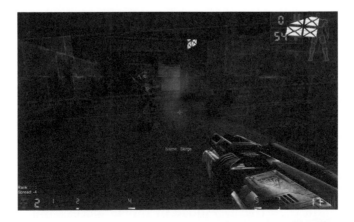

FIGURE 9.2 *Unreal Tournament* **(1999, Epic Games). (Courtesy of Epic Games.)**

FIGURE 9.3 *Star Wars: Jedi Knight—Dark Forces II™* (1997, LucasArts). (Courtesy of Lucasfilm Ltd. LLC©.)

Games like *Star Wars: Jedi Knight—Dark Forces II* (1997, LucasArts), meanwhile, pursued novel directions that combined first- and third-person perspectives in full 3D. *Jedi Knight*, a sequel to the 2D sprite/3D space *Star Wars: Dark Forces* (1995, LucasArts), expanded first-person shooter conventions by including the iconic Star Wars lightsaber and its cinematic range of attacks and defense. Since dynamic melee combat was difficult to control and appreciate in a first-person perspective, the game switched to a third-person perspective that allowed the player to see the game character and enemies in space (Figure 9.3). It also incorporated mechanics for character development such as upgrading abilities with The Force as well as a morality system based on the "light side" and "dark side"—elements that connected the game to trends of hybridization with role-playing game systems.

Other directions for full 3D included a focus on tactical gameplay involving methodically planned actions as seen in strategy games, which ran counter to the prevailing trends of the fast-paced "twitch" gameplay of mainline first-person shooters. The first-person shooters by Red Storm Entertainment, a game studio co-founded by American novelist Tom Clancy, used tactical gameplay to add a degree of sober realism to a genre dominated by exotic weapons and monsters. *Tom Clancy's Rainbow Six* (1998), centered on the missions of an elite anti-terrorist strike force. The game's design attempted to simulate the reality of armed combat, reflecting Clancy's literary focus on the tactical elements of modern warfare: running made accurate shooting difficult and a single bullet could kill. This "tactical first-person shooter" required the player to meticulously plan a route through each map and take into account their role as a squad member. Success, thus, required precisely executed actions. *Rainbow Six* became a major franchise and was later joined by *Tom Clancy's Ghost Recon* (2001), another first-person shooter that emphasized tactical gameplay.

Hybrid First-Person Shooter/Role-Playing Games at the Turn of the Millennium

The popularity of first-person shooters led to a number of unique design concepts that blended elements from several game genres. Role-playing game systems, in particular, were well suited for this mode of presentation as many dungeon crawling CRPGs were already presented from a first-person perspective (see Chapters 2 and 6). Early 2D sprite/3D space hybrids included *Strife* (1996, Rogue Entertainment) as well as many of the games form Looking Glass Studios (see below). In the later 1990s, developers took advantage of rapidly evolving 3D technologies by making the environments themselves an important part of role playing.

Looking Glass Studios and Its Offshoots

Looking Glass Studios was principally important for introducing new types of first-person 3D gameplay. While the studio created a number of innovative technologies, it was primarily known as a design-focused developer. Its reputation was established through the 2D sprite/3D space *Ultima Underworld: The Stygian Abyss* from 1992 (see Chapter 8), *Ultima Underworld II: Labyrinth of Worlds* (1993) and the sci-fi-themed *System Shock* (1994).[*] Looking Glass Studios continued to focus on game design with *Thief: The Dark Project* (1998), a title that proved to be a significant departure for fully 3D first-person games. Rather than clearing large rooms of enemies, as in *Doom* and *Quake*, players of *Thief* were discouraged from direct confrontation as the player was unable to withstand large amounts of damage. The game was designed for stealth-based gameplay that required a keen awareness of sound and the strategic use of shadows to navigate a darkly lit, medieval-themed world. A variety of arrows performed useful actions such as extinguishing torches, distracting enemies, and dampening the sound of footsteps. Players used cunning to slip past patrolling guards and undead foes, and were given nonlethal options for subduing enemies.

Each of the game's levels contained quests that ranged from stealing objects to escaping from captivity. The game-level design added another dimension to the play: it allowed the player to utilize multiple paths toward each mission's goal. Players, thus, had an uncommon degree of choice for how to approach the game's challenges. The game's minimal interface primarily consisted of an indicator that showed the player's degree of visibility

---

[*] *Ultima Underworld: The Stygian Abyss* was produced under the name Blue Sky Productions prior to a 1992 merger with Lerner Research. From 1992 to 1996, the merged studio was known as Looking Glass Technologies before changing names again to Looking Glass Studios.

to enemies and provided a high degree of immersion as it moved away from the information-dense windows seen in earlier FPSs and dungeon crawling CRPGs.

Looking Glass Studio's willingness to pursue 3D game concepts outside of established genres was continued by a number of its employees who departed the studio for new opportunities. Irrational Games was a studio formed in 1997 by former Looking Glass Studios developers Ken Levine, Robert Fermier, and Jonathan Chey. Amiably collaborating with their former employer and using the technology that powered *Thief*, Irrational Games released the highly acclaimed sci-fi horror game, *System Shock 2* in 1999 (Figure 9.4). *System Shock 2* was set on a derelict spaceship after a parasitic alien virus infected the crew and turned them into hostile hosts. The player, a lone soldier suffering from amnesia, was tasked with finding a way to stop the infection. The game drew heavily from CRPGs, which led to an uncommonly rich set of game systems for a first-person shooter: the player chose one of three character specializations, each with differences for gameplay. Players were able to upgrade physical stats and individual skills in areas such as weapons, psychic powers, and computer hacking ability; an inventory allowed them to collect items, some needing research prior to use; weapons required repair after repeated use and could be modified to change function.

In addition to cinematic cut scenes for narrative exposition, the game's simple but atmospheric environments drew the player in and told a story that allowed players to piece together the game world's events. For instance, living quarters with bloodstains and furniture serving as a makeshift blockade suggested a desperate, but doomed last stand. Many of the scenes included audio log devices with short monologs by crewmembers, a feature directly inherited from the first *System Shock* and ultimately related to the

FIGURE 9.4 *System Shock 2* **(1999, Irrational Games). (Courtesy of Night Dive Studios. www.nightdivestudios.com)**

text-based notes found on dungeon floors of CRPGs of the 1980s and 1990s. These audio log "breadcrumbs," together with scripted sequences that featured ghostly apparitions of crewmembers re-enacting moments of their lives, helped relay the story visually, aurally, and spatially. These narrative techniques, as well as character development, became signature elements in Irrational Games' later first-person shooters, *BioShock* (2007), *BioShock 2* (2010), and *BioShock Infinite* (2013).

The cyberpunk-themed *Deus Ex* (2000, Ion Storm*) represented a high point for the design of hybrid role-playing/first-person shooter games and proved to be influential on later titles. The player, as a member of a futuristic, anti-terrorist organization, undertook missions to disrupt the activities of hostile groups. The player learned, through the course of play, of larger machinations involving conspiracy groups such as the Illuminati and Majestic 12, which led to a narrative based on gray areas of tangled alliances.

The design of *Deus Ex* emphasized allowing the player to drive the gameplay, a feature motivated by executive producer and director Warren Spector's dissatisfaction with the linear nature of role-playing games. Drawing from his career as a producer for *System Shock*, the *Ultima Underworld* games, and titles in the *Wing Commander* and *Ultima* series, Spector and game designer Harvey Smith employed an organic approach to gameplay in *Deus Ex*. In more traditional CRPGs, character progression was represented by gradual increases in numbers such as hit points or ability scores. *Deus Ex* replaced this system with a simplified set of skills and abilities that demonstrated immediate and obvious improvements. The game's levels contained many choice-based features that allowed players to freely switch between the aggressive "guns blazing" style of *Quake* and the stealthy and nonconfrontational style of *Thief*. Locked doors could be opened in different ways: picking the lock, hacking the computer that controlled the door, or using explosives to destroy it. All of these gameplay choices carried different risks and were modified by the player's particular character progression. This ultimately provided a form of role-playing that maximized player control and proved to be a pivotal shift in developer attitudes about game design.

Cinematic Perspectives at the Turn of the Millennium

One of the most difficult challenges in adapting to 3D space was the presentation of the game space itself. Many fully 3D third-person games of the period were played from a camera position that followed the character through space, seen in games like *Tomb Raider*, *Crash Bandicoot*, the 3D adaption of Sonic the Hedgehog, *Sonic Adventure* (1998, Sonic Team),

---

* Ion Storm was established in 1996 in Dallas, Texas. Its founders included John Romero and Tom Hall, formerly of id Software. *Deus Ex* was created by Ion Storm's branch in Austin, Texas, which Warren Spector founded in 1997.

and skateboard trick simulator, *Tony Hawk's Pro Skater* (1999, Neversoft Entertainment). An alternative to the character-following camera presented the game space from multiple camera angles while the character moved through it.

Resident Evil (1996, Capcom), a zombie-themed survival game, similar to *Alone in the Dark* (see Chapter 8), employed perspectives influenced by horror films. *Resident Evil* was initially intended to be fully 3D, like other third-person games mentioned above. Problems associated with memory constraints and the difficulty of development for the then new PlayStation console, however, limited this vision. The game employed backgrounds consisting of static, pre-rendered, 3D images as a concession and required multiple camera perspectives since the images could not be presented from an infinite number of angles, as in a fully 3D game space. This was an advantage, however, as the fixed cameras helped build tension by presenting the space from unsettling angles, employing views that induced claustrophobia. In several instances, camera angles were deliberately set to obscure the presence of enemies, leading to the game's famous use of "jump scares." Another survival horror game, *Silent Hill* (1999, Team Silent), centered on unraveling the mysteries of a town perpetually shrouded in a dense fog. The game was fully 3D and allowed a player to explore the town, using the character-following camera associated with other third-person games. This view, however, was combined with unsettling, dynamic pans and tilts once the player entered narrow alleys or indoor spaces which contributed to the game's eerie psychological sense of horror.

One of the most sophisticated examples of cinematic space was Hideo Kojima's *Metal Gear Solid* (1998, Konami Computer Entertainment Japan), a 3D adaption of his earlier MSX computer game *Metal Gear* (1987, Konami). *Metal Gear Solid*, like its 2D predecessor, was based on infiltrating and avoiding detection by patrolling guards, rather than a strict focus on action elements. The game used a complex set of cameras that tracked with the player's movement and presented the game from a top-down perspective, which emphasized the gameplay's tactical nature and recalled the original 8-bit game perspective. As the player entered and exited spaces, peered around corners, and crawled into air vents, the camera automatically changed its perspective through quick zooms, tilts, and cuts that gave the player the best view of the game space. The effect of these constant but smooth transitions created a feeling of continuous space while allowing the game to integrate cinematic intensity into the gameplay itself.

LucasArts brought its expertise in adventure games to a fully 3D world with the 1998 Day of the Dead-themed and film noir-inspired, *Grim Fandango* (Figure 9.5). Led by developer Tim Schafer, it featured many of the traditional elements of the adventure game genre: a cast of unique characters, engrossing narrative, and puzzle-based gameplay. *Grim Fandango*,

FIGURE 9.5   *Grim Fandango*™ **(1998, LucasArts). (Courtesy of Lucasfilm Ltd. LLC©.)**

however, departed from convention by offering an alternative to the typical practice of roving with a mouse cursor, looking for the game's various "hot spots." Instead, keyboard controls moved Manny Calavera, a grim reaper/travel agent for the dead, through pre-rendered 3D spaces. The game used an innovative system that turned Manny's head toward important objects as he approached them, indicating their interactivity to the player. The lack of interface plus multi-camera presentation of the game space led to a decidedly cinematic experience. Unfortunately, the heyday of the adventure genre was rapidly passing in favor of action games in the late 1990s and early 2000s. This translated to poor sales for *Grim Fandango* despite glowing reviews. LucasArts, meanwhile, shifted away from adventure games in the years following, as Star Wars properties dominated the company in the early 2000s.

Games like BioWare's *Star Wars: Knights of the Old Republic* (2003, BioWare Corporation), injected a feeling of the cinematic into the role-playing game genre through modifying the traditional concept of a *combat round*. Combat rounds were a structure found in the tabletop version of *Dungeons & Dragons* that typically limited combatants to one action per round. Combat continued among the survivors of each round until hostilities ceased through death or other means. In *Knights of the Old Republic*, each combatant's turn was executed at regular intervals regardless of the actions of others, uncoupling actions from rounds. At any time, the player could pause gameplay, view the surroundings, and issue a sequence of specific actions to a party character and watch the results automatically play out. Thus, the combat sequences of *Knights of the Old Republic* exhibited a dramatic cinematic quality with lightsaber strikes and blaster fire happening simultaneously but allowing the player to engage in strategic decision-making (Figure 9.6).

FIGURE 9.6 *Star Wars: Knights of the Old Republic™* **(2003, BioWare Corporation). (Courtesy of Lucasfilm Ltd. LLC©.)**

Games and Game Design in the New Millennium

Changes in the Industry

The industry changed significantly in the late 1990s and early 2000s. Teams of a dozen or less people made games like *Doom* and *Super Mario 64*, but swelled to teams of hundreds in the 2000s as the larger scope of games required increasingly specialized knowledge. Game publishers undertook a massive buying campaign, which merged smaller studios and restricted pathways for game publication. Game budgets grew larger and development time expanded to 2–3 year cycles. The result was greater risk and more pressure to produce successful games, leading many developers to seek more conventional projects that guaranteed a return on investment. Developers also reduced their focus, becoming inseparable from certain franchises and types of gameplay. In this context, consoles emerged as a driving force for the industry. Although PCs provided the highest performance for 3D games throughout the 2000s, significant cost increases for game-related components and limited knowledge about hardware configurations among the

FIGURE 9.7 **Specialized controllers for *Donkey Konga* (2004, Namco Limited) and *Guitar Hero* (2005, Harmonix Music Systems).**

general population stunted mass-market appeal. Consoles were comparatively easier to operate and their improved 3D capabilities after the 2000s narrowed the gap with PCs.

For developers, the open architecture scheme of PCs that allowed multiple types of hardware and software configurations often resulted in compatibility issues that required additional development time. Consoles, with their fixed hardware configurations, eliminated many of these uncertainties and became increasingly attractive for content creators. Arcade games continued to lose influence: expansive 3D worlds enabling player freedom worked against the coin-operated business model based on high difficulty and fast failure. Arcade rhythm games like *Dance Dance Revolution* (1999, Konami), however, played to these strengths. Players became public performers by "dancing" on the machine's large platform in time with visual cues from the screen. Although games like *Dance Dance Revolution* and other rhythm-based games were popular on home consoles (Figure 9.7), the general ability of arcade titles to drive direction and innovation on home consoles had come to an end.

New Consoles and the Maturing of Games in the 2000s

Sega's Exit

Sony's PlayStation rapidly eroded both Nintendo and Sega's market share in Japan and North America through the 1990s. Sega, in response, again attempted to leapfrog its competitors with the sixth generation Dreamcast console, launched in Japan in 1998. The Dreamcast was lackluster in Japan due to Sony's new dominance, its North American launch in 1999, however, was more successful. The Dreamcast's more advanced hardware was vividly demonstrated in Yu Suzuki's *Shenmue* (1999, Sega AM2), an open world, third-person action/role-playing game set in the Japanese city of Yokosuka in 1986. The console's new abilities allowed the game to replicate many buildings and features from the actual city, including a population that followed daytime and nighttime schedules and weather patterns that conformed to historical data. The degree of interaction was also notable: players could dial individual numbers on a telephone, open cabinet drawers, and even visit an in-game arcade to play some of Yu Suzuki's earlier games such as *Hang-On* and *Space Harrier*. The momentum behind Sega's Dreamcast in North America, however, quickly evaporated after Sony's worldwide release of the PlayStation 2 in 2000. With Sega unable to capture the mass market for consoles, the company made the decision to discontinue the Dreamcast in 2001 and completely withdraw from the console market, becoming solely a software developer.

Nintendo introduced the GameCube, its second 3D-capable console, in 2001. It featured games that more fully refined Nintendo's iconic characters in 3D game worlds. Many of the GameCube's highly praised games, such as *Super Smash Bros. Melee* (2001, HAL Laboratory), *Mario Party 4* (2002, Hudson Soft Company), and *Mario Kart: Double Dash!!* (2003, Nintendo EAD), featured a strong multiplayer social element, as Nintendo cultivated an identity that was increasingly separate from the "hardcore" games of the PlayStation 2. This was further continued in 2006 with Nintendo's seventh generation, motion-controlled, Wii console, featuring *Wii Sports* (2006, Nintendo EAD), as well in 2012, with the eighth generation Wii U. Nintendo also led the handheld game market in the 2000s through its 2004 Nintendo DS and 2011 3DS. Both units consisted of dual screens that recalled the design of Nintendo's clamshell Game & Watch handhelds of the 1980s. The DS and 3DS were particularly popular in Japan, as they fit well with the country's reliance on public transportation and small living spaces. The units offered much of the same types of games as their larger television-based cousins; however, their portable nature also allowed them to be ideal for casual gameplay experiences.

Microsoft's Entry

Sega's 2001 departure from the console market benefitted both Sony and Nintendo and proved to be perfectly timed for the entrance of Microsoft's inaugural console, the Xbox. Microsoft's move into the console market was prompted by a fear that Sony's PlayStation 2, with its DVD-ROM and other features, would make inroads in the games, home entertainment, and home computer markets, threatening sales of its Windows operating systems. All signs pointed to a mainstream breakout and rapid expansion of the video games market. Microsoft, however, had little direct experience with developing games. Its most notable entertainment software were Windows pack-in games, *Solitaire* and *Minesweeper*; while the *Flight Simulator* series (see

Chapter 6) and RTS franchise *Age of Empires* rounded out Microsoft's retail presence.

Microsoft had, nonetheless, been connected to PC game development in the 1990s through DirectX, a bundle of software technologies that served as a universal communication tool between games and game-related hardware. One of the components of DirectX was Direct3D, which helped games "speak" the many "languages" of 3D accelerated graphics cards. Without needing to write instructions for individual pieces of hardware, Direct3D and its main competitor, OpenGL,* allowed game developers to focus on creating games and facilitated the PC's transition to 3D through the 1990s.

The concept behind Microsoft's Xbox console was to make it function like a PC. It utilized DirectX (which provided inspiration for the console's name), a Pentium III processor, hard drive, and graphics card. This made it developer friendly and provided the potential for a large library of third-party games. The Xbox was also intended to fulfill home entertainment needs with its DVD-ROM and surround sound capabilities, bringing it into direct competition with Sony's ambitions for the PlayStation 2. The machine's built-in broadband modem, at a time when access to broadband Internet in the United States was still extremely limited, signaled a commitment to a future of downloadable content and Internet-based multiplayer gameplay. Although Sega's Dreamcast featured a built-in dial-up modem for online interaction, the pace of development in Internet infrastructure quickly made its slower speed unattractive.

Microsoft was able to gain an immediate foothold through the Xbox's military sci-fi, first-person shooter, *Halo: Combat Evolved* (2001, Bungie). The majority of first-person shooters of the 1990s were developed for home computers prior to *Halo*, as their 3D graphics capabilities and hard drive storage significantly outperformed their contemporary home consoles. Although the earlier Nintendo 64 and Sony PlayStation received limited ports of games like *Quake* and featured notable original titles, such as *Golden Eye 007* (1997, Rare) and *Medal of Honor* (1999, DreamWorks Interactive), games with more complex 3D imagery and gameplay such as *Half-Life*, *Unreal Tournament*, and *Deus Ex*, were not possible on these units. *Halo*, as a launch title for the Xbox, represented a closing of the gap between console and PC games and helped establish the ascendancy of console-based first-person shooters. *Halo* further popularized a control scheme that appeared earlier in the PlayStation's *Medal of Honor* that relied on two analog sticks for control: the left, to move along the ground and the right, to control the horizontal and vertical view—a setup that replicated the WASD keyboard and mouse configuration on the PC. This separation of movement and view became the default

---

* The 1997 hardware-accelerated version of *Quake*, *GLQuake*, used OpenGL.

method of control for console-based 3D games throughout the 2000s and 2010s.

The Proliferation of Open World Gameplay

Sony, nonetheless, become the leader of the console industry in the early 2000s with a large library of third-party-developed games that appealed to a maturing demographic of players in their late teens and 20s. One of the platform's most successful games was *Grand Theft Auto III* (2001, Rockstar Games), a cinematic and stylish, third-person crime drama (Figure 9.8). *Grand Theft Auto III* featured a large borderless city in which players freely chose missions with specific goals or engaged in unstructured sandbox-like gameplay allowing for exploration and experimentation. These signature elements were inherited from the initial 2D top-down, *Grand Theft Auto* (1997, DMA Design) that, in turn, drew inspiration from games like David Braben and Iain Bell's space-trading *Elite* (see Chapter 6).

Details dominated *Grand Theft Auto III*'s 3D city; all of the game's vehicles could be driven and showed damage from collisions, inhabitants changed behaviors between day and night, weather patterns affected driving, elevated trains ran on regular schedules, and committing crimes led to intervention by the police. The game's mature, crime-based narrative combined with the ability to harm or kill the civilians of the city, however, generated considerable controversy that brought issues of violence in videogames back to the forefront of public discourse. The high production values and innovative nature of *Grand Theft Auto III*, nonetheless, helped propel its developer Rockstar Games to prominence and led to several sequels, one of which,

FIGURE 9.8 *Grand Theft Auto III* **(2001, Rockstar Games). (Courtesy of Rockstar Games.)**

Grand Theft Auto: San Andreas (2004, Rockstar Games), was the best-selling game over the lifespan of the PlayStation 2.

Fully 3D, open world games with sandbox elements, thrived on home consoles and PCs throughout the 2000s and 2010s, as new generations of technology allowed larger, more complex spaces. The inherent freedom-based gameplay was highly attractive to players. The first-person medieval-fantasy RPG, *The Elder Scrolls III: Morrowind* (2002, Bethesda Game Studios) delivered on the vision established in Bethesda's *The Terminator* from 1991 (see Chapter 8), as well as the preceding 2D sprite/3D space RPGs, *The Elder Scrolls: Arena* (1994) and *The Elder Scrolls: Daggerfall* (1996). Other notable open world games of the 2000s included Ubisoft's period piece franchise, *Assassin's Creed*, Volition's humorously quirky *Saints Row* series, and Sucker Punch Productions' superpowered, morality driven *InFAMOUS*. MMORPGs like *Ultima Online* (1997, Origin Systems), *EverQuest* (1999, Sony Online Entertainment), and *World of Warcraft* (2004, Blizzard Entertainment) too proliferated as the rapid spread of Internet access in the later 1990s and 2000s allowed thousands of players to form organizations and adventuring parties.

Reducing Load Times on Consoles

The amount of data associated with open world games created a technical problem for consoles. Early 3D open world games such as *Shenmue* typically loaded one sector of game space at a time (such as a specific neighborhood) and loaded another once a border had been reached. The constant display of load screens and gameplay interruptions, however, dispelled the illusion of continuous sprawling cities and landscapes. Disc-based console games of the 2000s remedied this through *streaming*. With streaming, data for the game's various sections were read from the disc in the midst of gameplay prior to reaching a border, resulting in the appearance of a seamless open world as seen in games like *Jak and Daxter: The Precursor Legacy* (2001, Naughty Dog) and *Shadow of the Colossus* (2005, Team Ico), among others previously mentioned. Many of the open world games featured level design that prevented a player from outrunning the console's streaming capabilities through including twists and turns in roads or other geographic barriers. Other games looking to reduce load times, but not employing an open world design, such as *Metroid Prime* and *God of War* (2005, SCE Santa Monica Studio), featured long hallways, staircases, or elevators between larger spaces that allowed the game data time to stream without interrupting gameplay.

The Emergence of Casual and Mobile Games

As storage capacity and processing power increased in the 2000s, developers tended to skew toward games with longer play sessions and complex narratives. Many catered to players who expected high production quality and intense game experiences. These tendencies among large budget games in the 2000s excluded many in the general population and eventually led to the opening of a new market space for games, described as "casual." Although definitions of casual games, like independent games (see Chapter 10), are not clear-cut, they are associated with ideas such as shorter lengths of play, broad appeal stemming from accessibility, a de-emphasis of violent gameplay, and a high degree of replayability.

As discussed earlier, Microsoft's *Solitaire* and *Minesweeper,* Maxis' *SimCity* and Cyan World's *Myst,* captured a wide variety of players outside of traditional marketing demographics. In particular, designer Will Wright built a reputation for open-ended "system simulation toys" with *SimCity* and other "Sim" games throughout the 1990s. Taking this concept further, Wright designed the life simulator, *The Sims* (2000, Maxis). This "virtual dollhouse" allowed the player to manage the day-to-day activities of a household of people called "Sims" (Figure 9.9). Like Wright's early games, *The Sims* did not have predefined goals, but allowed for free unstructured play through interactions with the game's many systems. Each of the household's semiautonomous Sims had different needs, such as food, fun, comfort, and room, which, when met, increased their happiness. Players could direct each Sim to pursue career goals, personal improvement, romantic relationships, and other activities. A key concept involved designing the Sims' space by buying and placing new items in the house, a form of creative free play limited only by the amount of money in the household. *The Sims* generated considerable sales. It overtook *Myst* as the best selling PC game and initiated a successful franchise of other Sims games and expansions throughout the 2000s.

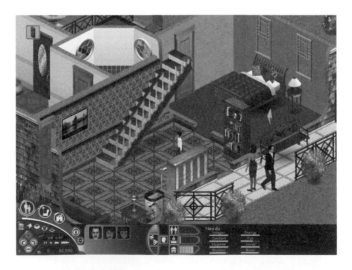

FIGURE 9.9 *The Sims* **(2000, Maxis). (Courtesy of Electronic Arts.)**

Although *The Sims* franchise was highly popular and garnered praise, the Internet and advent of mobile smartphones proved crucial for the breakout of casual games in the 2000s. Unlike the systems heavy *The Sims*, early browser-based casual games worked with a unique set of design constraints dictated by the state of Internet access at the turn of the millennium. Throughout the 1990s and first years of the 2000s, the majority of computer users relied on dial-up connections based on phone lines to access the Internet. The user manually initialized the computer's modem each time, leading to a series of beeps and static sounds and the phone line's occupation, for the duration of the connection. The limited speed of dial-up Internet access made the distribution of large files inefficient and unappealing. Mindful of data speeds, game developers sought to make the web more interactive and focused attention on creating small games with simple gameplay, delivered through web portals like MSN Gaming Zone and Yahoo Games.

One of the most successful of these games was PopCap Games' *Bejeweled* (2000). Programmed by Jason Kapalka, *Bejeweled* consisted of an 8×8 board of colored gems where the player swapped adjacent tiles to create a sequence of three or more gems of the same color. Once aligned, the gems disappeared and caused the stack above to fall, while a new set of random gems filled in the top. Gameplay continued until the player created a requisite number of matches to proceed to the next level, or could not create any more matches. The game also included a timed option to make matches as quickly as possible. *Bejeweled*'s "match three" tile-swapping gameplay was based on an earlier game called *Shariki* (1994) created by Russian programmer Eugene Alemzhin. *Bejeweled*, however, contained more appealing visuals, animations, and sound effects—features made possible by faster dial-up Internet connections at the turn of the millennium and the development of the Java programming language. Following the game's appearance on Microsoft's MSN Internet Gaming Zone web portal, PopCap adopted an unusual business model whereby it sold a "deluxe" copy of the free browser-based game on disc allowing play without an Internet connection (Figure 9.10). The ability to play *Bejeweled* "offline" appealed to dial-up Internet users and helped establish PopCap Games as a leader in the emerging casual games scene which led to other titles such as *Alchemy Deluxe* (2001), *Zuma Deluxe* (2003), and eventually *Plants vs. Zombies* (2009).

The context and design of casual gameplay changed dramatically after Apple's 2007 iPhone and 2010 iPad tablet computer. These mobile devices provided new forms of interaction in addition to portable computing and Internet connectivity. Multi-touch screens replaced physical buttons and allowed users to tap and swipe their finger anywhere on the screen. Competing smartphone and tablet manufacturers rapidly adopted the multi-touch screens making it the preferred interface for mobile devices. Casual game developers were quick to integrate these new button-less interactions

FIGURE 9.10   *Bejeweled Deluxe* **(2000, PopCap). (Courtesy of Electronic Arts.)**

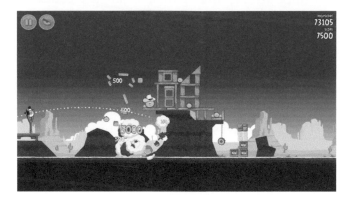

FIGURE 9.11 *Angry Birds* **(2009, Rovio Entertainment). (Courtesy of Rovio Entertainment.)**

into their games. PopCap's *Bejeweled* was among the launch games for the iPhone as the tile-switching mechanic was ideally suited for quick horizontal and vertical swipes rather than cumbersome cursor movement using a phone's numeric keys. Rovio Entertainment's physics-based puzzle game, *Angry Birds* (2009), likewise used swiping to aim and launch colorful bird characters from a slingshot (Figure 9.11). Using unique abilities for each bird type, players destroyed or knocked down structures in an attempt to eliminate a set of green pig targets.

Digital Distribution in the 2000s

Broadband Internet connections rapidly replaced dial-up Internet access in the 2000s, although dial-up was still used in certain sparsely populated areas. Broadband had a significantly larger capacity for data relative to dial-up service, allowing easier delivery of multimedia content, such as video and large files. In addition to speed, broadband connections were "always on," allowing for a constant stream of data, which led to a sea change in game distribution in the 2000s. In 2003, *Half-Life* developer Valve launched Steam, a broadband software delivery technology for home computers. Steam, in addition to selling Valve's games, performed checks that authenticated the legality of the games, helping to reduce software piracy. The system also automatically updated games with the latest patches and fixes, ensuring that all copies of games, such as *Counterstrike*, then the world's most popular online game, stayed up to date to prevent cheating and exploitation.

Steam established a significant foothold after the release of *Half-Life 2* (2004, Valve), as the game required the service in order to run. Highly successful, *Half-Life 2* expanded on its predecessor's style of continuous interaction through scripted sequences while expanding the feeling of the game's engrossing environments. It featured elaborate physics-based puzzles and other memorable sequences such as driving a makeshift buggy on an abandoned highway and operating an electromagnetic crane, both of which broke up the well-paced action. Steam, propelled by the overwhelming success of *Half-Life 2*, began selling games from third-party developers in 2005 and eventually became the largest source for the sale of home computer games. It also played a crucial part in the breakout of independent games (see Chapter 10).

Home consoles also pursued digital distribution. Services that allowed players to download games to their consoles had been in existence since 1981 with PlayCable for Intellivision, followed by numerous other services developed for Atari, Nintendo, and Sega home consoles. Many of these services experienced brief periods of success, but downloadable console games did not reach mass audiences until the explosive growth of broadband Internet. One of the key strategies for the Xbox centered on multiplayer gaming through Microsoft's online subscription service, Xbox Live. Especially popular with players of *Halo*, Xbox Live set a precedent for console connectivity in the 2000s as Microsoft managed the online component of games rather than placing the burden of creating network infrastructure on developers. This allowed a more uniform set of online parameters as well as the creation of an Xbox-based gaming community.

Microsoft expanded Xbox Live through the online marketplace, Xbox Live Arcade in 2004. Xbox Live Arcade's initial success depended on small but continuous purchases made by a large number of customers, just as in the penny arcades of a hundred years earlier. This prompted Xbox Live Arcade to feature short games that required a minimal investment of time to learn and play, such as ports of arcade games from the 1970s through 1990s, as well as games with more casual gameplay, such as *Bejeweled*.

Microsoft relaunched Xbox Live Arcade for the seventh generation Xbox 360 in 2005, closely followed by Sony's PlayStation Network Store in 2006, and Nintendo's 2008 Wii Shop Channel. The inherent connectivity of seventh generation home consoles accelerated trends of media convergence: players could purchase and play music, films, television shows, and other digital content. Streaming content from providers like Netflix, Hulu, YouTube, and others, completed the transformation of video game consoles into true home media devices, a trend that intensified in the eighth generation consoles of the 2010s.

Casual Games and Digital Distribution

Digital distribution allowed casual games to spread to all major mobile platforms as well as social media websites, such as Facebook. Many casual games distributed through online means were designed to follow the "freemium" business model. The freemium business model combined aspects of shareware (see Chapter 8) and elements of arcade game design as it gave away the game for free, but included limits on game features or limits on progress, which could be lessened through in-game microtransactions. The freemium model was successfully used for a number of casual games such as the management-based *FarmVille* (2009, Zynga) and the tile-swapping, match-three puzzle game *Candy Crush Saga* (2012, King). Both games employed gated progression: players waited hours to days for crops to grow before harvesting in *FarmVille*, while certain playfield obstacles prevented players from switching tiles in later stages of *Candy Crush Saga*. Players could pay a small fee to receive in-game items that subverted the normal rules and allowed instantaneous production of crops or the ability to destroy any tile without switching it.

Although the freemium model was highly influential, the field of casual games became vastly more diverse after the 2008 launch of Apple's App Store and Google's Google Play digital distribution hub. This coincided with the boom in independent games (see Chapter 10), as developers were given new channels of distribution and were freed to challenge entrenched notions of game design. A standout example was *Monument Valley* (2014, ustwo), a 3D puzzle game for mobile devices in which players guided a princess through a series of levels (Figure 9.12). The game's art and level design, inspired by M.C. Escher's optical illusions, required a player to consider all surfaces and aligned spaces in order to progress. Unlike puzzle-based games that focused on difficulty, *Monument Valley* was more of a minimalist aesthetic experience focused on the joy of interaction; a notion influenced by digital design firm ustwo's background in user experience. Instead of directions and tutorials on how to play, players were invited to discover the game through touch. Sliding and rotating the architectural elements of the game space created pleasing musical notes that blended with *Monument Valley*'s atmospheric

FIGURE 9.12 *Monument Valley* **(2013, ustwo). (Courtesy of ustwo.)**

soundtrack. Players could zoom in and not only gaze at the appealing blend of 2D graphic design and 3D architecture in the game space, but also take pictures of it as each level was intended to be an image worthy of framing.

Game Visuals and Gameplay Aesthetics in the 2000s and Beyond

The 2000s and 2010s witnessed a rapid evolution in game graphics as each new generation of hardware allowed developers to provide increasingly natural looking visuals. Some games pursued photo-realism outright, but most pursued a mix of stylized visuals with realistic lighting and texture effects. The complexity of 3D game models rose dramatically in both cases, as developers increased the number of polygons to provide more detail and to match new hardware capabilities. Character models in the 2010s, for example, were commonly created using polygon counts in the tens of thousands to hundred thousands. The increase in geometric complexity had a direct impact on how 3D models were constructed as well as how they were animated.

Character models of the mid to late 1990s, for example, were commonly created "by hand" using a few hundred polygons, resulting in the typical "boxy" look of the period's 3D models. Further, features such as arms and legs, were constructed from discrete pieces of geometry that overlapped with

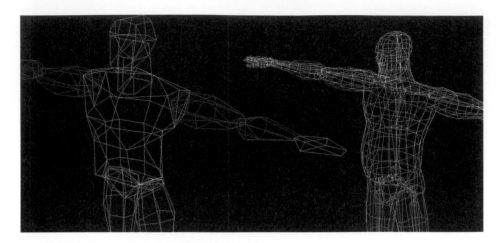

FIGURE 9.13 Common approaches to animating game characters in the late 1990s (left) and 2000s (right). The low polygon figure on the left is constructed from individual segments while the high polygon figure on the right is continuous and is animated through manipulating internal bones. (Courtesy of Mark Jarman.)

each other. The individual segments were grouped and given animation data, which produced movement. This stood in contrast to the later technique of creating a model made of a continuous set of polygons. To produce animation, characters were *rigged* using "bones" located inside the model to smoothly deform the high polygon surfaces and simulate actions such as elbow and knee bending (Figure 9.13). Rigging was generally avoided in earlier models since it was more computationally intensive. Further, the limited number of surfaces on low polygon 3D models typically did not bend subtly enough and created undesirable or unnatural effects. The visual differences between low polygon models constructed in segments versus a single high polygon model can be seen in *Star Wars: Jedi Knight—Dark Forces 2* (Figure 9.3) and *Knights of the Old Republic* (Figure 9.6), two games separated by only 6 years. In the later 2000s and 2010s, character models were often created through 3D scans of an actor's body while motion capture data provided more fluid and lifelike animation.

Realism in Surfaces

3D game visuals prior to the early 2000s relied heavily on *color* (also sometimes referred to as *diffuse maps*) that wrapped 2D images on 3D surfaces, to simulate a particular material. The 2D image could be anything; thus, color maps were able to turn the same simple cube into a wooden crate or a metal box. Color maps alone, however, were unconvincing, since surfaces remained flat and relatively featureless because of the low polygon count of early 3D models. The advent of *shaders*, however, significantly increased visual realism in games as they could alter the appearance of surfaces on 3D models.

FIGURE 9.14   The effects of pixel shaders on a character model from *Saints Row IV* (2013, Deep Silver Volition). From left to right model with: (1) wireframe model, (2) normal map, (3) color map, and (4) composite model with reflections and final details. (Courtesy of Deep Silver Volition.)

Bump maps were one of the earliest shaders that significantly refined game visuals as they simulated subtle surface irregularities and gave the illusion of height and depth on an otherwise flat surface. Statues made of stone, for example, showed pits and rough texture while cloth shirts exhibited the appearance of woven thread. Bump mapping, found as early as the PC-based, first-person, Jurassic Park tie-in *Trespasser** (1998, DreamWorks Interactive), was not widely adopted on consoles until after the release of the Xbox and GameCube, which both provided built-in support for the feature. *Normal maps* provided sharper detail by converting the surface of a high polygon 3D model to a 2D map and overlaying it on a low polygon model. This technique added more visual detail without adding more computation-intensive polygons. Shaders were also used to simulate the effects of light on models and the game environment through *specular maps*, which controlled the reflective properties of a surface, allowing highlights that automatically reacted to different light intensities (Figure 9.14). *Bloom* or *glow maps* simulated the illusion of extremely bright light bleeding past edges, while *after-images* produced a motion-blur effect for moving cameras and objects. The effect of bloom maps can be seen in the comparison of the lightsaber effect in Figure 9.3 versus Figure 9.6. Developers of the 2000s also met the growing demand for higher amounts of detail by using 3D scanning techniques to capture the fine points of faces, bodies, objects, and even entire environments. Face scanning, for instance, was used for certain characters of Valve's

---

* *Trespasser* was also notable for a number of unique gameplay elements intended to increase realism, such as physics simulation and the manual control of the character's arm that allowed the player to pick up and interact with many game world objects. Despite innovative ideas, *Trespasser* contained many performance issues and was not commercially successful. A number of the development team's key members were alumni of Looking Glass Studios, among them Seamus Blackley who later helped develop Microsoft's Xbox.

FIGURE 9.15 Characters from *Mass Effect* (2007, BioWare Corporation) created through face scanning technology. (Courtesy of Electronic Arts.)

Half-Life 2 as well as the Mass Effect series (Figure 9.15). Face scanning also became an integral part of sports games that featured recognizable sports figures such as the Madden NFL franchise.

Film-Like Gameplay in the 2000s

Unlike the film-heavy, interactive movies of the early 1990s (see Chapter 8), game developers of the 2000s sought more unique ways to combine the expressive strengths of film with the interactive aspects of games. Two of the most common cinematic elements in gameplay of the 2000s included *quick time events* and *set pieces*. Quick time events made narrative cutscenes more interactive as they incorporated sequences where the player watched actions unfold, but were required to press a certain button within a limited period of time to make progress. Quick time events, often tied to cinematic action sequences, allowed the button presses to resonate with the scene's tension. Yu Suzuki's *Shenmue*[*] featured segments where the main character chased fleeing criminals through the streets; when prompted by flashing icons, players pressed buttons to dodge pedestrians and vault over obstacles in their path. The consequences of failing quick time events in *Shenmue* included starting the sequence over again, the alteration of the game's story, and even player death. Quick time events

---

[*] *Shenmue* referred to these sequences as "quick timer events." The term was subsequently modified to "quick time event" likely due to its ease of pronunciation.

appeared in games throughout the 2000s and were used in genres ranging from action adventure such as *Uncharted: Drake's Fortune* (2007, Naughty Dog) to head-to-head fighting such as *Mortal Kombat X* (2015, NetherRealm Studios).

Set pieces, meanwhile, were special sequences that added narrative drama and spectacle to gameplay without interrupting it. Set pieces or set piece-like sequences were used in a number of earlier 2D and 3D games such as the lead up to the boss fights in *Star Fox*, the destruction of the Ceres Space Colony in *Super Metroid*, and the physics experiment gone wrong in *Half-Life*. On seventh and eighth generation consoles, set pieces reached more elaborate heights. In *Call of Duty 4: Modern Warfare* (2007, Infinity Ward), the player, aboard a helicopter, flees heavy combat only to witness the detonation of a nuclear device. The helicopter spins out of control and crashes; the player crawls through a city full of fire, debris, and collapsing buildings, then dies. Throughout the entire sequence, players maintained partial or complete control, bringing together the cinematic and interactive.

THE RETURN OF DEDICATED CONSOLES AND THE RETRO REVIVAL

Dedicated consoles made a brief return in the early 2000s in the form of "retro-styled" plug and play controllers and miniature versions of vintage consoles. The units used the same "Pong-on-a-chip" concept employed in dedicated consoles of the late 1970s (see Chapter 3) and typically featured collections of arcade and console games from the 1980s through the early 1990s (Figure 9.16). The popularity of the novelty units and their simple, pixelated games provided a counterpoint to the push for greater levels of visual realism and narrative complexity in the larger game industry. Elements of this "retro revival" and nostalgia for bygone game eras also surfaced in downloadable titles on online marketplaces (see above) as well as in the independent games movement (see Chapter 10).

(a)   (b)

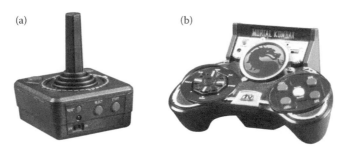

FIGURE 9.16   Retro units by Jakks Pacific. The Atari 10 in 1 TV Games (a) and Mortal Kombat Plug & Play TV Games units (b).

Criticism and Backlash against the Industry

Despite the significant advances in game visuals and game technologies, some developers became unhappy with the direction of the industry. From their perspective, they felt that games had become tantamount to amusement parks and exhibited "film envy" as visual spectacle trumped meaningful game design and gameplay experiences. Looking to advance games beyond current practice, these individuals chose to leave their positions and join the independent game development scene. There, they joined others with like-minded criticism of contemporary game design practices and explored unconventional or novel concepts. Many were attracted to independent games as they offered a sense of ownership over their projects. Smaller in scope, due to limited budgets and team sizes, independent games, nonetheless, steadily grew in popularity during the 2000s and achieved significant milestones in the 2010s. Not all of the energy behind independent games was fueled by a reaction against the practices of big budget game developers and publishers, but for many it was a significant motivator. Chapter 10 discusses elements of the development, directions, and breakout of the independent games scene.

Chapter **10**

Independent Games (1997-Present)

The Scratchware Manifesto and Dimensions of "Indie"

In the summer of 2000, a group of anonymous game designers published a three-part essay, *The Scratchware Manifesto*, on the abandonware archive site, Home of the Underdogs. The declaration delivered a scathing critique of practices in the digital game industry: it criticized publishers who chose game genres with safe investment returns over innovative ones, who made demands on workers with long periods of crunch time, and who shipped buggy games that resulted from rushed production schedules. The essay called for an alternative type of game described as "scratchware." It was to be accessible, high quality, replayable, short, and created by teams of three or less individuals with multiple skill sets. Scratchware games were to focus on 2D art, which allowed for economical and rapid development while providing the opportunity to explore untapped aesthetic avenues. Key to scratchware games would be their cost and method of distribution: $25 or less and deliverable without retailers, via the Internet. Each element was intended to break the practices of the game industry by producing easy-to-acquire games with greater novelty in design, at lower cost to players. In short, it was a rallying cry for the creation of independent games.

The growth of independent games in the mid to late 2000s appeared, on the surface, to have answered the manifesto's call. Many *had* operated at lower budgets and with smaller development teams; pixel art, 2D graphics, and other flat styles *did* allow for efficient development times and a critique of photorealistic 3D imagery; many independent game developers *were* able to exercise creative control, retain ownership, and develop ideas that large developers were not interested in pursuing. In addition to the growth of Internet distribution, alternative funding streams such as the crowd-funding site Kickstarter allowed developers to further bypass traditional methods of seeking bank loans or other forms of seed money.

The development of the contemporary independent games scene, however, was much more complicated than fulfilling the prescriptions from The Scratchware Manifesto. Motivations of individual developers varied, some were former industry professionals inspired by The Scratchware Manifesto, while others had no industry experience and simply saw an opportunity in a changing market. Promoters of independent games ranged from populist entities, like niche Internet communities to major corporate players like Valve, Microsoft, Nintendo, and Sony who actively promoted independent games based on their marketability to the larger gaming audience. Even the words "independent" and "indie" carried different connotations that ranged from games that were simply self-funded, self-published, and self-promoted, to games that provided deeply intellectual commentary and criticism. These complex and contradictory elements associated with independent games, nonetheless, created a vibrant context as the barriers for game creation became progressively lower throughout the 2000s.

The Early Independent Game Scene
Success with Shareware

As discussed in Chapter 8, shareware was a form of marketing in which users were able to try a limited version of a program before they bought the full edition. Despite the fact that most shareware games did not generate reliable funding and that the popularity of the model had declined significantly by the late 1990s, some shareware games earned enough to support their makers as full-time, independent game developers.

Jeff Vogel founded Spiderweb Software in the mid-1990s and specialized in the creation of CRPGs. Rather than compete with the detailed, pre-rendered graphics and recorded dialog of large budget games like *Diablo* or the 3D open world environments of *Daggerfall*, Vogel's games, such as *Exile III: Ruined World* (1997, Spiderweb Software) represented a continuation in the development of the 1980s Ultima-Style CRPGs (see Chapter 6). The games featured pixelated graphics, contextual details, and dialog delivered via windows of richly written text and, most significantly, a systems-heavy, tactical approach to gameplay involving party management. These older design elements were partnered with refinements to the interface and to the design of interaction that matched contemporary expectations, many of which were inspired by larger big budget games.

Unable to compete based on the superiority of its graphics, *Exile III* relied on shareware to allow potential customers to experience a portion of the game's engrossing narrative and evaluate the gameplay. Players who wanted the full version used a credit card to purchase a key code that unlocked the remainder of the game—a difficult setup, as banks in the mid-1990s were leery of online commerce. Nonetheless, the game found a niche audience that was substantial enough to earn *Exile III* two shareware *Game of the Year* awards. Vogel's later games in the Geneforge, Nethergate, Avadon, and Avernum series also succeeded by following the same model.

Other shareware independent games also received accolades. *Tread Marks* (2000, Longbow Games) combined armored tanks, racing games, and fast multiplayer, tournament-style, deathmatches similar to *Unreal Tournament* (Figure 9.6). The game's high-end 3D graphics, a rarity for independent games of the time, featured terrain that deformed with each explosion and other dazzling visual effects by Longbow Games' president and programmer, Seumas McNally (Figure 10.1). While *Tread Marks* was distributed as shareware the full version was sent through the mail on CD as the game was too large to directly download at the time through the predominant dial-up Internet connections.

FIGURE 10.1   A tank battle in *Tread Marks* (2000, Longbow Games). (Courtesy of Longbow Games.)

THE SEUMAS McNALLY GRAND PRIZE

Since 1999, the Independent Games Festival at the Game Developers Conference has given awards for games in categories for excellence in visual art, audio, design, and others including a grand prize for the year's "best game." Seumas McNally's *Tread Marks* was the second independent game to win the IGF's grand prize along with best design and best programming, raising its profile and eventually leading to a retail release through a publisher. McNally, however, tragically passed away in 2000 after a 3-year ordeal with Hodgkin's lymphoma only weeks after *Tread Marks* won the three awards. Shortly thereafter, the Independent Games Festival's grand prize was renamed "The Seumas McNally Grand Prize" in his honor and continues to be awarded annually to the year's best independent game.

Flash and 2D Freeware Games

Talented artists and programmers at the turn of the millennium also developed games for sheer creative enjoyment and released them free-of-charge as browser-based Flash games or as downloadable freeware. The typical small size and short game length made it easy to quickly enact changes and add content, leading to a vibrant development context as games could reciprocally influence and be influenced by each other over the course of different release versions. Web sites and online communities like Newgrounds, Jay Is Games, Kongregate, and the Independent Gaming weblog, helped establish an amateur game developer scene in the early 2000s by facilitating conversations among designers across the world and providing a means for dissemination.

Flash and Struggles for Legitimacy

Flash was one of the most popular development platforms available to amateur game designers for 2D games through the early 2000s. It was simple to use and had a visual-friendly layout. The prospect of company sponsorship in exchange for placing advertising banners in the games also helped draw developers to the platform and provided a small amount of revenue for independent game creation. The initial versions of Flash were focused on producing animation and supported clickable buttons; thus, the first set of Flash games consisted of minimally interactive "click games" that used mouse movement and clicking input. Using these capabilities, designers created simple shooting galleries, short narrative-based games with branching dialog choices, and even point-and-click adventures. Many amateur developers in the nascent Flash communities used pre-existing images and/or music taken from popular culture rather than original art and sound assets, leading to a "mash-up" aesthetic common to many games. Since dial-up modems imposed a practical limitation on the size of the games one could produce, most early Flash games typically contained only a few minutes' worth of gameplay.

Despite these limitations, some creators were able to exploit the abilities of Flash to create games with an unexpected depth of gameplay. Tom Fulp, who founded the Flash portal Newgrounds in 1995, also created one of the most sophisticated early Flash games, *Pico's School* (1999). The objective of *Pico's School* was to survive a school shooting perpetuated by ninjas and aliens disguised as Goth teenagers. Despite the game's theme, which pushed the limits of black humor and political correctness (like much of the content on Newgrounds), it exhibited a complexity of design and polish in presentation that was virtually unseen in amateur Flash game development. After a brief cutscene that introduced the game's setting, players of *Pico's School* could choose multiple pathways through the school's halls, have conversations that affected game outcomes and engage in boss fights, all of which were driven by simple mouse clicks.

Later versions of Flash added options that allowed the programming of advanced behaviors and interactions. Developers then created more ambitious games that led to a healthy Flash gaming scene focused on Fulp's Newgrounds site. Flash-based games, regardless of complexity, however, were seen as illegitimate relative to downloadable freeware games made in more traditional, software-creation programs. Honorific bodies charged with recognizing accomplishments in independent games such as the Independent Games Festival, for example, did not initially accept browser-based Flash game submissions for award consideration. Publishers, meanwhile, refused to port Flash games to consoles because they did not look or play like console games. Tom Fulp and Dan Paladin's Flash game *Alien Hominid* (2002), however, helped change these perceptions.

Alien Hominid (Figure 10.2), was a fast-paced action platformer in the style of 2D run 'n gun games like *Contra* and *Metal Slug* (1996, SNK). The game, like *Pico's School*, began with a brief, animated cutscene showing a flying saucer crash landing on Earth and the alien pilot's encounter with a friendly boy. Gameplay, after the introduction, launched into chaotic, side-scrolling, shooting action, as waves of FBI men in black streamed in from the sides, attempting to capture and study the alien. The technical ability of the game was beyond expectations for Flash games: players could jump, duck, fire their alien blasters in four directions, and move in a highly responsive manner. There was great variety in gameplay: players could receive brief power-ups for their guns, earn extra lives, destroy moving cars, and fight gigantic boss characters. *Alien Hominid* also featured a distinctive art style created by game artist Dan Paladin. Rather than the simple geometric shapes or mouse-drawn graphics of Flash games of the time, Paladin used a stylus and drawing tablet, which led to the game's hand-drawn, cartoon-like visuals. While the single-level Flash game could be completed in a

FIGURE 10.2 **The Flash version of** *Alien Hominid*. **(Courtesy of Newgrounds/The Behemoth.)**

number of minutes, *Alien Hominid* became one of the most popular games on Newgrounds and received millions of plays.

Alien Hominid's online release caught the attention of John Baez, an environment artist who worked for the same company as Dan Paladin. Since few games then available for consoles looked and played like *Alien Hominid*, Baez saw potential in releasing it in console version. When Baez and Paladin were both laid off, Baez convinced Paladin and Fulp to pursue full-time independent development. The result was The Behemoth founded in 2003. The Behemoth secured a publisher and *Alien Hominid* was reworked and expanded for commercial release on consoles and handhelds in 2004 and 2005. It was the first adaptation of a browser-based Flash game to game consoles. Although the Behemoth felt *Alien Hominid* would only generate niche appeal, it gained popularity across a wide audience due to its retro-style gameplay and unique visuals, proving to publishers that independent games could be financially successful despite a radical deviation from expectations.

The improved capabilities of Flash also allowed game designers to add new sensations of speed and velocity in moving objects. Raigan Burns and Mare Sheppard of Metanet felt that the development of 2D platforming games had been cut short by the industry's rush to adopt 3D graphics, leading to *N* (2004, Metanet), a freeware platforming game developed in Flash that featured a visually abstract ninja (Figure 10.3). Inspired by the classic computer platformer *Lode Runner* (1983, Brøderbund Software, Inc.) as well as other contemporary freeware games, *N* required the player to navigate increasingly difficult, single-screen puzzle-like levels collecting gold, while avoiding the game's many cleverly placed hazards.

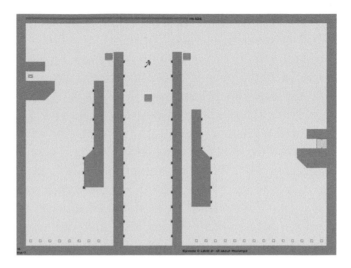

FIGURE 10.3   An early level in *N* (2004, Metanet Software). (Courtesy of Metanet Software Inc. www.metanetsoftware.com)

N was unconventional in its radical simplicity: the visuals were predominantly black and gray abstract shapes while controls were limited to horizontal movement and jumping. The game, nonetheless, contained depth, as its "elastic" feel of the jump and run provided the player with a sense of acceleration through space. This provided new opportunities for level design, as the player could use the built-up inertia to jump and sail through the air of levels with unconventionally far off platforms and hazards. *N* also included an editor that, like the earlier *Lode Runner*, allowed users to create and distribute new levels. Many community-designed levels were included in the game's version 2.0, making the play experience of *N* a community project within the online Flash-based game scene.

N, like *Alien Hominid*, gained a significant online following that resulted in millions of plays and was similarly ported to home consoles, handheld systems, and online digital marketplaces. Both won Audience Choice awards at the 2005 IGF and *Alien Hominid* also won for Technical Excellence and Excellence in Art. This recognition brought Flash-based games further legitimacy and created a path for the commercial release of later games originating in Flash such as *flOw*, *Super Meat Boy*, and *VVVVVV*.

Japan's Doujin Soft and Freeware Scene

Unlike independent games in North America in the early 2000s, *doujin soft*, Japan's rough equivalent of independent games, had highly developed channels that allowed game developers not affiliated with large companies to bring their games to customers. *Doujin soft* games, like many Flash games, were small, self-published, hobbyist projects that commonly used pre-existing images, characters, and sounds from popular culture such as *manga* and *anime* series. Many of these Japanese hobbyist games, however, were openly sold at specialized retail locations and conventions, despite their use of trademarked characters. *Doujin soft* game makers worked in all genres but many gravitated toward visual novels and classic 2D games such as RPGs, shoot 'em ups and platformers. The 2D pixel art, head-to-head fighting game, *Melty Blood* (2002, Type-Moon/Watanabe Seisakusho), for example, was created with characters from the visual novel *Tsukihime* and followed many of the design conventions established in Capcom's 2D fighting games of the later 1990s. The high production values and anime-inspired flair earned it instant praise among the PC-based *doujin soft* community and a version was brought to the arcades and published on home consoles. Other games in the *Melty Blood* series also received mass publication, however, *doujin soft* games were typically unavailable outside of Japan due to their extreme niche appeal, distribution in physical form, limited locations, and difficulties in obtaining internationally compatible formats.

While *doujin soft* was regarded as commercialized "fan work," several Japanese game developers released a number of games with original design concepts and graphics as freeware, many of which had a significant influence on the developing North American independent games scene. Shoot 'em up games were particularly well suited for experimentation with new ideas since established game mechanics could be modified in simple ways that produced innovative changes in gameplay. Hikoza Ohkubo's freeware *Warning Forever* (2003, Hikware) consisted solely of boss fights but utilized a unique system in which every boss evolved different offensive capabilities depending on how the player destroyed its predecessor (Figure 10.4). Kanta Matsuhisa (a.k.a. "Omega") designed *Every Extend* (2004), which replaced the ability to shoot with a single-use, self-destruct mechanic employed by

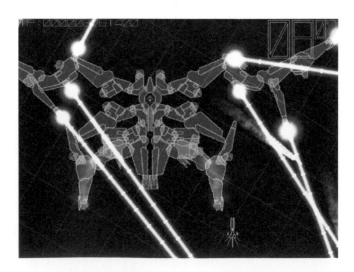

FIGURE 10.4 *Warning Forever* **(2003, Hikware). (Courtesy of Hikoza Ohkubo.)**

the player to create explosive chains among moving formations of enemies. Kenta Cho, one of the most prolific designers of the Japanese freeware game scene, gained recognition for innovative shooters like *TUMIKI Fighters* (2004, ABA Games), which allowed the player to collect the parts of fallen enemies and use them as upgraded firepower and armor. Many of Cho's other shoot 'em up games, such as *Parsec 47* (2003), *Torus Trooper* (2004), and *Gunroar* (2005), also gained a wide following.

While many freeware shoot 'em ups influenced North American game developers, Daisuke Amaya's 2004 adventure game, *Doukutsu Monogatari* or *Cave Story*, proved to be a galvanizing title. *Cave Story* was developed over the course of 5 years and featured an unusually large amount of content for a freeware game. It contained a complex cast of characters situated in an engrossing narrative represented through bright, pixilated visuals. The game's concept grew from Amaya's admiration for the original 1986 *Metroid* that allowed players to explore and learn about the gameworld through their own actions. According to Amaya, this approach made each of the player's accomplishments, whether major or minor, meaningful. *Cave Story* represented a design form that has since been dubbed *Metroidvania*, games that drew inspiration from the construction of space and flow of gameplay seen in action platformers *Metroid* and *Super Metroid* as well as *Castlevania: Symphony of the Night* (1997, Konami). In *Cave Story* like many other Metroidvania games, players crisscrossed and backtracked through large, continuous 2D game spaces and attempted to find power-up items that opened previously closed areas for play. This approach to design emphasized game mechanics as the functions of the various weapon and item upgrades were directly worked into progression through the game.

The art, design, and scope of *Cave Story* caught the immediate attention of Japanese freeware aficionados in North America. Within a month, these communities created a translation hack that brought *Cave Story* to English-speaking audiences. Word of *Cave Story* spread rapidly online: it led to ports to various operating systems, playthrough videos on YouTube, and numerous dedicated fan sites. Although *Cave Story* was not completely unique among Japanese freeware games, it struck a chord in North American independent communities and became seen as the embodiment of "indie": a labor of love created entirely by a single designer, which utilized a retro visual style and focused on game mechanics.

Freeware Experiments with Games and Art

The mid-2000s saw a number of "art games" that used recognizable genres and mechanics but downplayed the traditional challenge-based elements of gameplay, favoring instead the communication of an experience or concepts between creator and player. As many of the games were unconventional with limited initial commercial appeal, they were frequently released as freeware.

Art games, however, eventually gained a sufficient audience to warrant commercial release and success for a few in the later 2000s and 2010s.

Although developers focused on different elements between art and games, they overwhelmingly made interactivity a primary focus as it distinguished games from other forms of media. *Samorost* (2003) was a short point-and-click adventure created in Flash that carried a thread of the surreal through its photo collage visuals and gameplay. The game, created by Czech film student, Jakub Dvorský, as part of a thesis in animation for the Academy of Arts, Architecture and Design in Prague, undercut many of the point-and-click genre's foundations on logical puzzle solving. The game, instead, placed an emphasis on interactive animations. Play focused on directing a small space elf in a quest to divert an asteroid on a collision course with his home (Figure 10.5). An early section of *Samorost*, for example, featured a verdant mountain landscape that was inhabited by a group of people working near a ski lift. The player's goal, unknown, was to activate the ski lift and allow the space gnome to ski down the hill. To accomplish this, the player needed to click on a hookah-smoking man three times: allowing the man to consume the substance and drop the pipe, which the player then used as a key to start the ski lift and continue on to the remaining puzzles. This illogical thought process invited the player to click on multiple elements of the game space and thus trigger a variety of incidental animations. Through exhibition at art shows and its availability online, *Samorost* received significant recognition among both art and game communities.

Dvorský founded Amanita Design as a freelance design studio after he graduated, but continued to create short Flash games, some commissioned by Nike and Polyphonic Spree. Amanita Design pushed back against what it saw as the game industry's unwillingness to experiment and its overemphasis

FIGURE 10.5 *Samorost* **(2003, Amanita Design). (Courtesy of Amanita Design. (C) Samorost by Amanita Design, www.amanita-design.net)**

on 3D, when it introduced its first retail game *Samorost 2* (2005), which followed the same surreal style of the original. It earned numerous awards and, although short, was successful enough to support Amanita Design as a full-time, independent game developer.

Although Amanita Design did not consider its works "art," a number of other game designers consciously created games as art. Belgian developers and digital artists Auriea Harvey and Michaël Samyn, founded Tale of Tales in 2002 seeking to directly engage the audience not through museums or galleries but online through interactive digital art. One of Tale of Tales' early projects, *The Endless Forest* (2005), began as a commission by the *Grand Duke Jean Museum of Modern Art* in Luxembourg and consisted of an MMORPG in which the player controlled a deer running through a fairytale-like forest. The game featured none of the quests or goals typically associated with other MMORPGs: it was, instead, a live performance space. Players interacted with individual elements of the forest and with each other, in a sense of pure play. *The Endless Forest* did not allow players to converse with each other directly; the only mode of in-game communication was a series of emotes and other actions triggered through buttons on an action bar, reminiscent of the interfaces in popular MMORPGs such as *World of Warcraft*. The game could also function as a screensaver, launched during periods of inactivity, and allowing a player to wander the forest for brief periods in a relaxed state.

Tale of Tales created a number of other titles through the late 2000s, which, like Amanita Design, were commercially sold. *The Graveyard* (2008), for example, allowed the player to direct the movement of an old woman in a black and white graveyard to a park bench. Upon sitting, the old woman appeared to have an introspective moment as the game camera showed a close-up of the woman's face superimposed on the gamespace. This action, or lack thereof, continued for as long as the player chose, creating a shared moment with the game character. Following the period of introspection, the player directed the slowly moving old woman out of the graveyard. While the game was entirely free, a commercialized version introduced the random possibility of the old woman's death which otherwise undercut the game's gentle pace with an unexpected and sudden event.

One of the most celebrated freeware art games was Jason Rohrer *Passage* (2007). *Passage* presented life from young adulthood through old age and death, in the span of 5 minutes, using a screen resolution of 100×16 pixels (Figure 10.6). The interactive *memento mori*, or meditation on the inevitability of death, was created as an entry to the Gamma 256 event sponsored by Kokoromi, a Montreal-based group dedicated to the promotion of artistic and experimental digital games. In *Passage*, players could chose to go through the digital life alone or with a digital partner, and explore a large space that was visually limited to a narrow band of pixels. In a simple but thought-provoking manner, the right portion of the band became sharper as

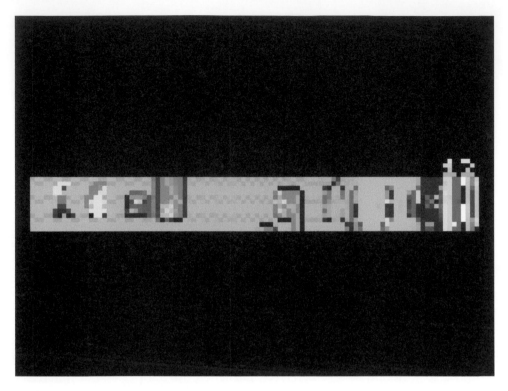

FIGURE 10.6 *Passage* **(2007). (Courtesy of Jason Rohrer.)**

the character aged, representing a clearer view of one's future and ultimate fate. This was countered with increased haziness on the left portion of the screen, as memories of the past became more distant.

Unlike the works by Tale of Tales, *Passage* melded symbolism with traditional game mechanics and featured a score accumulator that ascended as one progressed, representing the richness of one's life. The score could increase by journeying with a partner, as well as through the discovery of life-enriching treasure chests in hidden areas of the gamespace. Thus, the player could make many choices on how to spend the 5-minute life. Nonetheless, as the game functioned as a *memento mori*, the accomplishments gained during the life ultimately meant nothing and did not prevent the character's death, no matter how high the score. *Passage* received praise for its simple yet deeply profound message expressed as a game. It was among the first group of games added to the Museum of Modern Art's permanent collection of videogames established in 2012.

The Mainstream Breakout of Independent Games

In 2005, game industry veterans Greg Costikyan and Johnny Wilson launched Manifesto Games, an online marketplace with digital distribution for computer-based independent games. Born from the spirit of The Scratchware Manifesto (of which Costikyan anonymously contributed to under the name "Designer X"), Manifesto Games was an attempt to provide a home for niche games that would not receive shelf space in retail locations. Thus, games with unconventional or truly innovative ideas could find an audience and help break what Costikyan and Wilson saw as stagnation in the games market. Unfortunately, Manifesto Games was unable to attain the mass of developers and customers needed to support the site and it was shut down in June 2009. Ironically, it was large companies like Valve Corporation, Sony, Microsoft, and Nintendo that completed the work of bringing niche games to players and helped foster the breakout of independent games precisely when Manifesto Games shut its doors.

Steam and Independent Games

As discussed in Chapter 9, Valve's Steam marketplace became one of the main refuges for computer games amid the greater popularity of console gaming and shrinking computer game offerings by retailers. In addition to selling digital-only games, Steam hosted some of the earliest breakout independent game titles. With Valve's high esteem among modding communities coupled with the central role of PCs in game development, Steam quickly became one of the preeminent places for the sale of independent games.

One of the first independent games available on Steam was Introversion Software's *Darwinia* (2005), a winner of the IGF Seumas McNally Grand Prize. *Darwinia* combined multiple modes of gameplay, including elements reminiscent of RTSs and arcade shoot 'em ups, into an experience that defied traditional definitions of genre. The player managed the action of units and gathered resources, but gameplay concentrated on shooting enemies in a manner similar to the Golden Age arcade games, *Robotron 2084* and *Centipede*. The game's story of repelling a virus invasion from within a computer and saving a group of indigenous digital entities was enhanced by visuals that drew inspiration from films like *Tron* through its gridded world of faceted polygons (Figure 10.7).

Steam's basis on home computers allowed independent game developers to take full advantage of the mouse as an input device. Mark Healey's *Rag Doll Kung Fu* (2005), another early independent game on Steam, was a tongue-in-cheek fighting game that parodied kung fu films of the 1970s. Healey, a professional within the game industry, created *Rag Doll Kung Fu* in his spare time out of a desire to design a ridiculous game. Using the mouse, players kicked, punched, and jumped by grabbing and snapping the limbs of the game's puppet-like, 2D rag doll characters.

FIGURE 10.7 *Darwinia* **(2005, Introversion Software). (Courtesy of Introversion Software.)**

The mouse was prominent in Amanita Design's first full-length game, *Machinarium* (2009), which built on the studio's momentum from the *Samorost* games and helped in the revitalization of the dormant point-and-click adventure genre. In *Machinarium*, the player directed a small robot on a quest to rescue his robot girlfriend and stop a group of evil robots from bombing the city. *Machinarium* was unlike the simple "click game" approach of the studio's previous titles. It utilized a more conventional approach to point-and-click adventure games with more logical puzzle solving and the use of items collected and combined from an inventory. *Machinarium*, however, retained the studio's emphasis on animation and unique 2D visuals by using a digital version of cut-out animation and placing characters in atmospheric, hand-drawn environments (Figure 10.8). Like the studio's earlier point-and-click games, the player never experienced defeat in the form of death: progress was interrupted only through the inability to decipher the puzzle, a concept the developers had taken from *Myst*. Amanita Design continued its Flash-based, point-and-click adventures through *Botanicula* (2012), which was a return to form as it emphasized playful exploration over logical puzzle solving and used visuals focused on nature and microbial life. Point-and-click adventures were further strengthened with other games such as *Primordia* (2012, Wormwood Studios) a game created in the style of LucasArts adventure games of the 1990s.

FIGURE 10.8 *Machinarium* **(2009, Amanita Design). (Courtesy of Amanita Design. (C) Machinarium by Amanita Design, www.amanita-design.net)**

Console Manufacturers Pursue Independent Developers

Aside from *Alien Hominid* and a handful of other titles, non-puzzle-based independent games did not have a significant presence on consoles until the popularization of online marketplaces and game services such as Microsoft's XBLA, Sony's PSN, and Nintendo's Wii Shop Channel (see Chapter 9). Following the success of casual titles such as *Bejeweled*, console-based online game services built a library of small, downloadable independent games with arcade-like gameplay and niche appeal. Many had already won awards from the IGF or received other forms of recognition; characteristics that posed a minimal financial risk compared to the predominant big budget games.

Two early independent game releases on the PlayStation Network, *flOw* (2007, thatgamecompany) and *Everyday Shooter* (2007, Queasy Games) featured gameplay that was familiar and easy to understand while employing innovative mechanics and visuals. In *flOw*, the player directed a bioluminescent organism through deep-sea waters in search of creatures to devour (Figure 10.9). The organism grew in complexity as it consumed like *Blockade* and *Snake* (see Chapter 3), allowing the player to dive deeper to hunt larger, more challenging prey. *FlOw*, unlike conventional game design, allowed the player to adjust the game's difficulty by traveling into deeper or shallower waters at will. This simple design concept subverted the convention of game difficulty that grew greater the longer one played. This more gentle form of difficulty progression, combined with the game's minimalist graphics and tranquil soundtrack, created a Zen-like play experience that promoted feelings of relaxation rather than tension.

FIGURE 10.9 *flOw* (2007, thatgamecompany). (Courtesy of Sony Interactive Entertainment America LLC.)

FlOw's unique gameplay was based on a Flash game designed by Jenova Chen, a University of Southern California graduate student, to accompany his MFA thesis. Chen sought ways to quickly induce "flow" in players, a psychological state of total absorption and optimal task performance entered only when a task is neither too difficult nor too easy. Based on this concept, the Flash game contained the "Embedded Dynamic Difficulty Adjustment" system mentioned above that gave players direct control over the game's difficulty. Thus, players, regardless of individual skill, could theoretically experience a flow state.

Sony's other early independent hit was *Everyday Shooter* by Jonathan Mak. *Everyday Shooter* closely followed the twin-stick shooter format popularized in Eugene Jarvis' Golden Age arcade game, *Robotron 2084*, as gameplay consisted of shooting and maneuvering around enemies in an enclosed, top-down perspective game space. The game was distinctive for its conceptual nature and abstract aesthetics, as Mak designed the game along the lines of a music album composed of game levels for musical tracks. During play, each destroyed enemy unleashed an abstract explosion of color and a short set of acoustic guitar notes that meshed with each level's minimalist songs. Each level of *Everyday Shooter*, like tracks on an album, featured different sounds, color themes, and rules for interacting with the enemies. The stages were influenced by Japanese freeware shoot 'em ups, including *Every Extend*, *Warning Forever*, and the games of Kenta Cho. The end result was an interactive, improvisational soundscape that made the player a creator of music through gameplay (Figure 10.10).

Beat 'em up independent games made an appearance on Microsoft's XBLA with The Behemoth's *Castle Crashers* (2008) and James Silva's *The Dishwasher: Dead Samurai* (2009, Ska Studios). *Castle Crashers* used the core gameplay seen in the Famicom/NES title, *River City Ransom* (1989, Technōs Japan) but added traditional RPG elements of experience points, a leveling system, inventory items, and weapon upgrades. The game's four-player

FIGURE 10.10 *Everyday Shooter* **(2007, Queasy Games). (Courtesy of Sony Interactive Entertainment America LLC.)**

cooperative mode, isometric perspective, brightly colored protagonists and large-scale boss fights recalled The Behemoth's earlier *Alien Hominid* as well as the licensed beat 'em ups of the early 1990s by Konami and Capcom. The hand-drawn art style of Dan Paladin, meanwhile, presented a fresh and comical take on the pixel art-dominated genre. *The Dishwasher: Dead Samurai* was created when James Silva won Microsoft's inaugural Dream Build Play competition aimed at courting independent developers. Silva's independent game development career began in 2001 with the shareware *Zombie Smashers X*, another isometric beat 'em up also inspired by *River City Ransom*. The 2D gamespace in *The Dishwasher: Dead Samurai*, however, was filled with hypercharged, over-the-top bloody action that, like *Castle Crashers*, was rendered in a hand-drawn art style.

The title that brought the most attention to independent games, both within and outside of the context of gaming, was Jonathan Blow's *Braid* (2008, Number None, Inc.). *Braid*'s gameworld and design referenced platformers like *Super Mario Bros.* with piranha plants in green tubes and the ability to defeat enemies by jumping on them, however, at its core *Braid* was a series of unique logic puzzles solvable by speeding up or reversing the flow of time. Players who fell into a pit or ran into an enemy could simply reverse time and make the appropriate adjustments to prevent death. Following Miyamoto's approach to platformers, Blow created complexity in gameplay by individually layering simple systems and behaviors. Rather than power-ups, however, the player encountered different sets of mechanics for the puzzles of each world: levels with objects immune to the effects of time manipulation, levels where time moved forward and backward as the player moved right and left, and levels that granted the ability to create a localized bubble of slow time, all of which were accompanied by the basic rewind mechanic.

The depth of game design seen in *Braid* was matched by its introspective and mature narrative. The game involved a search for a kidnapped princess, but deconstructed this typical trope and focused instead on the difficulties encountered in an adult relationship. It explored concepts of doubt, the obsessive search for fulfillment, conflict in mastering one's drives and ambition, the inability to reverse mistakes, and growth resulting from learning from mistakes. The themes were connected in varying degrees to gameplay and *Braid*'s mechanics: mistakes and learning from them, for example, was explicitly connected to the game's main rewind mechanic. *Braid*'s highly lauded art was created by David Hellman and rendered in an expressive, painterly style that further reinforced the focus on subjective human experience. The game's music, also a departure from the traditional 8-bit, chip tune beats, featured string instruments, drums, and soft piano suites that Blow had licensed from a music provider.

Braid's success stemmed from its contrast of intellectual puzzle solving, emotional storytelling, and unique art and musical style, qualities that helped legitimize independent games and their developers in the mainstream. For a number of years 2D puzzle-platformers with unique art styles and mechanics proliferated across online marketplaces and proved to be highly popular; many, like *Braid*, explored themes related to the human condition. *Limbo* (2010, Playdead) featured a black and white expressionist world with a heavy emphasis on brooding. Terry Cavanagh's *VVVVVV* (2010) featured a gravity-flipping mechanic and imagery recalling the color palette of the Commodore 64 computer. Mike Bithell's *Thomas Was Alone* (2012), focused on moving a colorful cast of characters, represented as geometric shapes, through various maze layouts, while the protracted *Fez* (2012, Polytron Corporation) used pixel art graphics and a game mechanic that allowed the player to rotate the 2D game world on an axis. Other 2D games of the time such as *Super Meat Boy* (2010, Team Meat), and the Bit Trip series used brightly colored pixel art, often ironically, to enhance the fast-paced, frantic gameplay.

The meteoric rise of independent games in the mainstream reached a fevered pitch with *Journey* (2012, thatgamecompany). *Journey*, like thatgamecompany's earlier *flOw* and follow-up, *Flower* (2009), challenged notions about videogames by focusing on emotional experiences over competitive or combative gameplay. The game's concept involved a spiritual pilgrimage to a distant mountain, partially inspired by the monomyth of the "hero's journey," formulated by the prominent scholar of mythology, Joseph Campbell. According to Campbell, the hero's journey began by departing from the ordinary and entering a world of supernatural wonder where the hero encounters challenges, emerges victorious, and returns home with new powers or abilities. In the game *Journey*, the player entered a world full of ancient monuments that had been claimed by the desert (Figure 10.11). The game's environment created feelings of awe as it artfully used a range of colors matched with large landscape vistas dominated

FIGURE 10.11 *Journey* **(2012, thatgamecompany). (Courtesy of Sony Interactive Entertainment America LLC.)**

by a distant mountain. The distant mountain beckoned the player toward it and, through the course of play, allowed the player to gain insight into the world's mythology. After a number of dangers, the player reached their final goal and returned to the game's beginning in preparation for another journey.

In addition to its stylized visuals and immersive environments, *Journey* was praised for its unique gameplay that allowed pairs of strangers to not only embark on the arduous journey together, but also to forge an emotional bond with one another. This was accomplished through a number of art and design choices. Players saw their companion as they saw themselves. Outward signs of difference were removed, as each player was an identical abstracted figure wearing a robe and trailing scarf. The game allowed players to temporarily fly in the air, an ability which was depleted with each flight but could be recharged by the player's proximity to each other, providing motivation to stay together. The game featured shared experiences that elicited feelings of joy and ranged from playfully sliding together down long pathways made of sand, to feelings of tension and fear as enemies threatened the characters, requiring them to hide, together, in makeshift shelters. Most poignantly, players could keep each other warm during the final snowy ascent up the mountain by walking closely together. Similar to Tale of Tales' *The Endless Forest*, players in *Journey* could not directly speak to each other; the only outward form of communication was through a single sound that varied in volume. Underscoring the gameplay was a superb soundtrack that changed with the game's many moods, providing an essential emotional cue for the players.

Although other multiplayer games such as the MMORPG, *World of Warcraft*, contained cooperative gameplay between strangers, magic items or currency incentivized most group tasks. *Journey*'s focus on exploration and discovery, rather than personal gain, allowed players to progress with a different mindset. Despite its unconventional features such as noncompetitive gameplay and a focus on emotion, *Journey* was popular among players and helped illustrate the rapid changes and diversification of gaming in the early 2010s.

Success beyond "Games"

The independent gaming landscape became increasingly diverse and specialized as games without goals or traditional concepts of winning and losing found commercial success in creative sandboxes and first-person narrative adventures.

Creative Sandboxes

Sandbox games allowed players freedom of play through building virtual worlds and gained their highest profile with the independent titles, *Garry's Mod* (2006, Facepunch Studios) and *Minecraft* (2011, Mojang). Community input during each game's development, as well as after official release, was key to their success. The Steam-based *Garry's Mod* by Garry Newman, began in 2004 as a free mod for Valve's *Half-Life 2*. Players were granted access to the game's library of character and object models and could change their properties, weld them together, and manipulate them in space. The Source engine for *Half-Life 2*, designed with a special emphasis on physics, allowed players of *Garry's Mod* to set up elaborate Rube Goldberg-like machines, create moving vehicles from parts, erect buildings, and execute other experiments. Valve approached Newman in the hope that a stand-alone version with enhanced capabilities could be produced. Over time, *Garry's Mod* grew into a unique multiplayer platform as players could import user-created maps as well as add *their own* mods and items to the game. In addition to creating animated movies and designing games within the game, players created everything from cinemas that allowed groups to virtually watch YouTube videos together to elaborate role-playing worlds where players chose from a variety of professions, bought property, and earned income. As such, the popularity of *Garry's Mod* depended wholly on community involvement to continuously generate new, creative content.

Swedish programmer Markus "Notch" Persson released the alpha version of *Minecraft* in 2009 as a "toy" that allowed players to stack pixelated blocks and create structures in randomly generated worlds. *Minecraft*, although simple, generated a significant amount of attention as players engaged in pure, creative unstructured play similar to *Garry's Mod*. Persson's vision for his game, however, was much greater. During its development between 2009 and 2010, *Minecraft* featured new additions such as multiplayer support, monsters, items, a crafting system, and a more structured "survival mode" of gameplay which required the player to find or create food and shelter while dealing with monsters that came out at night. Like *Garry's Mod*, the development of *Minecraft* was strongly influenced by its growing and devoted fan base as Persson polled the community concerning the development of upcoming features, responded to feedback, and implemented popular requests in the game.

One of the results of this collaborative approach led by Persson, resulted in the formation of the expansive crafting system, which allowed players to refine materials gathered from the world such as wood, stone, and diamonds and create a variety of objects like weapons, decorative household items, and tools. The game grew to include systems for cultivating plants and trees, breeding animals, building structures, and making programmable creations using switches, motors, and simple logic statements. *Minecraft,* unlike previous RPGs with crafting systems, contained no instructions for how to combine materials or even what was possible for players to create. The unconventional approach attracted numerous players who felt that the larger game industry had sacrificed the element of challenge for an emphasis on accessibility. "Hard-core" players reveled in the opportunity to decipher the game's systems through experimentation, the results of which were published on community-created wiki pages. This knowledge base, wholly generated and shaped by the community, created a sense of shared ownership.

The influence of *Minecraft* was felt strongly in the proliferation of random generation, crafting systems, and survival-based gameplay in wilderness settings in independent games during *Minecraft*'s several-year development. Further, the construction-based systems and flexibility offered through mods facilitated *Minecraft's* expansion beyond the confines of games into other applications. Teachers utilized the *MinecraftEdu* educational mod to teach core competencies in elementary and middle schools while the Danish Geodata Agency created a model of the entire country of Denmark in a 1:1 scale, complete with roads and buildings with the help of map data and algorithms.

Narrative Exploration

Narrative exploration games further expanded and challenged the definition of games by virtually eliminating the mathematical core that governed rules and strategy. Instead the games emphasized mood and narrative leading to interactive experiences based on complex emotions. Related to art games, narrative explorations often focused on the human condition by combining philosophical thought with storytelling that moved beyond the power fantasy themes commonly represented in commercial digital games.

The ready availability of mod tools for first-person shooters, in particular, allowed a greater sense of narrative immersion through near total control over character movement. In many ways, these games represented the continuation of the ideas featured in *Myst* and its sequels through the elimination of player death.

One of the first major titles of narrative exploration games produced in this context was *Dear Esther* (2012, The Chinese Room). *Dear Esther* began as a free mod for *Half-Life 2* in 2008 and after winning numerous awards, was turned into a stand-alone game by British developer, The Chinese Room. Rather than action or puzzle-based gameplay, *Dear Esther* was an immersive mood poem situated on a deserted island located in the Hebrides off the West coast of Ireland. The game's atmosphere was dark and brooding with stormy clouds, a constant wind, and brief but haunting musical themes that played at certain points. The game's main feature was the narration of a letter to a woman named Esther, delivered in randomly selected segments throughout the player's island wanderings. This experimental form of interactive narrative created a shifting ambiguity of interpretation concerning the identity of the player's character as well as the order of the events described as each playthrough yielded a different set of readings.

The concept of balancing narrative with interactivity was explored in a number of other games of the time as well. *Proteus* (2013), by British designer/programmer Ed Key and American composer David Kanga, eschewed traditional narrative entirely and focused on the experience of traversing an abstract natural world, where falling leaves, animals, and rain created musical sound effects. The environment in *Proteus* transitioned through four seasons, each with its own color palette, music, and set of sound effects (Figure 10.12). The contrast, for example, between the vibrant color, abundant animals, and active music of summer, with the muted palette, stillness, and minimal music of winter, artistically reinforced notions of change and

FIGURE 10.12   Ed Key and David Kanga's *Proteus* (2013). (Courtesy of Ed Key.)

FIGURE 10.13 An unpredictable player is given a line to follow in *The Stanley Parable* (2013, Galactic Cafe). (Courtesy of Galactic Cafe.)

the cycles of the natural world that reflected Key's interest in Taoist philosophy. As the game randomly generated the game space, each playthrough and each season led to a unique musical narrative of one's wanderings.

Gone Home (2013, The Fulbright Company), designed by a team featuring former game industry professionals, featured a story set in 1995 that revealed its engrossing narrative through the examination of objects in an empty house. Using limited narration, the game dealt with a number of real-world relationship conflicts and elements of prejudice, rather than supernatural or fantastic elements. *The Stanley Parable* (2013, Galactic Cafe) originated, like *Dear Esther*, as a mod for *Half-Life 2*, but took a different approach by humorously deconstructing narrative and interactivity in games. The player, as an unremarkable office worker named Stanley, moved through a mundane setting of cubicles and break rooms while a narrator prompted player choices with a story told in the past tense. Players could either defy or follow the narrator's words through their choices and subsequent actions, creating a form of nonverbal communication with the game's narrator. Players who continuously frustrated the narrator with their choices experienced a number of surreal fourth wall-breaking situations including, among others, the game attempting to reassert control through placing a bright yellow line on the ground for the player to follow (Figure 10.13). This, however, fails as the line itself becomes disorderly and freely scrawls paths on the walls and ceiling.

Meeting Challenges in the Contemporary

The success of games like *Braid*, *Journey*, and *Minecraft* coupled with a number of industry professionals forming their own studios, the ease of accessing online tutorials, and the spread of game design curricula in universities, contributed to a dramatic rise in the number of people involved

FIGURE 10.14 *Everybody's Gone to the Rapture* **(2015, The Chinese Room). (Courtesy of Sony Interactive Entertainment America LLC.)**

in independent game development in the late 2000s and 2010s. As a result, the environment became more competitive and new challenges centered on discoverability became a significant barrier to success. The derivative and mediocre comingled with the thoughtful and excellent, stoking fears of an independent game market collapse that would mirror the North American console crash of 1983.

As a result, certain independent game developers attempted to distinguish themselves by increasing the production value of their games. The first-person investigation game *The Vanishing of Ethan Carter* (2014, The Astronauts) and The Chinese Room's narrative exploration game, *Everybody's Gone to the Rapture* (2015), for example, used high resolution photorealistic imagery with complex lighting effects, professional music composers, and larger production teams (Figure 10.14). Other solutions included developing games for the new generation of consumer model, virtual reality headsets such as in *Keep Talking and Nobody Explodes* (2015, Steel Crate Games), a cooperative game in which players wearing an HMD needed to defuse a bomb while receiving instructions on how to do it from others reading from a manual. The requirement, however, for greater technical complexity, longer development times, and larger production budgets, began to carry many of the same financial risks as big budget games. Other avenues of independent game design will undoubtedly emerge in the coming years as the market continues to mature.

Bibliography

Alexander, L. 2012. Inside the Making of Alone in the Dark. Retrieved August 22, 2014, from http://gamasutra.com/view/news/165360/GDC_2012_Inside_the_making_of_Alone_in_the_Dark.php.

Altice, N. 2002. *I Am Error: The Nintendo Family Computer/Entertainment System Platform. Platform Studies* (1st ed.). Cambridge, MA: The MIT Press.

Amaya, D. 2011. The Story of Cave Story. *GDC Vault.* Retrieved October 18, 2016, from http://www.gdcvault.com/play/1014621/The-Story-of-CAVE.

Antoniades, A. 2009. Monsters from the Id: The Making of Doom. Retrieved August 22, 2014, from http://www.gamasutra.com/php-bin/news_index.php?story=21405.

Baer, R. 2005. *Videogames: In the Beginning.* Springfield, JN: Rolenta Press.

Bell, A. G. 1978. *The Machine Plays Chess? Pergamon Chess Series.* Oxford: Pergamon Press.

Bowery, J. 2001. Spasim (1974) The First-Person-Shooter 3D Multiplayer Networked Game. Retrieved December 3, 2013, from http://web.archive.org/web/20010410145350/http://www.geocities.com/jim_bowery/spasim.html.

Brand, S. 1972. Spacewar: Frantic life and death among the computer bums. *Rolling Stone,* 7, 50–58.

Brand, S. 1974. *II Cybernetic Frontiers.* New York, NY: Random House.

Bueschel, R. M. 1988. *Pinball 1: Illustrated Guide to Pinball Machines, Volume 1 Bagatelle to Baffle Ball 1775–1931, The Origins of Pinball and the "depression Baby" Boom* (Vol. 1). Wheat Ridge, CO: Hoflin Publishing Ltd.

Bueschel, R. M. 1996. *Arcade Sports Games.* Fountain Valley, CA: Coin-Op Classics Magazine.

Bueschel, R. M. 1997. *Encyclopedia of Pinball Vol 2: Contact to Bumper 1934–1936.* Novato, CA: Silver Ball Amusements.

Bueschel, R. M. and Gronowski, S. 1993. *Arcade 1: Illustrated Historical Guide to Arcade Machines.* Wheat Ridge, CO: Hoflin Publishing Ltd.

Caulfield, A. and Caulfield, N. 2011. *Sonic: The Birth of an Icon.* UK: Gracious Films.

Colley, S. n.d. Steve Colley Describe's Maze's Earliest History at NASA Ames. Retrieved March 14, 2016, from http://www.digibarn.com/history/04-VCF7-MazeWar/stories/colley.html.

Colmer, M. 1976. *Pinball: An Illustrated History.* London: Pierrot Publishing Limited.

Costa, N. 1988. *Automatic Pleasures: The History of the Coin Machine* (1st ed.). London: The Bath Press.

Cotton, B. and Oliver, R. 1993. *Understanding Hypermedia: From Multimedia to Virtual Reality.* London: Phaidon Press.

Crogan, P. 2011. *Gameplay Mode: War, Simulation, and Technoculture.* Minneapolis, MN: University of Minnesota Press.

Dillon, R. 2011. *The Golden Age of Video Games: The Birth of a Multi-Billion Dollar Industry.* Boca Raton, FL: Taylor & Francis Group, LLC.

Donovan, T. 2010. *Replay: The History of Video Games.* East Sussex, UK: Yellow Ant.

Eales, R. 1985. *Chess: The History of a Game.* New York/Oxford: Facts on File Publications.

Edwards, B. 2007. The History of Civilization. Retrieved March 14, 2016, from http://www.gamasutra.com/view/feature/129947/the_history_of_civilization.php.

Edwards, J. 2013. BEJEWELED: The Definitive, Illustrated History of the Most Underrated Game Ever. Retrieved March 14, 2016, from http://www.businessinsider.com/the-history-of-bejewled-2013-9.

Eisler, C. 2006. DirectX Then and Now (Part 1). Retrieved July 2, 2016, from http://craig.theeislers.com/2006/02/20/directx-then-and-now-part-1/.

Essinger, J. 2004. *Jacquard's Web: How a Hand-Loom Led to the Birth of the Information Age* (Vol. 1). Oxford: Oxford University Press.

Ferrell, K. 1990. Memory arcade. *Compute!*, 12(5), 72–75.

Flower, G. and Kurtz, B. 1988. *Pinball.* Secaucus, NJ: Chartwell Books.

Fox, M. 2012. Space Invaders Targets Coins. Retrieved July 2, 2015, from http://www.numismaster.com/ta/numis/Article.jsp?ArticleId=24643.

Galaxy, B. 2002. *Collecting Classic Video Games.* Atglen, PA: Schiffer Publishing, Ltd.

Graetz, J. M. 1981. The origin of spacewar. *Creative Computing*, 5, 56–67.

Hafner, K. and Lyon, M. 1998. *Where Wizards Stay Up Late: The Origins of the Internet.* New York: Touchstone.

Halter, E. 2006. *From Sun Tzu to Xbox: War and Video Games.* New York: Thunder's Mouth Press.

Herlands, W. B. 1941. *Operation of Pinball Machines in the City of New York.* New York: Department of Investigation.

Hjorth, L. 2011. *Games and Gaming: An Introduction to New Media.* Oxford: Berg.

Igarashi, K. 2014. There and Back Again: Koji Igarashi's Metroidvania Tale. Retrieved October 18, 2016, from http://www.gdcvault.com/play/1020822/There-and-Back-Again-Koji.

Jones, H. B. 1976. *Coin-Operated Amusement: An Historical and Technological Survey.* Chicago, IL: Bally Manufacturing Corporation.

Katz, A. 1984. Lucasfilm premieres first two games: Can it become a force in electronic gaming? *Electronic Games*, 2(14), 21–24.

Kent, S. L. 2001. *The Ultimate History of Video Games: From Pong to Pokemon and Beyond—The Story behind the Craze That Touched Our Lives and Changed the World.* Roseville, CA: Prima Publishing.

Klepek, P. 2005. Down with Publishers!: The Men of Manifesto Games Explain Their Plan for Revolution. Retrieved March 15, 2016, from http://www.1up.com/news/publishers.

Kohler, C. 2004. *Power-Up: How Japanese Video Games Gave the World an Extra Life*. BradyGames.

Kohler, C. 2006. *Retro Gaming Hacks*. Sebastopol, CA: O'Reilly Media, Inc.

Kurtz, B. 2004. *The Encyclopedia of Arcade Video Games*. Atglen, PA: Schiffer Pub.

Kushner, D. 2004. *Masters of Doom: How Two Guys Created an Empire and Transformed Pop Culture*. New York: Random House.

Laister, N. 2006. *Pennies by the Sea: The Life and Times of Joyland Amusements, Bridlington*. St. Albans, UK: Skelter Publishing LLP.

Langston, P. S. 1985. The Influence of the UNIX Operating System on the Development of Two Video Games. Retrieved October 18, 2016, from http://www.langston.com/Papers/vidgam.pdf.

Langston, P. S., Fox, D., Arnold, S., Morningstar, C., Gilbert, R., and Falstein, N. 2014. Lucasfilm Games Postmortem. Retrieved September 4, 2015, from http://www.gdcvault.com/play/1020557/Classic-Studio-Postmortem-Lucasfilm.

Leone, M. 2012. The Man Who Created Double Dragon. Polygon. Retrieved March 14, 2016, from http://www.polygon.com/2012/10/12/3495124/the-man-who-created-double-dragon.

Levey, S. 2010. *Hackers: Heroes of the Computer Revolution*. Sebastopol, CA: O'Reilly Media, Inc.

Loftus, G. R. and Loftus, E. F. 1983. *Mind at Play: The Psychology of Video Games*. New York: Basic Books, Inc.

Mace, S. 1984. *Atari Unveils Lucasfilm Games; Star Wars Company Touts "Edge of the Art" Sound, Graphics*. InfoWorld, 6(23), 12.

Mallinson, P. 2002. Games That Changed the World: Ultima Underworld. Retrieved October 18, 2016, from https://web.archive.org/web/20090303101150/http://www.computerandvideogames.com/article.php?id=28003.

Mäyrä, F. 2008. *An Introduction to Game Studies: Games in Culture*. London: Sage Publications.

Michel, H. 1966. *Scientific Instruments in Art and History*. New York, NY: The Viking Press.

Miller, R. 2013. Classic Game Postmortem: Myst. Retrieved October 18, 2016, from http://www.gdcvault.com/play/1018048/Classic-Game-Postmortem.

Montfort, N. and Bogost, I. 2009. *Racing the Beam: The Atari Video Computer System*. *Platform Studies*. Cambridge, MA: MIT Press.

Moschovitis, C. J. P., Poole, H., Schuyler, T., and Senft, T. M. 1999. *History of the Internet: A Chronology, 1843 to the Present*. Santa Barbara, CA: ABC-CLIO, Inc.

Nasaw, D. 1993. *Going Out: The Rise and Fall of Public Amusements*. New York, NY: Basic Books.

Nedeski, S. 2010. Interview Don Daglow: The First Console Wars How He Survived it. Retrieved March 15, 2016, from http://www.criticalgamer.co.uk/2010/06/07/interview-don-daglow-the-first-console-wars-and-how-he-survived-it/.

Nielsen, J. 1990. *Hypertext and Hypermedia*. Boston, MA: Academic Press.

Nintendo of America, Inc. 2011a. Iwata Asks: New Super Mario Bros. Volume 1. Retrieved March 14, 2016, from http://iwataasks.nintendo.com/interviews/#/wii/nsmb/0/0.

Nintendo of America, Inc. 2011b. Iwata Asks: Volume 5: Original Super Mario Developers. Retrieved January 1, 2016, from http://iwataasks.nintendo.com/interviews/#/wii/mario25th/4/0.

Perry, D. C. 2006a. XBLA: Greg Canessa Interview, Pt. 1. Retrieved March 15, 2016, from http://www.ign.com/articles/2006/07/26/xbla-greg-canessa-interview-pt-1.

Perry, D. C. 2006b. XBLA: The Arcade That Microsoft Built. Retrieved March 15, 2016, from http://www.ign.com/articles/2006/08/02/xbla-the-arcade-that-microsoft-built.

Perry, D. C. 2006c. XBLA: The Greg Canessa Interview, Pt. 2. Retrieved March 15, 2016, from http://www.ign.com/articles/2006/08/02/xbla-the-greg-canessa-interview-pt-2.

Rorher, J. 2007. What I Was Trying to Do with Passage. Retrieved March 15, 2016, from http://hcsoftware.sourceforge.net/passage/statement.html.

Ryan, J. 2011. *Super Mario: How Nintendo Conquered America*. New York, NY: Penguin Group.

Sharpe, R. C. 1977. *Pinball!*. New York, NY: Dutton.

Sheffield, B. 2011. Tekken's Harada Reveals The Roots of This Seminal Series' Systems. Retrieved March 14, 2016, from http://www.gamasutra.com/view/news/126687/Tekkens_Harada_Reveals_The_Roots_Of_This_Seminal_Series_Systems.php.

Smith, R. 2008. *Rogue Leaders: The Story of LucasArts*. San Francisco, CA: Chronicle Books.

Snezana, N. 2010. Interview Don Daglow: The First Console Wars How He Survived It. Retrieved March 15, 2016, from http://www.criticalgamer.co.uk/2010/06/07/interview-don-daglow-the-first-console-wars-and-how-he-survived-it/.

Temple, K. 1991. *Pinball Art*. London: H.C. Blossom.

The Scratchware Manifesto. 2000. Retrieved March 15, 2016, from http://www.homeoftheunderdogs.net/scratch.php.

Tresca, M. J. 2011. *The Evolution of Fantasy Role-Playing Games*. Jefferson, NC: McFarland & Company, Inc.

Vendel, C. and Goldberg, M. 2012. *Atari Inc.: Business is Fun*. Carmel, NY: Syzgy Press.

Wardrip-Fruin, N. and Montfort, N. 2003. *The New Media Reader*. Cambridge, MA: MIT Press.

Wichman, G. 1997. A Brief History of "Rogue". Retrieved March 14, 2016, from http://www.wichman.org/roguehistory.html.

Williams, J. M. 1978. Antique mechanical computers part 3: The Torres chess automaton. *Byte*, 3(9), 82–88.

Wolf, M. J. P. 2001. *The Medium of the Video Game*. Austin, TX: University of Texas Press.

Wyatt, P. 2012a. The Making of Warcraft. Retrieved March 14, 2016, from http://www.codeofhonor.com/blog/the-making-of-warcraft-part-1.

Wyatt, P. 2012b. Tough Times on the Road to Starcraft. Retrieved March 14, 2016, from http://www.codeofhonor.com/blog/tough-times-on-the-road-to-starcraft.

Index